A SOCIOLOGY OF THE ABSURD

A SOCIOLOGY
OF THE ABSURD

Stanford M. Lyman
UNIVERSITY OF CALIFORNIA, SAN DIEGO

Marvin B. Scott
SONOMA STATE COLLEGE

FOREWORD BY

Rom Harré

LINACRE COLLEGE, OXFORD

New York

APPLETON-CENTURY-CROFTS
EDUCATIONAL DIVISION
MEREDITH CORPORATION

Preface

The "Sociology of the Absurd" is a new approach to the fundamental question that first animated sociological inquiry: How is social order possible? In contrast to the evolutionist and functionalist perspectives, we envisage social order in the meaning social "actors" attach to events, persons, self, and others. The Sociology of the Absurd introduced in this book is both subjective and rigorous, empirical and yet devoid of the dehumanizing effect of mathematical representation.

The book is organized in the manner of a theoretical introduction and prolegomena. Our fundamental position is detailed in the introductory chapter, "Toward a Sociology of the Absurd." This is followed by chapters that illustrate its facets and formulate concepts providing successive sets of angular perceptions on the original presentation. Beginning with the argument that social order is the product of human construction, subsequent chapters point up the game-like features of social interaction (Chapters 2 and 3), the ecological settings and their meaning(s) in human association (Chapter 4), the nature and types of accounts by which humans prevent untoward acts from being followed by social chaos (Chapter 5), the character associated with risky activity (Chapter 6), the fears that follow from man's conception of his dramatic possibilities (Chapter 7), and the temporal distinctions that mark man's passage along the ways of life (Chapter 8).

The authors have come to share the perspective presented here from different specialities in the discipline. Lyman is a specialist in Non-Western social organization, especially that of the Chinese and Japanese, and in race and ethnic relations in general. Scott's areas of interest include sociological theory and the study of deviance. The collaboration has in every way been a joint effort, combining the specific perspectives and specialties of the two authors and producing in the process a new emergent that stands apart from the particular backgrounds of the individual authors.

The papers presented here have been read by and discussed with a great many colleagues, and our debt to them is beyond payment. Moreover, some of those with whom a brief, intense conversation later resulted in improvement of our work have been obscured by faulty memories and thus will go unsung, though their ideas are not forgotten. We are especially grateful to Erving Goffman whose brilliant monographs on social relations and human behavior are both an inspiration and a challenge, and whose critical advice at nearly every stage of this work added immeasurably to its quality. That small fraternity of scholars known as ethnomethodologists—Harold Garfinkel, Harvey Sacks, Aaron Cicourel, and Jack Douglas—have influenced us directly and by example. We are also indebted to Donald Ball for his critical reading and other helpful assistance at various stages in the manuscript's development. At a late stage in the manuscript's development we were aided considerably by discussions with Rom Harré of Oxford University. Joyce Scott deserves a special word of thanks for both her instrumental and expressive contributions to the present work.

Portions of this manuscript appeared in *Social Problems*, *The American Sociological Review*, *The Journal of Health and Social Behavior*, and *Sociology and Everyday Life* (edited by Marcello Truzzi, Englewood Cliffs, N.J.: Prentice-Hall, 1968) to whose editors we gratefully acknowledge our appreciation for permission to reprint them here.

S.M.L.
M.B.S.

Foreword

New waves of thought have an odd habit of starting at many different points at once. Lonely innovators suddenly find themselves among a great company of like-minded persons, *to whom they have never spoken or written before*. This fact deserves our astonishment. How is it possible? The new view of the meaning of Wittgenstein's philosophy,[1] the critique of social psychology by the new post-positivist philosophy of science, and now the sociology of the absurd makes just such a convergence, and one particularly worthy of our surprise and interest. I had read, and been delighted by a paper called "Accounts."[2] Here was social science done for the first time in a way which theoretical considerations had made me suppose to be correct.

Chance enabled me to compare my reasons, deriving from the failure of logical positivism as a philosophy of science, with Lyman and Scott's grounds for their innovatory attack in "Accounts." My reasons and their grounds were enormously different, though our conclusions were mutually supporting in an astonishing way. Does this make the convergence more significant? Only a new epistemology of the absurd could answer that question. Yet the fact of the convergence of many lines of thought in these fields is indubitable.

---

[1] S. Toulmin, *Encounter*, 1969.
[2] Reprinted in this volume.

For Lyman and Scott society is a structure of relationships which is essentially linguistic, and which is ephemeral in the sense that it is always constructed anew. It is not a matrix within which men move, nor a system of causes actuating them in ways of which they are unaware. Life is a sequence of episodes, in which people achieve some measure of understanding, and influence, but which has no independence, and, in a sense, no existence. Much of the capability which a man exercises in his relationships with others comes and goes from episode to episode. All this implies a wholly new view of human nature, which is paradoxically, the common view. Men are not chemicals with fixed powers and capabilities, explicable by reference to fixed natures. They are not like elemental gases, whose behavior can be represented by functions of independent parameters. The sociology of the absurd repudiates the atomistic, parametric view of human beings *as a tool for understanding their social interactions.*

Scientists need not produce laws as a result of their studies. They might, instead, in some fields, be the *entrepreneurs* of understanding. The upshot of an investigation might be a set of concepts with which episodes can be understood. The use of the concepts may provide no general knowledge, no expectation of future behavior. But it may make each episode intelligible in itself. Perhaps the creation of such a conceptual scheme is the proper ambition of social sciences. In their idea of the "game" model, and particularly in their paper, "Accounts," Lyman and Scott are generating and studying intelligibility, understanding and the like. Here is one of the places of the interaction of the new sociology with contemporary Oxford philosophy, since one of the results of that movement has been a delineation of systems of concepts actually in use in and among men for understanding and describing what is done by themselves and others. And for commenting upon those doings. "Accounts" studies, in a preliminary way, the crucial socio-linguistic mechanisms for rendering behavior intelligible. The sociology of the absurd can have no other ambition but to add to the tools of intelligibility. Looking at interactions as a game is a contribution to "accounting." From this point of view, a social scientist is no more than the chief negotiator in the game of life. He has seen more, suffered more, and, through his professional training, he has had more vicarious experience, but his role lies *inside* the episodes he makes intelligible.

Getting inside human situations has been called "participant observation," but, in a way, that is not what Lyman and Scott have in mind, though they use the phrase. For that phrase connotes a mode of participation which is self-conscious, a false entry into alien ways of life. What the new sociology and social psychology require are the skills of novelists, poets and playwrights. They demand the power to live with some awareness of the situations, negotiations, linguistic interactions, changing capabilities and powers, through which one lives. It is the art of standing aside from one's own life that provides the material. The genius of Goffman, to whom Lyman and Scott rightly and frequently refer, is the capability to see his subjects as he sees himself. But our interaction with our human environment, and our very identifications of such features of our lives as our emotional state, are linguistically mediated. To learn the name of a feeling is to become capable of experiencing it, to learn a mode of assessment of our situation among people is to acquire a certain situation amongst people. So we return to the central place of language in human life.

The reader of this book will find no sociological theory here, that is, no hypothesis as to the hidden causes of social fact and social change. In consequence, the role of experiment in the sociology of the absurd is wholly different from its role in the mythical and hence unrealizable sociologies of the parametric, atomistic model. The laboratory is but another situation, and the experiment but another episode, within which the "scientist" dwells, negotiating his own identity and providing his own excuses and justifications. And all he gets back in response are the excuses and justifications of his subjects.

The realization of this truth has been the source of the final strand in the sociology of the absurd to which I would like to draw attention, namely, its connection with the barbarously named ethnomethodology of Garfinkel. Only in crisis and social breakdown are tacit conventions revealed. As I would like to say social life has something of the character of a ritual, though a ritual for which no definitive liturgical texts can be found. "To garfinkel" is to behave in a socially outrageous fashion, so as to provoke in those involved a realization of the liturgical structure of the normal episode. But the drastic character of the episodes to which the founder of ethnomethodology has given his name is really no part of the sociology of the absurd. We can come to see what roles we play and the rules to which we tacitly subscribe, and even to recognize our expertise in presenting ourselves in various ways, in an awareness of the ordinary course of life.

One misses certain influences that might be here, particularly that of Lorenz. But this is the first book of the new sociology. A corresponding social psychology is now to be looked for.

Rom Harré
Linacre College, Oxford

Contents

A SOCIOLOGY OF THE ABSURD

1

Toward a sociology of the absurd

A new wave of thought is beginning to sweep over sociology. Aspects of the wave have been given an assortment of names—"labeling theory," "ethnomethodology," and "neo-symbolic interactionism"—but these do not cover its entire range of critique and perspective. A new name must be found to cover a concept which presents not only a unique perspective on conventional sociology but is also a radical departure from the conventional.

We feel an appropriate name is *the Sociology of the Absurd.*

The term "absurd" captures the fundamental assumption of this new wave: *The world is essentially without meaning.* In contrast to that sociology which seeks to discover the *real* meaning of action—a sociological reality, such as the *functional* meaning of social behavior—this new sociology asserts that all systems of belief, including that of the conventional sociologists, are arbitrary. The problems previously supposed to be those of the sociologist are in fact the everyday problems of the ordinary man. It is he who must carve out meanings in a world that is meaningless. Alienation and insecurity are fundamental conditions of life—though they are experienced differently by individuals and groups—and the regular rehumanization of man is everyman's task.

The Sociology of the Absurd draws its philosophical inspiration from existentialism and phenomenology. The works of Edmund

Husserl are particularly crucial to its originating ideas.[1] Moreover, the interpreters of Husserl—especially Alfred Schutz[2] and Maurice Merleau-Ponty[3]—are major sources of intellectual perspectives, fundamental concepts, and promising insights. On the basis of its debt to phenomenology and existentialism the Sociology of the Absurd might be called an existential phenomenology for sociology.

From existentialism the Sociology of the Absurd derives its emphases on human freedom and the life-long process of "becoming"; on the nexus between the reality which is "out there" and the man who is thinking, feeling, apprehending "inside" himself; and on the broader view of man as an integral being, composed not only of *cogito*, but also of feeling, sensing, and apprehending. Finally, on the basis of existentialist thought the Sociology of the Absurd restores the individual to his rightful place as the principal agent of action, the central subject of sociology. Together with Kierkegaard, Sartre, and Jaspers, the sociologists of the new wave seek to place man at the center of study—as he already is in fact at the center of thought and action.[4]

From phenomenology, the Sociology of the Absurd derives its emphasis on certain aspects of human activity, such as intentionality, consciousness, and subjective meaning. Human intentions, contrary to the position of the Watsonian behaviorists, are definable to both social actors and their observers, not by some special technique

[1] Edmund Husserl, *Phenomenology and the Crisis of Philosophy*, N.Y.: Harper Torchbooks, 1965. See also *The Phenomenology of Internal Time-Consciousness*, Bloomington and London: Indiana University Press, 1964. These two works will introduce the reader to Husserl's style and general orientation. For an explication, interpretation and extension of Husserl's philosophy, see *Phenomenology: The Philosophy of Edmund Husserl and Its Interpretation*, edited by Joseph J. Kockelmans, Garden City, N.Y.: Doubleday Anchor, 1967.

[2] Alfred Schutz, *Collected Papers*, The Hague: Martinus Nijhoff, 1962, 1964, 1966. Three volumes. Edited by Maurice Natanson, Arvid Brodersen, and I. Schutz, respectively. See also Schutz's *The Phenomenology of the Social World*, translated by George Walsh and Frederick Lehnert, Evanston, Ill.: Northwestern University Press, 1967.

[3] Maurice Merleau-Ponty, *The Structure of Behavior*, Boston: Beacon, 1963; *In Praise of Philosophy*, Evanston, Ill.: Northwestern University Press, 1963; *Sense and Non-Sense*, Evanston, Ill.: Northwestern University Press, 1964; *The Primacy of Perception and Other Essays*, Evanston, Ill.: Northwestern University Press, 1964; and *Signs*, Evanston, Ill.: Northwestern University Press, 1964.

[4] See Edward A. Tiryakian, *Sociologism and Existentialism*, Englewood-Cliffs, N.J.: Prentice-Hall, 1962, 71–76.

possessed solely by experts or mystics, but rather by means of the most ordinary—but as yet not fully understood—mechanisms of perception carried on in everyday life.[5] Human consciousness should be the principal object of study in sociology, and this has been suggested in the work of Max Weber[6] and in the early formulations of Parsons' theory of action.[7] But methodological problems restricted research, and it has not yet excited the intellectual interest it deserves.

Phenomenology, and especially existential phenomenology, appears to have laid the basis for a solution to the methodological problem of subjective knowledge and objective existence, and in this the new sociology finds a grounding for new research. As Tiryakian has observed, existential phenomenology "seeks to elucidate the existential nature of social structures by uncovering the surface institutional phenomena of the everyday, accepted world; by probing the subterranean, noninstitutional social depths concealed from public gaze, by interpreting the dialectic between the institutional and the non-institutional. . ."[8]

Now what specifically is the nature of human action from the viewpoint of the Sociology of the Absurd? Action consists of the pursuit of ends by social actors capable of deliberating about the line of activity they undertake and of choosing among alternatives to the same end. This does not mean that men always precede action by deliberation. This is manifestly not the case. What it does mean is that men are capable of giving an account of their actions either as preactivity mental images of the action, its consequences and meanings, or as post hoc retrospective readings of completed acts. As images either before or after completion, these constructions emerge as statements made by the actor which give meaning to his actions.[9] These constructions are not unintelligible to others.

---

[5] Edmund Husserl, "The Thesis of the Natural Standpoint and Its Suspension," in Kockelmans, *op. cit.*, 68–79.

[6] Max Weber, *The Theory of Social and Economic Organization*, N.Y.: Oxford University Press, 1947, 88.

[7] Talcott Parsons, *The Structure of Social Action*. Glencoe: The Free Press, 1949, 79–81, 732–33, 750–51.

[8] Edward A. Tiryakian, "Existential Phenomenology and the Sociological Tradition," *American Sociological Review*, 30 (October, 1965), 687.

[9] See G. E. M. Anscombe, *Intention*, Ithaca: Cornell University Press, 1966, 1–61.

Most important, these statements constitute the actual meaning, though not necessarily the cause, of these actions, and thus are the basic data of the new sociology. Instead of adopting an undisguised skepticism of what humans say—a skepticism deeply rooted in the positivist and behaviorist traditions—the Sociology of the Absurd rejects the question of the truth value in face of the significance of the meaning value of these statements. In this respect the new sociology draws on yet another new intellectual strand, that introduced by the ordinary language philosophers who now contribute so much to linguistics and psychology.[10]

It follows from the emphasis on freedom and becoming in existentialist thought that human action should be considered, as Parsons once put it, "voluntaristic."[11] Without this idea of voluntarism, human activity would be "mere behavior."[12] Instead, in concert with Parsons' early view of the theory of action,[13] the sociologist of the Absurd sees activity in discernible units of action—episodes, encounters, situations—to which the actor gives meaning; meaning beyond merely the sense of a set of physical objects. Thus humans are not necessarily the creatures of social or psychological forces—class, caste, race, or deep-lying unconscious states—which *determine* their behavior in the situation. The age-old problem of freedom versus determinism is not a problem of objective philo-

[10] For an introduction to ordinary language philosophy, see Antony Flew, editor, *Logic and Language, First Series*, Oxford: Basil Blackwell, 1960. Our own thinking on language and meaning has been strongly influenced by the following Ludwig Wittgenstein, *Philosophical Investigations*, Oxford: Basil Blackwell, 1959; J. L. Austin, *Philosophical Papers*, Oxford: Clarendon Press, 1961; Gilbert Ryle, *The Concept of Mind*, N.Y.: Barnes and Noble, 1949; and D. S. Shwayder, *The Stratification of Behavior*, N.Y.: Humanities Press, 1965. Anthropologists are far ahead of sociologists in their recognition of the fundamental importance of the study of language. See John J. Gumperz and Dell Hymes, editors, *The Ethnography of Communications*, a special publication of the *American Anthropologist*, 66 (December, 1964). Whatever recognition sociologists have given the study of language falls under the rubric of "sociolinguistics." For a sampling, see William Bright, editor, *Sociolinguistics*, Hague: Mouton, 1966.

[11] Parsons, *op. cit.*, 10–12, *et passim*.

[12] For a general discussion, see Edward C. Devereux, Jr., "Parsons' Sociological Theory," *Social Theories of Talcott Parsons*, edited by Max Black, Englewood Cliffs, N.J.: Prentice-Hall, 1961.

[13] For an analysis of the early and more recent changes in Parsons' frame of reference, see John Finley Scott, "The Changing Foundations of the Parsonian Action Scheme," *American Sociological Review*, 28 (October, 1963), 716–35.

sophy but rather of the actor's construction of reality, his image of freedom and constraint. The Sociology of the Absurd conceives of man as being constructed—and of constructing—social reality in every situation. From this point of view mental illness, for instance, is a social construction, not an absolute, unambiguous disease.[14]

If life consists of encounters, episodes and engagements among persons pursuing goals of which they are consciously aware, or about which they can be made aware, then it appears that the fundamental structure of human action is *conflict*. This is true even if individuals are pursuing the same ends, since each is out to maximize his own interests. Thus, even two lovers in an erotic embrace, as Simmel once noted,[15] may be regarded in conflict since each may be seeking to outdo the other in demonstrating affection or providing the other with feeling. If one begins with the conception of human action as interpersonal conflict, two important implications (for theory) follow. The first concerns the kind of model of *interaction* most useful for the analysis of the social world; the second is the heuristic model of *man* most fruitful for the analysis of interaction.

Concerning the first, it seems that a *game model* is most suited for the analysis of interaction as our conception of the game model derives from the conception of man as a goal-seeking, voluntaristic, intentional actor. It follows from these characteristics that in any engagement he will employ, more or less consciously, stratagems and tactics to attain the end intended. It also follows that others participating in the engagement may be viewed as allies, opponents, or neutrals according to the goal sought and the means employed. The game model, we hold, is fruitful for the analysis of all social interactions, but it is especially so for the study of problematic statuses, such as homosexuals, paranoids, minorities, and the stigmatized in general. In the following essays we have emphasized the game model, including a discussion of the nature and types of games, the role of game-strategy behavior in understanding the sick and stigmatized, the relation of spatial considerations to game strategies

[14] See Thomas Szasz, *The Myth of Mental Illness*, N.Y.: Delta, 1967. See also Michel Foucalt, *Madness and Civilization*, N.Y.: Pantheon, 1965.

[15] Georg Simmel, "The Adventure," *Georg Simmel, 1858–1918*, edited by Kurt H. Wolff, Columbus: Ohio State University Press, 1959, 249–252.

and personal identities, and the type of character and self-presentation associated with strategies and tactics.

With regard to the second, the Sociology of the Absurd assumes a model of man in conflict—with others, with society, with nature, and even with himself. Even though much of sociology has refused to adopt this conception of man,[16] it recommends itself as the most powerful *heuristic* device for the study of man-in-society.[17] In passing it may be noted that the recent findings in animal ethology—especially the works of Konrad Lorenz[18]—lend a curious kind of support to our conception. More significant, however, are the fruitful settings for intellectual problems provided by the adoption of this model of man. By beginning with the assumption that social life is one of conflict, it follows that every social situation is problematic for those involved. With this model the sociologist must continually search for mechanisms that permit the production—and reproduction in a continuous series of engagements—of stable, uniform and persistent interaction.[19] Thus the sociologist is induced by this model to persistently try and solve the riddle that originally set the discipline in motion: how is society possible? The sociologist must view man as the maker and remaker of social existence, as the producer and reproducer of stable engagements, as the craftsman of society and the ever-renewed social order.

---

[16] Tiryakian has argued that existentialism might benefit from the sociological conception of man as interdependent. "Sociologism, to reiterate an earlier point, does not view the relation between the individual and society as one marked by conflict, for it stresses ultimately the needs and contributions of each to the other." See *Sociologism and Existentialism, op. cit.*, 167. Our conception is that the conflict between individual and society, or individual and individual may not be "marked," although sometimes it is, but it is always present, though sometimes repressed or hidden from view. Further, though men may "ultimately" contribute to one another's needs, they act out relations which are full of conflict in the actual episodes of their lives.

[17] A conflict model was employed by early sociologists derived from their awareness of the conflicts between classes, races, and states. See for example Ludwig Gumplowicz, *Outlines of Sociology*, edited by Irving L. Horowitz, N.Y.: Paine-Whitman, 1963. A modern sociology of conflict has been urged by Lewis Coser. See his *The Functions of Social Conflict*, Glencoe: The Free Press, 1956, and *Continuities in the Study of Social Conflict*, N.Y.: The Free Press, 1967.

[18] Konrad Lorenz, *On Aggression*, N.Y.: Harcourt, Brace and World, 1966.

[19] Thus the value of Sigmund Freud's *Civilization and Its Discontents* is not to be found in its empirical validity, but rather in its conception of man in opposition to society and thus in a position to regard all social situations as problematic.

The Sociology of the Absurd does not aim at building a "social system." Indeed system building would go against the grain. This new sociology is perhaps best characterized as a conceptual style of theoretical ideas and sensitizing concepts tied together not by logic or system, but rather by the underlying existential-pheno-menological assumptions stated above. In this respect it is worth contrasting the Sociology of the Absurd with functionalism.[20]

The Sociology of the Absurd stands in opposition to func-tionalism on five major contentions. First, functionalism is interested in understanding human action in terms of forces unperceived by the actor. Functionalism assumes a determined world inhabited by creatures who are for the most part unaware of the forces that shape their destinies and who live by the illusion and self-deception of their own imagined freedom. The Absurd, on the contrary, holds that there is an existential continuum between freedom and deter-minism constructed and reconstructed by the social actors indivi-dually or in concert. Thus some men are more free than others; some are more constrained than they know. The Absurd is con-cerned with man's intentions and consciousness, with his "felt" state of freedom or fatalism, and with the consequences that flow therefrom.

Second, functionalism holds that the various parts of society are non-arbitrary since they contribute to the integration of the whole. The Absurd, on the other hand, holds that all elements of society are arbitrary. These elements have no fixed, stable, and irreducible meaning. They certainly are not part of an organic system with a built-in end purpose—homeostasis. This imagery of society which functionalism inherited from Aristotle and his followers lends itself to the radical separation of events from pro-cesses, and in many cases to a peculiar sociological emphasis on processes detached from events or particular episodes.[21] The Absurd emphasizes the individual and the episodic—the event—

[20] For a clear and systematic statement on functionalism, see Robert K. Merton, "Manifest and Latent Functions," in *Social Theory and Social Structure*, N.Y.: The Free Press, 1968, 73–138.

[21] See Kenneth E. Bock, *The Acceptance of Histories*, Berkeley: University of California Press, 1956, 49–56; and Marvin B. Scott, "Functional Foibles and the Analysis of Social Change," *Inquiry*, 9 (1966), 205–14.

and perceives this as the factor emerging from the participants' social construction of reality.

Third, functionalism regards the social order as rooted in a basic interdependence and cooperation. As the functionalists see it, men, through the socialization process, internalize norms, and fit into roles. These roles, in turn, are meshed together to form interlocking role-sets, or institutions. Aside from our disagreement with the empirical validity of this interpretation (we believe, for example, that society in the modern complex world is better described as a collection of conflicting subcultures,[22] which in their relations manage to maintain some pattern of stability by the employment of social mechanisms as yet imperfectly understood by sociologists), we hold that the functionalist perspective is heuristically weak because it begs the basic question for which sociology was founded. By assuming cooperation and interdependence *a priori*, by pressing society on to a teleological Procrustean bed, by conceiving of society as an organism or a mechanism, functional theory cannot make the social order problematic; it can assume that society is possible but not *discover* how it is possible.

Fourth, because functionalism sees man as a determined creature played upon by forces largely seen "as through a glass, darkly," it opts to study man from the point of view of the observer. Functionalism pays little attention to the perceptions made by men about their own activities. Rather it regards these as founded on ignorance of the real forces that shape human action.[23] The Absurd on the other hand rejects the *a priori* existence of a determined world discoverable by sociologists. It regards man as an actor who builds up his actions on the basis of his goals and of his continuing attempts to define and redefine the situation. Thus, the social world is studied from the point of view of the actors who construct it.

Finally, functionalism postulates a common value system in society. We hold, on the other hand, that in modern complex societies there are few if any common, binding values. Values and norms are pluralistically applicable on the basis of situations,

[22] See Milton M. Gordon, *Assimilation in American Life*, N.Y.: Oxford University Press, 1964, 132–232.

[23] The point is nicely made by Floyd Matson, *The Broken Image*, N.Y.: Braziller, 1964, 54–101.

persons, and times.[24] Thus what is crucial is the definition of the situation. And this definition is not simply "given." Rather, it is a bargain struck for the time being by the participants in the episode. For values to be employed, for norms to be operational, there must be "negotiation" of situations and identities, and obviously the participants have significant stakes in this negotiation. Only when these interactants are agreed upon who they are and what they are do they give and receive accounts—excuses and justifications—the linguistic devices that shore up fractured social situations.

Because we cannot assume value consensus, we have a second reason for supposing the social world to be problematic. Every investigation carried out under the aegis of the Sociology of the Absurd is approached with a sense of astonishment that a social order exists. *The puzzle, the mystery of how social order somehow emerges from the chaos and conflict predicated by the inherently meaningless is the motive for the study of social phenomena.*

Much sociology has been motivated by social meliorism.[25] Although we might laud the endeavors to improve the world, and certainly recognize the multi-faceted problems in modern societies, for several reasons we cannot subscribe to the thesis that social engineering or social change is the primary objective of the Sociology of the Absurd. First, no sociological enterprise directed at healing the social ills, improving the body politic, or salvaging cultural remnants can approach the subject from the standpoint of the Sociology of the Absurd. A consciously naïve but intellectual inquiry into how social order is possible supersedes questions of policy and priority in such a manner as to make the latter not only irrelevant but also a hindrance.

Second, once sociologists consciously adopt meliorism as their principal objective, they seek to influence policy-makers. Influence requires a rhetoric calculated to convince those in power that one has both the appropriate ideas and the techniques with which to make the studies that are convincing to policy makers. Thus, the policy-oriented sociologist is more likely to be inclined to low-level

[24] See Joseph Fletcher, *Situation Ethics*, Philadelphia: The Westminster Press, 1966.

[25] See C. Wright Mills, *The Sociological Imagination*, N.Y.: Oxford University Press, 1959, 84–90.

theorizing, quantification, axiomatic system building, and whatever other rhetorical stratagems are likely to be persuasive.[26]

Finally, sociological meliorism is a contradiction of the nature of man and society as assumed by the Sociology of the Absurd. Meliorism, were it to be the aim of sociology, assumes that sociologists are philosopher-kings, or to put it more accurately, philosophers *of* the people and advisers *to* the kings. The sociologist of the Absurd is simply an observer of the social scene and thus does not suffer from the conceit and arrogance of the social engineer who would reshape the world according to what he lays down as "objective" ethics.

It follows from this, however, that the sociologist of the Absurd can maximize his observations and reflections in the freest of societies. Such a society is not one in which the practicing social scientist is restricted in his opportunities for observation. This does not mean a society devoid of privacy, but one in which the sociologist takes his chances to see what he can see, observing the nooks and crannies, crevices and interstices as well as the broad range of open spaces and public situations. A society marked by police regulation and extensive sumptuary legislation is unlikely to produce much good sociology, just as it is unlikely to produce much excellent art or literature.

It would be untrue, however, to say that restricted societies are unamenable to sociological inquiry. The sociologist of the Absurd must be a careful observer in any situation, and his awareness and exact description of the political, legal, social, and moral restraints on the individual is part of his task. He must, insofar as possible, apprehend the exact definition the individual has of his own freedom and of the constraints upon it in every encounter, so that he can, as part of his description, locate the person precisely in the continuum between humanism and fatalism. He must uncover ideology and utopia in each man, wish and transfiguration in each situation. The sociologist of the Absurd, by his very description of society, by his everlasting unfolding and illumination of the modes and styles of social order, can summon men to build the world of their dreams, but he cannot build it for them.

Although the Sociology of the Absurd is a new wave, it grows

[26] We are indebted for this point to Jack Douglas.

out of contemporary issues and new ideas in other arenas of progressive thought and action. Undoubtedly one of the most important of these is the Theatre of the Absurd, a school of dramatic thought limned by such names as Beckett, Ionesco, and Genet. Indeed our definition of the Absurd derives from Ionesco's in his essay on Kafka: "Absurd is that which is devoid of purpose. . . . Cut off from his religious, metaphysical, and transcendental roots, man is lost; all his actions become senseless, absurd, useless."[27]

If the Theatre of the Absurd illustrates the meaninglessness of the world, the Sociology of the Absurd *describes* man's constant *striving for meaning* in the face of the faceless Monolith. The Sociology of the Absurd emphasizes the episodic in man's life; it deemphasizes, though it does not discount, the predecessors and successors of contemporary man. It sees man as Simmel saw some men and Camus saw all men—as strangers. Thus Simmel wrote:

If wandering is the liberation from every given point in space, and thus the conceptional opposite to fixation at such a point, the sociological form of the "stranger" presents the unity, as it were, of these two characteristics. . . . The stranger is thus being discussed here, not . . . as the wanderer who comes today and goes tomorrow. . . . He is fixed within a particular spatial group, or within a group whose boundaries are similar to spatial boundaries. But his position in this group is determined, essentially, by the fact that he has not belonged to it from the beginning, that he imports qualities into it, which do not and cannot stem from the group itself.[28]

And Camus:

A world that can be explained by reasoning, however faulty, is a familiar world. But in a universe that is suddenly deprived of illusions and of light, man feels a stranger. His is an irremediable exile, because he is deprived of memories of a lost homeland as much as he lacks the hope of a promised land to come. This divorce between man and his life, the actor and his setting, truly constitutes the feeling of Absurdity.[29]

---

[27] Quoted in Martin Esslin, *The Theatre of the Absurd*, Garden City: Doubleday Anchor, 1961, xxi.

[28] Georg Simmel, "The Stranger," *The Sociology of Georg Simmel*, Glencoe: The Free Press, 1950, 402.

[29] Quoted in Esslin, *op. cit.*, xix.

Simmel characterizes the stranger as an awe-inspiring, fearsome contributor; Camus as a victim of the irrelevant past and unpromising future. The sociologist, seeing man as the stranger, emphasizes the problematic nature of his existence. Essentially a contemporary, the stranger must struggle to establish the meaning of each new moment, even if only to get through it and be confronted by the next moment, and the next. Further he must sort out his relationships, appropriately sharing his affections between strangers and brothers, acquaintances and lovers. He is annoyed by the importunity of unwarranted fellowship; estranged by the coldness of unrequited affection; threatened by the powers of the mighty; frightened by the terror of the unknown; and doomed by the inevitability of death. And always he is confronted with life—things, events, people—which demand responses, require interpretation, cry out for meaning. Thus the Sociology of the Absurd studies existential man, the creature who strives after sense in a senseless world.

The development of the Sociology of the Absurd has just begun, and it is impossible at this time to predict its future. But it is worthwhile to review its intellectual past, identifying its principal predecessors and acknowledging the more prominent of its contemporaries. The most important precursors of the Sociology of the Absurd are Machiavelli, Max Weber, Georg Simmel, and Alfred Schutz. Its principal contemporaries are Erving Goffman and Harold Garfinkel. Edmund Husserl, Jean-Paul Sartre, Maurice Merleau-Ponty, and Ludwig Wittgenstein have given it philosophical inspiration. Our task will not to be review the perspectives of these men, but rather to show what aspects of the work of its initial forebear—Machiavelli—have contributed to the growing body of thought on the Absurd.

NICCOLO MACHIAVELLI (1469–1527)

For the past five hundred years Machiavelli has received a bad press. Shakespeare called him the "murderous Machiavel," outdone in planned villainy only by the unredeeming evil of the

Duke of Gloucester. Leo Strauss referred to Machiavelli as anti-Christian and a teacher of evil.[30] And Bartholemew Landheer defines Machiavellianism as "the doctrine of the state as an institution of brute power."[31] Yet, Maurice Merleau-Ponty begins his perceptive essay on Machiavelli with the probing question, "How could he have been understood?"[32]

Machiavelli's infamy rests largely on his best known work, *The Prince*.[33] This book may be (and has been) read as a handbook on how to fool friends and influence people, a sort of Dale Carnegie for rogues. Public life, Machiavelli argues, consists largely of deceptions, lies and broken promises. Since ordinary men tend not to think in terms of multiple realities, they can be made to believe in illusions which are mere chimeras and calculated performances.

If one were to search for that arena of social conduct that best epitomizes the essence of life, one would find it—according to Machiavelli (and later, reasserted by Freud)—in eros. The erotic relations of man and woman are the paradigm of all social relations. For Machiavelli man is in a potential relationship between the world's *fortuna* and his own *virtu*. "*Virtu*," as Hannah Arendt has noted, "is the response summoned up by man, to the world, or rather to the constellation of *fortuna* in which the world opens up, presents and offers itself to him, to his *virtu*."[34] And as Machiavelli points out, "Fortune is a woman, and if you wish to master her, you must strike and beat her, and you will see that she allows herself to be more easily vanquished by the rash and the violent than those who proceed more slowly and coldly."[35] Machiavelli here sounds much like his disciple, the Marquis de Sade. For both, love is not only the three-fold syndrome of deceptions, lies, and broken promises, but more fundamentally a relationship of domination and subordination. In a love relationship one party imposes his or

[30] Leo Strauss, *Thoughts on Machiavelli*, Glencoe: The Free Press, 1958.
[31] Bartholomew Landheer, "The Universalistic Theory of Othmar Spann," in *An Introduction to the History of Sociology*, edited by Harry Elmer Barnes, Chicago: University of Chicago Press, 1948, 388.
[32] Maurice Merleau-Ponty, "A Note on Machiavelli," *Signs*, *op. cit.*, 211.
[33] Niccolo Machiavelli, *The Prince*, N.Y.: Washington Square Press, 1963.
[34] Hannah Arendt, *Between Past and Future*, N.Y.: Viking Press, 1968, 137 (revised edition).
[35] Machiavelli, *op. cit.*, 114.

her will upon the other, and the other submits. Moreover, love has a game-like quality, involving covert conflict and clandestine deception so that, as Willard Waller—a modern Machiavellian in our sense—has described it, love takes on the characteristic of pluralistic ignorance, setting forth a fundamental condition for game-theoretic analysis:

A and B begin an affair on the level of light involvement. A becomes somewhat involved, but believes that B has not experienced a corresponding growth of feeling. and hides his involvement from B, who is, however, in exactly the same situation. The conventionalized "line" facilitates this sort of "pluralistic ignorance," because it renders meaningless the very words by means of which this state of mind could be disclosed.[36]

One of Machiavelli's contributions to the Sociology of the Absurd is his understanding that, as with love, all human relations have the qualities of a game. Although ordinary men might not perceive this ubiquitous quality, the prince has to do so in order to persevere. Thus, Machiavelli is not as opposed to humane qualities as some have supposed. Rather, as Merleau-Ponty has observed,[37] he qualifies his humanism with a perception of the forms in which these qualities may be realized or subverted. Machiavelli writes, "a prince should seem to be merciful, faithful, humane, religious, and upright, and should even be so in reality; but he should have his mind so trained that, when occasion requires it, he may know how to change to the opposite."[38] The prince must have that situational hyper-consciousness, which, we have elsewhere noted, is the requirement of a true game-strategic player in life.[39]

Perhaps the most important of Machiavelli's contributions to the Sociology of the Absurd is his understanding that theory and method are not unrelated activities. Although some earlier admirers of Machiavelli have credited him with being the father of social

---

[36] Willard Waller, "The Rating and Dating Complex," *American Sociological Review* (October, 1937), 727–37. Reprinted in Logan Wilson and William Kolb, editors, *Sociological Analysis*, N.Y.: Harcourt, Brace & Co., 1949. Quotation from p. 617.

[37] Merleau-Ponty, "A Note on Machiavelli," *op. cit.*

[38] Machiavelli, *op. cit.*, 77.

[39] See "Game Frameworks" and "Paranoia, Homosexuality and Game Theory," appearing here as chapters 2 and 3.

science and one of the first users of historical method, these two compliments are undeserved.[40] However, Machiavelli has been unusually neglected for his perceptive commentary on the similarity between the artist and the theorist, and in particular his implicit suggestion of the inextricable linkage between methods employed and theories adduced.[41] Like the painter who can look up from the valley to perceive the mountain or down into the plain from a high peak to see the valley, the social theorist must have an *optimum distance* from his subject in order to see it accurately.[42] It is not dispirited "objectivity," as the term today is vulgarly employed, that Machiavelli advocates, but rather a passion chastened by the perspective of unalloyed clarity. His social theorist is neither king nor commoner, but something in between—an observer who adopts the stance appropriate to the subject matter at hand. Machiavelli might rightfully be credited with a fleeting but fundamental recognition of the positive functions of marginality[43] for social observation and also with some awareness of that method appropriate to the Sociology of the Absurd—participant observation.[44]

Machiavelli developed his methodology further in his *History of Florence*. In this methodology we find all the elements of the modern Sociology of the Absurd: the perspective of optimum distance, the empathic identification with each of the persons in an encounter in terms of their respective environments, a non-ideological stance, and the game model of social interaction. As Wolin has described his methodology:

Machiavelli's technique was to set out a situation where conflicting class interests were involved, and then, through the mouth of some partisan

---

[40] See Harry Elmer Barnes, "Ancient and Medieval Social Philosophy," in Barnes, *op. cit.*, 22–24; Emory S. Bogardus, *The Development of Social Thought*, N.Y.: David McKay, 1960, 196–98; Sheldon Wolin, *Politics and Vision*, Boston: Little, Brown, 195–238; Arendt, *op. cit.*, 136–7.

[41] Wolin, *op. cit.*, 202–3.

[42] Machiavelli, *op. cit.*, xxxvi.

[43] Although it tends to emphasize the unfortunate aspects of marginality, the best discussion is still Everett V. Stonequist, *The Marginal Man*, N.Y.: Russell and Russell, 1961.

[44] For an excellent discussion—but one which does not mention Machiavelli—see Severyn T. Bruyn, *The Human Perspective in Sociology*, Englewood Cliffs, N.J.: Prentice-Hall, 1966.

spokesman, proceed to argue the best case possible for each interested group. Regardless of the party, whether proletarian or patrician, the versatility of the new science enabled it to enter imaginatively into any particular position, analyzing the problems as they appeared from that perspective and indicating the course of action which would satisfy the interest in question. . . . It is easy to see from this why many critics have argued that Machiavelli fallaciously assumed international politics to be simply a chess game. . . . But one might also suggest that this was inevitable, given the versatile and detached quality of the new science: for the essence of chess is that it is a science applicable to either side of the board. This can be put another way by saying that the vantage point which Machiavelli sought for political theory was to come from its being inspired by a problem orientation rather than an ideological orientation. A problem has several facets, an ideology a central focus.[45]

The stance taken by Machiavelli's social theorist suggests the principal assumption of the Sociology of the Absurd—that the world has no objective meaning. One can study the social world from the point of view of the superior or the subordinate; of the lover or his mistress; of the bourgeoisie or the proletariat; of management or labor; of the deviant or the person who labels him deviant, and so on. What is important is that one should have a perspective, but the particular perspective employed is irrelevant to the rectitude of theorizing. One can make true statements from any perspective, including those not consonant with any available ideology.

But a familiar objection to this might be raised: Doesn't a particular perspective distort the reality under consideration? Surely there is a distortion in the perspective of the labelled deviant, as much, perhaps, as that in the person doing the labelling. Is it not necessary to find some objective perspective so that the social scientist can obtain the *essential* meaning of the social world and the connecting links in social relations? Virtually all the classical and contemporary theorists searched for the objective meaning and connecting threads of human relationships. For Adam Smith, they are tied together by an "invisible hand"; for the French *philosophes*, by the ineluctable laws of progress; for Marx, by the locomotive of history; for Merton by functional interdependencies.

[45] Wolin, *op. cit.*, 203.

For Machiavelli, in contrast, all such ideas about the structure of the world are as illusory as the fortresses with which fearful princes deluded themselves into a false sense of security.[46] Machiavelli, we believe, is the father of the Sociology of the Absurd because of his insistence on the essential meaninglessness of the world and his perception of how most men impute a meaning to their illusions, that is, construct social realities out of the shreds and patches of their experiences and memories.[47]

Machiavelli's conception of man's response once he has recognized that the world is meaningless is not that of Camus' anti-hero, who gives up his vale of tears in a brave act of suicide, or Joseph Heller's anti-hero, who engages in puckish black humor and a hedonistic destruction of shibboleths.[48] As the world reveals its arbitrariness, as *fortuna* unfolds before man, he increases his commitment to its challenge, his intense interest in its investigation, his desire for action. That, we believe, lies behind the activities of the sixteenth century Calvinists described by Weber.[49] The Calvinist conception of life and afterlife revealed a God who ruled the universe arbitrarily and without counsel or advice, or subjection to the pleas of those over whom he exercised his majestic authority. Calvinists responded to this not by resignation, suicide, or hedonism, but rather by an intensive search for signs of their election or damnation, signs of that over which they had no control whatsoever. Weber thus suggested that when the world reveals its meaninglessness, the men who discover this plunge into a course of action, undertake enormous risks, enter into a world of adventure which creates meanings out of the void, the discovery of which originally set them in motion.

Another precursor of the Sociology of the Absurd, Simmel,

---

[46] Machiavelli, *op. cit.*, 92–97. For an excellent discussion, see Wolin, *op. cit.*, 211–15. Although Machiavelli often employed the terminology that implied society perceived as an organism, these pictures were, as Wolin (*ibid.*, 214) has suggested, "palimpsests." At other times Machiavelli described political bodies in language translatable into that of physics, *ibid.*, 214.

[47] For a modern statement, see Peter Berger and Thomas Luckmann, *The Social Construction of Reality*, Garden City: Doubleday, 1966.

[48] Joseph Heller, *Catch-22*, N.Y.: Simon and Shuster, 1961.

[49] Max Weber, *The Protestant Ethic and the Spirit of Capitalism*, London: Allen and Unwin, 1930.

perceives the *adventure* in the same light.[50] The adventure exists outside routine time and place, is disconnected from everyday affairs. In its periodicity and episodes, the adventure gives zest and meaning to life. Simmel's disciple, Robert E. Park, points out that modern urban man is confronted by such a variety of rapid social changes taking place before his eyes that meanings are no longer stable.[51] As a result men everywhere search for adventure, thrills, novelty. In the process they break down the old forms of social organization and create new meanings.

If there are no immutably stable reference points in the social order, then the obvious place to begin the construction of a social theory is with the nature of man himself. We begin with man's two most salient characteristics: he is an animal; and he is capable of symbolic reflection. As an animal, man is fundamentally sexual, as Freud has argued so convincingly; he is possessed of aggressive impulses, as Lorenz has shown us in his pan-zoological studies[52]; and he is inclined to possess and dominate territory, as Ardrey, drawing upon a range of ethological investigations, has pointed out.[53] In short, man is a naked ape.[54] Of course man is different from the other animals. He is, in Marston Bates' phrase, a "glutton" and a "libertine"; that is, he seems to be more sexual, more aggressive, and more insatiable in his desire to possess things and dominate people.

More important, the fundamental difference between man and beast is that the former is gifted with imagination and the mechanism—language—by which he can symbolize and communicate his desires, feelings, and thoughts. With his imagination he not only constructs social life, but also multiplies his wants, enhances his desires, and pictures his possibilities. In a sense, his imagining power makes him insatiable, for he is always capable of conjuring up new images of those things he does not possess or control. Man is constantly moving, searching for objects to fulfill his desires, be they

---

[50] Simmel, "The Adventure," *op. cit.*, 243–46.

[51] Although this point is reiterated throughout his work, see especially Robert E. Park, "Community Organization and Juvenile Delinquency," in *The City*, Chicago: University of Chicago Press, 1967, 99–112.

[52] Lorenz, *op. cit.*

[53] Robert Ardrey, *The Territorial Imperative*, N.Y.: Atheneum, 1966.

[54] Desmond Morris, *The Naked Ape*, N.Y.: McGraw-Hill, 1967.

sexual, aggressive, or territorial. But the supply always seems to be limited. This, properly, is the starting point of all investigations. Man's searching interest in domination and control puts him into conflict with other men. This conflict would be a war of all against all unless some kind of order were established. The fundamental sociological question is that posed by Hobbes and reiterated by Simmel: How is social order possible?

From the point of view of man this question can be rephrased: How can man obtain what he wants without suffering terrible losses, defeats, subjugation, or death? For Machiavelli man gets what he wants through *virtue*. Virtue is the character that man summons up in the face of the world. One of the most important elements of virtue is "respect." Machiavelli's *Prince* is a guidebook for the establishment and maintenance of *respectability*. That Machiavelli should be concerned with respectability may seem strange. But the strangeness dissolves when we consider that respectability is more a function of appearances than realities, more a consequence of what is seen than what is known. As Machiavelli put it, ". . . for mankind in general judge more by what they see than by what they feel, every one being capable of the former and but few of the latter. Everybody sees what you seem to be but few really feel what you are: . . ."[55]

For man, then, achieving ends involves managing appearances. Instead of an open presentation of self, there is the masked exhibition of *persona*. Masks are the faces we assume appropriate to the situation. The ability to adopt an appropriate face, and to drop it or change it as exigencies require is not equally distributed among mankind. For Machiavelli it was a marvelous gift if a commoner possessed it, but a requirement for a prince. Modern sociology and world realities have gone further. Robert E. Park recognized that wearing a mask with ease was often a function of cultural orientation.[56] Negroes in America have found that not merely maintenance of status but preservation of life itself is at stake when one must mask realities with appearances.[57] The physically disabled

[55] Machiavelli, *op. cit.*, 78.
[56] Park, "Behind Our Masks," *Survey Graphic*, 56 (May 1, 1926), 135–39.
[57] See the perceptive poem by Paul Laurence Dunbar, "We Wear the Mask," in Arna Bontemps, *American Negro Poetry*, N.Y.: Hill and Wang, 1963, 14.

and morally disreputable must somehow manage a respectable appearance from out of their spoiled identities.[58] Modern society has democratized Machiavelli's morality.[59] Today every man must be a prince.

Two major lines of thought flow from Machiavelli's recognition of the primacy of appearances over reality. The first is found in the work of a modern student of *virtu*, Erving Goffman. Goffman's social actor, like Machiavelli's prince, lives externally. He engages in a daily round of impression management, presenting himself to advantage when he is able, rescuing what he can from a bad show. His everyday life consists of interaction rituals, employing deference and demeanor, saving his own and someone else's face, inhibiting actions that would spoil the fun in games, being intimate when occasion demands, maintaining his distance when proximity would be unwise, and in general being continuously alive to the requirements of behavior in public places.[60]

Machiavelli's prince and Goffman's social actor have no interior specifications. Rather, situations specify them. Or, as Goffman has put it, "not men and their moments. Rather moments and their men."[61] Machiavelli is not opposed to the humane qualities in man—indeed he states that princes should possess them. But man's success arises not from the presence or absence of humanity, but rather from the strategic employment of appearances. In short, it does not matter whether men *are* virtuous; what counts is whether they can appear to be so when it matters. Shakespeare, through the lips of the archvillain of all literary time, placed the *persona* ahead of the self, the performance ahead of the reality, and in doing so captured the *general* qualities of Machiavelli's and modern society's man:

[58] Goffman, *Stigma*, Englewood Cliffs, N.J.: Prentice-Hall, 1963.

[59] Simmel, "The Metropolis and Mental Life," in *The Sociology of Georg Simmel, op. cit.*, 409–24.

[60] Goffman has explored these phenomena in a series of brilliant monographs: *The Presentation of Self in Everyday Life*, Garden City: Doubleday Anchor, 1959; *Encounters*, Indianapolis: Bobbs-Merrill, 1961; *Asylums*, Garden City: Doubleday Anchor, 1961; *Behavior in Public Places*, N.Y.: The Free Press of Glencoe, 1963; *Interaction Ritual*, Garden City: Doubleday Anchor, 1967.

[61] *Ibid.*, 3.

Why I can smile, and murder whiles I smile,
And cry "Content" to that which grieves my heart
And wet my cheeks with artificial tears,
And frame my face to all occasions. . . .
I'll play the orator as well as Nestor,
Deceive more slily than Ulysses could,
And, like a Sinon, take another Troy.
I can add colours to the chameleon,
Change shapes with Proteus for advantages,
And set the murderous Machiavel to school.

It is this imagery, misunderstood, that leads to the humane
scholar's condemnation of Machiavelli. But this is surely to misread
not only Machiavelli, but Shakespeare as well. Shakespeare employs
the art of feigning and impression management not only in his
character Richard III but also in some of his most heroic figures.
Hamlet is perhaps the most outstanding, a man who in pursuit of
justice in a corrupt kingdom, at first feigns madness, masks his
unfilial feelings, and pretends coldness toward his betrothed, and,
despite his artfulness, wreaks havoc in the very process of gaining
his end. And in this we find Machiavelli's fundamental point. Life
is chancy and, even if a man be suited to his time, *fortuna* may turn
against him. Far in advance of the modern revision of the debate
over freedom and determinism,[62] Machiavelli saw that man was
neither free nor fated, but only what he and particular situations
demonstrate his condition to be. "I judge," Machiavelli wrote in
discussing this age-old debate, "that it may be assumed as true that
Fortune to the extent of one half is the arbiter of our actions, but
that she permits us to direct the other half, or perhaps a little less,
ourselves."[63] Against Fortune's demanding control, Machiavelli
poses man's potential use of the best of stratagems. As Merleau-
Ponty has observed this is a humanism of free men, suitable not to
a utopia but to the problematic realities of worldly affairs:

If by humanism we mean a philosophy of the inner man which finds
no difficulty in principle in his relations with others, no opacity whatsoever

[62] See Matson, *op. cit.*, 175–272.
[63] Machiavelli, *op. cit.*, 110.

in the functioning of society, and which replaces political cultivation by moral exhortation, Machiavelli is not a humanist. But if by humanism we mean a philosophy which confronts the relationship of man to man and the constitution of a common situation and a common history between men as a problem, then we have to say that Machiavelli formulated some of the conditions of any serious humanism.[64]

Goffman has also explored Machiavelli's second sense of *virtu*. The second meaning of *virtu*, the Greco-Roman sense of the term, refers to valor, strength and manliness. In this sense to be virtuous is to be forthright, courageous, and bold. For Latins it is summed up in the term *machismo*. This kind of virtue finds its principal form in the voluntary effort to subdue fortune. It involves what Goffman calls *action*.[65] The opportunities for action provide the situations in which men can demonstrate character. Action, in the fullest sense, calls for *courage*, carrying on a line of action in the face of perceived danger; *gameness*, sticking to an activity despite setbacks, pain, and exhaustion, by sheer grit; *integrity*, resisting the temptations of more profitable inducements which, if accepted, would thwart one's original aim; *gallantry*, the maintenance of manly courtesy in the midst of conflict; and *composure*, the maintenance of emotional control, poise, and self-possession in the face of challenges to these emotional states.[66] However, if character is a function of action situations, men who find themselves outside the action realm are under challenge to prove what is not readily demonstrable, while those immersed in action are required to continuously demonstrate what the occasion demands.

Although, as Machiavelli knew, the two senses of *virtu* are not mutually exclusive, their forms may appear separately or even as alternatives to one another. Thus for Machiavelli a prince might obtain his kingdom by strength and valor, but maintain it by establishing respectability. For those without the capacity to establish respectability, valor and strength may be an effective substitute. Of course the appearance of valor is often enough of a substitute for the real thing to be efficacious. And one of its most salient characteristics

---

[64] Merleau-Ponty, *op. cit.*, 223.
[65] Goffman, "Where the Action Is," *Interaction Ritual, op. cit.*, 149–270.
[66] *Ibid.*, 218–29.

is that element of composure once associated with sophistication and the blasé appearance, today called keeping "cool."[67] This aspect of character is part of the qualities of an action situation and yet one that can be created, staged, or generated to produce character. Thus children exhibit poise by maintaining a casual appearance while riding a merry-go-round, college administrators maintain an outward calm in the face of attacks by militant students, and adolescents establish character by cool composure in the heat of a rumble.

For some people, however, life presents the peculiar problem of allowing few opportunities for a show of respectability or valor. These are the people without the opportunity to exercise *virtu*, the hostages to fortune. As Machiavelli has written, "Fortune . . . displays her power where there is no organized valor to resist her, and where she knows that there are no dikes or walls to control her."[68] Such people are the oppressed, the down-trodden, the people who walk in despair. But there are more. Shakespeare has created the minor characters, the archetypical ones are Rosencrantz and Guildenstern, whose lives are but reflections of the actions or commands of others. Such persons live in an anomic world, not knowing whether life is a function of chance, opportunity, or fate. They have their entrances and their exits, but these are determined and involuntary—all else is waiting and wondering.[69] The modern Sociology of the Absurd widens the scope of its dramaturgic net to include not only the star performer and his exercise of *virtu*, but also the minor player and his hopeless victimization by fate.

Goffman also has adopted the specific unit of investigation derived from Machiavelli's conception of social life—the episode. Since the world is created anew is each encounter, it is precisely these engagements that form the comprehensible units for sociological investigation. Machiavelli indicated this in his discussion of the relationship between the prince's success, the spirit of the times, and fortune:

I say that we see a prince fortunate one day, and ruined the next, without his nature or any of his qualities being changed. . . .[T]he prince

---

[67] See "Coolness in Everyday Life," appearing here as chapter 6.
[68] Machiavelli, *op. cit.*, 111.
[69] For a relevant theatrical presentation of these ideas, see Tom Stoppard's play, *Rosencrantz and Guildenstern Are Dead*, N.Y.: Grove Press, 1967.

who relies entirely upon fortune will be ruined according as fortune varies. I believe, further, that the prince who conforms his conduct to the spirit of the times will be fortunate; and in the same way will he be unfortunate, if in his actions he disregards the spirit of the times. For we see men proceed in various ways to attain the end they aim at, such as glory and riches: the one with circumspection, the other with rashness; one with violence, another with cunning; one with patience, and another with impetuosity; and all may succeed in their different ways.[70]

From this perspective we can see that in analyzing occasions and encounters, moral norms on their own are meaningless and arbitrary. Any other set would do. The specific morality that emerges is a case of interplay between man's nature, the meaning of the situation, and chance. This interplay is the focus of study— not the interior specifications of man, alone; or the external real meaning of the situations, alone; or the chance probabilities, alone. Thus, it is the episode, which comprehends all three, that must, in all its complexity, be the proper focus of study.

But an objection might be raised. Doesn't this weight the study on the side of the over-dramatized image of man?[71] Does not Goffman's social actor possess too much input of dramatic finesse, strategic ingenuity and tactical genius to be a proper model for mankind? Has not Goffman, in swinging the pendulum away from Parsons' over-socialized view of man,[72] moved too far in the direction of an over-dramatized image of man?[73] We would not presume to answer this question for Goffman, but instead would only point out that Machiavelli's concept of man-in-episodes takes account precisely of this all-too-human problem. It is not that all men are clever calculators constantly matching wits with other men, or that they all boldy stride out with stratagems to challenge fate. Rather they succeed or fail according to whatever they can do and its effects on situation and chance. As Machiavelli put it:

[70] Machiavelli, *op. cit.*, 111–112.

[71] See the perceptive essay by Simmel, "The Dramatic Actor and Reality," in *The Conflict of Modern Culture and Other Essays*, N.Y.: Teacher's College Press, 1968, 91–7.

[72] See Dennis H. Wrong, "The Over-Socialized Conception of Man in Modern Sociology," *Psychoanalysis and Psychoanalytic Review*, 49 (Summer, 1962), 53–69.

[73] See Sheldon Messinger, *et al.*, "Life as Theater: Some Notes on the Dramaturgic Approach to Social Reality," in *Sociology and Everyday Life*, edited by Marcello Truzzi, Englewood Cliffs, N.J.: Prentice-Hall, 1968, 7–18.

This also causes the difference of success; for if one man, acting with caution and patience, is also favored by time and circumstances, he will be successful; but if these change, then will he be ruined, unless, indeed, he changes his conduct accordingly. Nor is there any man so sagacious that he will always know how to conform to such change of times and circumstances; for men do not readily deviate from the course to which their nature inclines them; and, moreover, if they have generally been prosperous by following one course, they cannot persuade themselves that it would be well to depart from it. Thus the cautious man, when the moment comes for him to strike a bold blow, will not know how to do it, and thence will he fail; while if he could have changed his nature with the times and circumstances, his usual good fortune would not have abandoned him.[74]

Thus Machiavelli saw that failure might be founded on man's sense of continuity, on his unchanging nature, which could not respond efficaciously to the times or the situation. Machiavelli's social man is not devoid of history, memory, or biography, as some critics of episodic analyses have supposed. The episode does not arise full-blown without connections to past or future. Rather man brings to it his memories, perceptual apparatus, and wishes, hopes and dreams. And if he has no particular wishes or goals in an episode, he may just muddle through it, piecing it together as he goes, and, perhaps, not reflecting too much about it.

The second line of thought that follows from Machiavelli's emphasis on appearances, engagements, and the interplay between man's nature, the situation and fate, is "ethnomethodology"—the sociological approach associated with the work of Harold Garfinkel.[75] Ethnomethodology is a new—and for many, strange[76]—approach to the analysis of social phenomena. The rather inelegant term refers to the study of the procedures (methodology) employed by everyday man (ethnics) in his effort to meaningfully cope with the world. Otherwise put, it seeks to give an organized account of the routine grounds for everyday action. Although Garfinkel has not acknowledged any influence from Machiavelli and derives his

---

[74] Machiavelli, *op. cit.*, 112.

[75] Garfinkel, *op. cit.*

[76] See the reviews of Garfinkel's *Studies in Ethnomethodology* by Guy E. Swanson, Anthony F. C. Wallace, and James S. Coleman in *American Sociological Review*, 33 (February, 1968), 122–130.

conceptualizations from the sociological philosophy of Alfred Schutz,[77] ethnomethodology starts with that same assumption that informs the Sociology of the Absurd and owes its intellectual origins to Machiavelli's view of the world: Nothing in the social world has an inherent meaning. Meaning consists only of that which is imputed by people to persons and objects, as they go about their daily lives trying to make sense of the world.

Ethnomethodologists contend that the subject matter of sociology is not some "raw" reality "out there," whose nature the sociologist discovers by the methods of natural science. Rather, the subject matter of sociology consists of the way people in the world have constructed and continue to construct the "out there." Hence, unlike the conventional sociologist who routinely employs the "established" concepts of the discipline—age, sex, race and class— and who regards social facts—education, enthnicity, and suicide— as unambiguous, the ethnomethodologist would insist that any usage of these concepts or recognition of these facts should correspond to the use that ordinary members of society make of them. Any explanation in terms of categories intelligible solely to sociologists is not valid.

Ethnomethodologists have employed some of their best efforts in a critique of the conventional sociologists' use of official statistics.[78] To the extent that the sociologist accepts these statistics as symbols of the "raw" reality which he wishes to understand, he fails to grasp the fundamental issue of the meaningless world. Thus suicide rates are not raw data; they are constructions of realities made by officials who must categorize dead bodies.[79] The first order of business, then, in a sociological analysis of suicide, is the discovery of how a corpse becomes a suicide. Despite the many sociological studies of suicide, this prior task has hardly been undertaken.[80]

[77] See especially Schutz, "Common Sense and Scientific Interpretation of Human Action," *Collected Papers, I, op. cit.*, 3–47.

[78] See Aaron Cicourel, *The Social Organization of Juvenile Justice*, N.Y.: Wiley, 1968, 27–29, 248, 290, 330.

[79] Jack Douglas, *The Social Meanings of Suicide*, Princeton: Princeton University Press, 1967, 192–96.

[80] See, however, Harold Garfinkel, "Practical Sociological Reasoning: Some Features in the Work of the Los Angeles Suicide Prevention Center," in *Essays in Self-Destruction*, edited by Edwin S. Shneidman, N.Y.: Science House, 1967,

The ethnomethodologist neither takes the world for granted nor imposes his *a priori* categories upon it. Instead he insists that the world be treated as problematic. He starts by making the world strange.[81] Making the world strange is the most efficacious way of getting to the "background expectancies" of everyday life—what Durkheim called the non-contractural conditions of contract. These understandings underlie the social world and are pushed to the back of human consciousness until something happens—a nasty surprise—which brings them to the forefront of awareness. The background expectancies are demonstrable by experiments which violate the conditions of trust that circumscribe human affairs. Trust is a readiness to act in the face of the omnipresent ambiguity and vagueness of meaning in the belief that things will become comprehensible. The background expectancies and conditions of trust constitute the general parameters with which one may analyze the episode. Thus ethnomethodology provides not only a critique of conventional sociology but a specification of the elements needed to study the basic unit in the Sociology of the Absurd.

The most appropriate way to gather data for use in studies of the Absurd is by unobtrusive observation of natural settings or by examining reproductions of natural settings—movies, taped conversations, and so on. Just as Machiavelli's prince is best studied in his everyday situations, so today's democratized prince cannot really be comprehended by survey research.[82] He must be studied in his natural habitat—the world, that senseless void where he continuously strives for meaning, undertakes action, wreaks havoc, and, in the very processes of so doing, recreates again and again. It is the meaningless-world-made-meaningful which is the strategic research site for the Sociology of the Absurd.

171–187; and Harvey Sacks, "The Search for Help," *ibid.*, 203–223. See also Marvin B. Scott, "New Rules for Suicide Students," *Psychiatry and Social Science Review*, 2 (October, 1968), 21–4.

[81] See Harvey Sacks, "Sociological Description," *Berkeley Journal of Sociology*, VIII (1963), 1–16.

[82] See Aaron Cicourel, *Method and Measurement in Sociology*, N.Y.: The Free Press, 1964, 106–107, 114–120.

2

Game frameworks

Until recently game theory was confined almost solely to "pure" mathematical analysis of decision-making in a two-person, zero-sum situation in which absolute conflict of interest, total rationality of players, mutual knowledge of the outcomes, and mutual agreement on the rank order of preferences were assumed *a priori.* The sociological criticism of this abstract and formalistic analysis as non-empirical and hence of limited use has led to tentative rethinking, bringing closer together theoretical and empirical models.[1] As a result of these efforts, it is now possible to treat social situations—in which two or more persons or groups are in communication with one another and are engaged in goal-directed action—in terms of a game-theoretic framework, at least in its simple social-psychological form.[2] Our task here is to specify the

[1] The rise of game theory and its recognition in sociological thought is discussed by Jessie Bernard in several essays. See "Where is the Modern Sociology of Conflict?" *American Journal of Sociology,* 56 (July, 1950), 11–16; "The Theory of Games of Strategy as a Modern Sociology of Conflict," *American Journal of Sociology,* 59 (March, 1954), 411–424; "Some Current Conceptualizations in the Field of Conflict," *American Journal of Sociology,* 70 (January, 1965), 442–454. For a good sampling of the range of interest and approach associated with the "game theory" perspective, see Martin Shubik, editor, *Game Theory and Related Approaches to Social Behavior,* N.Y.: Wiley, 1964.

[2] A most important borderline figure, bridging both traditional game theory and social-psychological concerns is T. C. Schelling. See his *Strategy of Conflict,* N.Y.:

elements of this framework and to typify the games played by ordinary actors in everyday life.

The minimal arena of game action is the social situation which Goffman has designated variously as a "focused gathering," an "encounter," or an "engagement."[3] The characteristics of a focused gathering are that two or more persons have come into one another's visual and audial presence, and have granted one another mutual rights of cognitive and communicative recognition and response. Such situations may be distinguished from those gatherings in which persons are physically co-present but are not privileged to interact—for example, the occupants of an elevator during the course of its journey. Such a gathering, designated by Goffman as "unfocused," is irrelevant to our present consideration.

Although a focused gathering is the minimal arena for game action, it is not the only one. Some of the most fruitful analyses of games have come from the study of nations posed against one another in some sort of competition.[4] Their physical co-presence was not at issue nor were their respective power elites required to be in a literal eyeball-to-eyeball confrontation. What is required for game action to proceed is that two or more persons or groups (and here we include nations, or more properly, power elites of nations) be consciously aware of one another, be cognitively focused on one another, and be in a position to communicate in some mutually intelligible, or seemingly intelligible, manner. Thus, games may be played by persons separated in space but connected

---

Oxford Galaxy, 1963. For an effort to apply game theoretic notions to social-psychological problems, see John W. Thibaut and Harold H. Kelley, *The Social Psychology of Groups*, N.Y.,: Wiley, 1959. A recent theoretical statement is provided by James S. Coleman in "Games as Vehicles for Social Theory," Johns Hopkins University: Report from the Center for the Study of Social Organization of Schools, 1968. See also Clarice S. Stoll, "Player Characteristics and Strategy in a Parent-Child Simulation Game," Johns Hopkins University: The Center for the Study of Social Organization of Schools, Report No. 23, 1968. While the above mentioned works have influenced our thinking, our greatest indebtedness is to Erving Goffman. In fact, the present paper may be read as an effort to extend the theoretical ideas in his unpublished manuscript, "Communications and Strategic Interaction."

[3] Erving Goffman, *Encounters*, Indianapolis: Bobbs-Merrill, 1961, 7–19.

[4] Such, for example, is the controversial work by Herman Kahn, *On Thermonuclear War*, Princeton: Princeton University Press, 1960.

by communicating media, such as telephones, telegraph, mail or messenger services. Examples include chess matches played by mail; the series of letters between sweethearts that culminate either in a marriage proposal or what American soldiers call a "Dear John" letter; and "hotline" interchanges between agents of national powers that result in, say, a declaration of war or a decision to relax one's vigil in a tense situation.

Interactants identify the game in play—although, of course, they do not usually think in game-playing terms—by comprehending, perceiving, or guessing what each is seeking to achieve. In other words, the interactants become cognizant of the goals that each has chosen, or is about to choose, by their respective lines of action. This is what is presumably meant by "rationality" in the game-theoretic framework, though this term has been subjected to considerable ambiguity and abuse by game theorists.[5] Awareness that other social actors have goals, and a varied but finite set of means through which to realize them, constitutes the primary prerequisite for game action. It is one of the meta-understandings that underlie all game action. Absence of such awareness constitutes one principal condition under which game action may not proceed.[6]

When the actors recognize that they are in a particular game they figuratively bracket the situation into an immediate situational awareness context.[7] A frame of reference and perspective is thus established which defines the meaning of persons and objects, and which also designates the historical events and biographical identities that will be brought into play. This frame constitutes a social

[5] For a discussion on this point, see Bernard, "The Theory of Games . . .," *op. cit.*, 413–415; and Schelling, *op. cit.*, 3–6, 14–15, 143–150, 278–290.

[6] Part of this and the following section on face games appeared in slightly modified form in the authors' "Accounts, Deviance and Social Order," in *Deviance and Respectability*, edited by Jack Douglas, N.Y.: Basic Books, 1970, 89–119.

[7] The following draws on the work of Goffman, Alfred Schutz, and Anselm Strauss. The "frame" approach is suggested by Goffman in "Fun in Games," *Encounters, op. cit.*, 19–35. The typification of identities is a central element in the sociological theory of Alfred Schutz, *Collected Papers*, Vols. I and II, Hague: Martinus Nijoff, 1962, 1964. The negotiation of identities, awareness contexts and other relevant concepts are discussed by Anselm Strauss in *Mirrors and Masks*, Free Press of Glencoe; and (with Barney Glaser), "Awareness Contexts and Social Interaction," *American Sociological Review*, 29 (October, 1964), 669–679.

boundary, a set of basic limitations, a unit of background expectancies that determine the sense that will be accorded to everything
within it.

These important ideas may be restated thus: Once the interactants have defined the game framework, they can interpret with
mutual understanding—or, as we shall show presently, when more
than one game is going on simultaneously, with complementary
and interlocking understanding—the meaning of the actions taking
place. Further, they can decide what behavior shall be included in
the attended sequence of events and what behavior may be excluded if it occurs.

Depending on the game in progress, the same event can have
different meanings. First, we may distinguish game-inclusive from
game-exclusive meanings. The former are events which, should they
occur, "count" (as it were) toward the outcome. Some events,
though they happen during the temporal period of a game and in
the presence of other players, are absolutely outside the frame of
reference of the game. They have the same status with respect to
games as accidents or unwarranted intrusions—they are present but
not accounted for.

Secondly, we may differentiate the several kinds of meaning
the same event may have, when it is counted in the game perspective. The meaning attached to a game-inclusive event—and,
incidentally, to a game-inclusive object as well—depends upon the
prior meanings that categories of events or objects have been assigned.
These prior meanings are established in tacit negotiation of the
game identity. Consider the possible meanings of a slip of the
tongue. In one kind of game, it may be seen as just the cue needed
by alter to uncover a much-sought fact; in another kind of game,
it might be a source of embarrassment; in still another game, it
might be taken as a humorous happening; finally, in a certain kind
of game, it might be seen as an indicator that an opponent is
weakening. Events are thus defined in a game-specific sense.

Just as events are defined in a game-specific sense, so *time* also
is perceived in relation to the game. In an encounter in which
definite goals are sought by the interactants, a notion of the beginning and end of the play is, in the typical case, shared. Thus in a
game of chess, players are constrained by the rules of the game to

regard it as ended when one player has placed the other's king in checkmate. Such an event can occur early or late in the course of the game; but regardless of the particular moment, that event constitutes the end of the game. After "checkmate," chess stratagems no longer count. The fact *that stratagems end upon mutual agreement is a crucial aspect of the trust accorded by players to one another.*[8] This is the case whether the game is chess, courtship, or war.

In addition to the understanding that there is a beginning and an end to game play, agreement also exists as to those periods allowed as "time out."[9] The latter is characterized by a mutually agreed suspension of the frame of reference negotiated at the outset of the game. Such a period may be characterized by a non-serious or irreverent attitude toward those very objects which in the period of game play were taken seriously and respectfully, or by activities having no relevance to the game at hand. Competitive courtship provides numerous illustrations, as for example, when rival suitors sit down to a cup of coffee and discuss trivial matters or matters entirely unrelated to their fierce rivalry for the same woman. Of course such "time out" periods are subject to subversion by the interactants, a situation occasioned when one or both opponents in a competitive game utilizes the "time out" for scoring points, preparing stratagems, strengthening forces, or striking in secret. "Time out" may provide the most strategic moment to poison an opponent's coffee.

The game itself may be conceived as consisting of a series of moves and countermoves. When the players are conscious of a game context for their behavior their own vocabulary may reflect this awareness, as when a spy confides to his assistant that "it is their move next."

When actors are aware that the behavior pattern in which they are involved is a game, they tend to have a sense of sequentiality about their own and their coparticipants' acts. For example, when

---

[8] The notion of trust is used here in accord with the one developed by Harold Garfinkel in "A Conception of and Experiments with 'Trust' as a Condition of Concerted Action," in *Motivation and Social Interaction*, edited by O. J. Harvey, N.Y.: Ronald Press, 1963, 187–238.

[9] For a discussion on this point, see Sherri Cavan, *Liquor License*, Chicago: Aldine Press, 1966, 9–12, 236–238.

one person seeks to find out information from another who desires to withhold that knowledge, their mutual acts appear as a series of covering and uncovering moves. Similarly when people are primarily interested in protecting their identities against spoilage, their acts are likely to take on the character of face-supporting and protective moves. Each move carries with it a host of strategies and counterstrategies, some of which are likely to go undetected by the players.

The game situation is a highly complex state of affairs. Its complexity lies precisely in the three kinds of contingencies inherent in goal-oriented behavior. The first involves the dynamics of game behavior itself. During the course of any game, the interactants will continually indicate by their behavior that they are in the game, out of the game permanently or temporarily, that they understand or do not understand that they are in a game, or that they are changing the nature of the game they are in. The communication concerning any of these states is transmitted in a variety of clues and cues—some obvious, other subtle; some recognized, others missed. That any player will know what is happening depends on his receptivity and perceptivity to ongoing behavior, and on past experience and its meaning to him in the game context.

Secondly, the complexity of interaction in game behavior arises from the paired mutuality or complementarity of symbolic interpretation. Thus to make but a single opening "move" of a game ego—call him John—must decide in what game he is participating, what game alter—call her Marsha—is playing, what game Marsha thinks John is playing, and what orientation John has toward his imputed interpretation of Marsha's and his own behavior. When third and fourth parties are added, the game becomes much more complicated. Complexity and causes for error in perception thus arise because of the very nature of human interaction, that is, the mutual mirror images and interpretation of the players.[10] By increasing the number of players (and thus of mirror images), complexity and potential misconceptions are enhanced.

[10] For an empirical test, see Sheldon Stryker, "Conditions of Accurate Role-Taking," in *Human Behavior and Social Processes*, edited by Arnold Rose, Boston: Houghton-Mifflin, 1962, 41–62.

Third, the interactants may be coparticipants in different games at the same time without confusion. For example, two scholars engaged in research on the same topic might meet and carry on a colloquy in which one seeks to maintain the "face" of both himself and the other, while the other seeks to establish a more secure relationship. The face-saving moves of the former may so interlock with the intimacy-creating moves of the latter that each will interpret the behavior of the other as complementary and co-ordinative, and both will end the encounter believing that the sought-after goals were achieved.[11] Thus, awareness by one player that the other is playing a different game does not necessarily result in confusion. Rather such a situation is more likely to produce conflict in which stratagems for controlling the situation or avoiding the unwanted outcome, and tactics of game-switching, are likely to ensue. Conflict, including deadly engagement, is usually carried on in a game context. Only when collective behavior of the type described under such headings as "extraordinary popular delusions"[12] or the "madness of crowds" occurs can we suggest that the game framework is fractured—and even then it may be only a partial fracture.[13]

Confusion and a state of anomie may arise when one inter-actant cannot fathom any meaning from the other's behavior and thus is left in a state of diffuse anxiety. Such a state is likely to occur when the interactants employ entirely different and mutually impenetrable universes of discourse and gesture. Examples of such

[11] There is a potentially proactive and serendipitous quality about such games which occurs when the players discuss the game at a later date and reveal to each other for the first time the conscious motives for their respective moves. They then discover that different but non-mutually exclusive goals were sought. At such discoveries each actor is likely to indicate his surprise by saying, in effect: "But I thought you were doing that to...." And the other is likely to say, "And to think that I thought you were...." And so on. An example of considerable interest is the relationship between "Agnes," a pseudo-intersexed person, and the physicians and sociologist interested in her problem. See Harold Garfinkel, "Passing and the Managed Achievement of Sex Status in an 'Intersexed' Person, Part I," and "Appendix," *Studies in Ethnomethodology, op. cit.*, 116–185, 285–288.

[12] Charles Mackay, *Extraordinary Popular Delusions and the Madness of Crowds*, Boston: Page and Co., 1932.

[13] See Herbert Blumer, "Collective Behavior," In *New Outline of the Principles of Sociology*, edited by Alfred McClung Lee, N.Y.: Barnes and Noble, 1946, 167–224; and Neil J. Smelser, *Theory of Collective Behavior*, N.Y.: The Free Press, 1962.

a condition are found in the autobiographical literature of travellers[14] and immigrants,[15] and in the accounts of persons held captive in a totally unfamiliar society.[16] A lesser state of anxiety, but of the same general type, sometimes occurs when persons of different ethnic, class, or status groups find themselves in situations where they must interact.[17] Even a state of anxiety, however, can lend itself to a game-strategic outlook as when a player determines that, whatever happens, he will not lose his composure,[18] or when he decides that his own anxiety is an element in a game the object of which is to confuse and demoralize.[19] Thus, for analytical purposes, the state of anomie must be regarded as but a potential element in a game situation.

A GAME TYPOLOGY

Although game situations are subject to abrupt or gradual shifts, and although one game may interpenetrate another, it is

[14] See, for example, Etsu Inagaki Sugimoto, *A Daughter of the Samurai*, Rutland, Vt.: Charles E. Tuttle, 1966.

[15] Numerous instances are reported in William Carlson Smith, *Americans in the Making*, N.Y.: Appleton-Century, 1939.

[16] An excellent example is *Equiano's Travels*, edited by Paul Edwards, N.Y.: Praeger, 1966, originally published in 1789, especially 30–31.

[17] A nice example involving race is related by the Negro poet M. Carl Holman, "The Afternoon of a Young Poet," in *Anger and Beyond*, edited by Herbert Hill, N.Y.: Harper and Row, 1966, 135–153. For numerous insights about social class in this respect, see W. Lloyd Warner and Paul S. Lunt, *The Status System of a Modern Community*, New Haven: Yale University Press, 1942. For a full-scale description of a game orientation between teacher and student involving the former's imagination of the embarrassment and anxiety he was causing the latter, see Willard Waller, *The Sociology of Teaching*, N.Y.: Wiley Science Editions, 1965, 326–332. A fictional account of mystification in what, in our terms, would be called an information and exploitation game, is brilliantly presented in Herman Melville, "Benito Cereno," *Great Short Works of Herman Melville*, N.Y.: Harper and Row, 1966, 182–259.

[18] This point is examined in detail in our essays, "Coolness in Everyday Life" and "Stage Fright and the Problem of Identity," which appear in this volume as chapters 6 and 7.

[19] The structure of Negro verbal contests provide many examples. See Roger D. Abrahams, *Deep Down in the Jungle*, Hatboro, Penn.: Folklore Associates, 1964, 41–64, 89–98.

possible to distinguish four game types: face games, relationship games, exploitation games, and information games.

For any concrete situation these games are functionally interdependent, empirically overlapping, but analytically distinct. Thus in any encounter it is possible to analyze behavior in terms of these four games. The game typology provides a framework by which an organized account of episodic social action may be produced.

Games may be distinguished according to the goals sought. In face games each participant maneuvers to maximize his own realization of a valued identity, while seeking an equilibrium that will permit others to do likewise. In relationship games, the participants seek to create, maintain, attenuate or terminate personal relations. In exploitation games, the participants seek to maximize their positions of power and influence vis-à-vis one another. In information games, the participants seek to conceal and uncover, respectively, certain kinds of knowledge. The goal orientations expressed here are designated in an abstract and general sense. In any concrete situation there would be a specific content and usually a sense of time and place attached to these goals.

Face games[20]

In face games two objectives, either singly or together, are sought. One may be described as *defensive*, in which a player seeks to protect his own identity against damage or spoilage; the other is *protective*, in which a player seeks to prevent any damage or spoilage to the identity of the other player(s). Often enough, activities undertaken on behalf of one of these goals require attendance to the effect of the other.

Face games, then, are those which involve preventing damage to one's own or another's identity or the salvaging of honor when it has been impugned. In the encounter where the face game is played, one may detect an *interchange* which (as Goffman suggests) has certain formal properties that indicate its beginning, playing

[20] This section leans heavily on Erving Goffman's "On Face Work," *Psychiatry*, 18 (August, 1955), 213–231.

time, and termination. There are at least two participants, and the acts or "moves" occur as a serialized taking of "turns." The game event—signaling that a face game is about to begin—is an occurrence that openly damages the identity of one of the persons. This occurrence can be initiated by the person damaged by the deed, or by another person. The event must be one that casts manifest doubt and negative evaluation upon the self that has been presented so far in the encounter. Thus a person may make a remark that is interpreted by others present to be beyond and beneath the character that he represents himself to be; he may indicate lack of motor skills or body control previously associated with his character; he may reveal incapacity to carry out tasks with which he has been previously identified; or he may give way to an emotional state which is regarded as unsuited to his general character.

But whether a face game will be initiated or not is always problematic. Several general considerations[21] will determine if an act is seen as untoward, and if a call or anticipated call for an account will be forthcoming—these being two conditions necessary for generating a face game.

To begin with, one or more of the participants in an encounter may be seeking *excitement*, which can easily be generated by "calling down" or "sounding" another. One may even fabricate another's wrongs and challenge him to an accounting—all for the sake of whipping up some "action." Thus, the youthful tough turns in anger on another accusing him (falsely) of bumping, of not watching where he is going, and demanding an apology. Should the innocent fail to respond apologetically, the situation for action (i.e., excitement) is generated. And insofar as one desires the increased excitement of a heated face game, hot action may be provided by challenging those persons in authority-endowed roles. For this kind of action, then, students can turn to the administration; inmates, to the staff; and juveniles, to the police.

If the players perceive an encounter as an opportunity or risk to gain or lose face, we have a second factor determining whether a

---

[21] In exploring these considerations, we are closely following the leads of Erving Goffman. See "Where the Action Is" in *Interaction Ritual*, Garden City, N.Y.: Anchor Books, 1967, especially 239–258.

face game will ensue. A certain kind of conduct on the part of the other might threaten or violate one's self-definition, sense of rightful place, or honor. Thus, an untoward action may be perceived not only as a breach of situational propriety, but also as an insult to the character of other participants in the situation. To spit on a person in a New York subway is not only a violation of a city ordinance, but also a violation of the victim's sense of honor. Typically, however, the challenge-to-honor act is more subdued. Through the slightest of cues—a look, a smile—a person tests the other's willingness to engage in moral combat, or decides whether the insult deserves notice as a character challenge.

A final feature influencing the initiation of a face game involves the restorative actions of those present in the encounter. Again, no more than a look or a word need be necessary to cue another that he must avoid or cease an activity lest he find himself in fateful moral combat. The very presence of others—witnesses before whom one wishes to enhance one's own face or destroy that of another— will affect whether an act is perceived as untoward, or worthy of initiating a character contest, or both.

In short, whether a face game will ensue depends on the *meaning* ascribed to various actions. This meaning in turn "derives in part from the orientation the player brings to them and the readings he retrospectively makes of them."[22]

In any case, the game itself is begun by a challenge, a "move" made immediately after the untoward event. One or more of the parties present calls attention to the offensive deed, designates the person responsible, and calls for an admission of responsibility or a statement or deed of exculpation. The challenge is one to the "face" (i.e., a valued element of the identity) of one of the participants. Response to the challenge may take the form of an offensive move against the challenger, or an offering of apology, explanation, or justification for the deed in question. When the offending party attacks the challenge itself or the challenger, the game is escalated to a counterattack on the "face" of the challenger. Such a counterattack must be responded to by withdrawal of the original challenge, accompanied either by appropriate face-saving statements, or by

[22] *Ibid.*, 244.

abject retreat (and, hence, loss of face by the challenger) or by a counter-challenge.

Here, however, we are concerned with the salvage of face; hence we shall deal with those instances in which the response consists of an *offering* by which the player in question hopes to restore the characterological *status quo ante*. Emphasis here may be placed either on the untoward event itself, as when a person challenged about an offensive story insists that it was "merely" a joke, or that it had no meaning with respect to persons present or those with whom they intimately identify;[23] or on the actor, as when our storyteller insists that he "must have been drunk," "didn't know what he was doing," or, in jest, claims to be a true representation of the reprehensible self exhibited by the telling of the story.

An alternative or supplementary strategy is compensation, penance and self-punishment. By these acts the offender, though unable to establish his innocence, indicates to his co-participants in the interchange that he is rehabilitated and ready to re-enter the group, if not as his old self, at least as one who has paid the penalty for his offensive deeds, and is thus cleansed of guilt and no longer required to feel shame. Moreover, he indicates by such acts that he is solicitous for the feelings and sensibilities of others, and that when—however unintentionally—he has injured someone or the entire group, he is willing to acknowledge fault and accept or even execute judgment on his untoward act.

When self-punishment is included, the actor signals to the others his calculation of the gravity of his offence and of the punishment appropriate to it, should it be taken seriously. Statements such as "I could kick myself," "I hate myself when I do things like that," and "I ought to be shot," express a layman's calculation of the punishment suitable to social crime[24]—for in the arena of face interaction, there are no crimes without victims.

[23] An example is the joke that slurs a racial group. In polite circles, it seems to be necessary to preface such a joke by an explanation or apology not only to the parties listening, but also, vicariously, to the offended racial group, whether any of its members are present or not.

[24] In very serious breaches, the individual may take the ultimate recourse of suicide in an effort to project a new and more favorable image of self. For a discussion along these lines, see Jack Douglas, *The Social Meanings of Suicide*, Princeton, N.J.: Princeton University Press, 1967, 284 ff.

Often enough, as the previous examples suggest, the offending party will overstate the punishment for his deed, and by such exaggerations invite the offended parties to assure him that "it wasn't that bad," and that "he shouldn't be so harsh with himself." By executing judgment and sentence on himself, the offender re-establishes the code of ritual which his deed has threatened, and indicates that he is a supporter of the code, as vigilant as his fellows concerning its violation, and is as willing to punish violators, including himself, as they are.

After the offering is made, the next move is up to the challengers and their allies. If face is to be restored, they must accept the offering and indicate that equilibrium is re-established. As suggested in the discussion of the offering above, the offender can so phrase his move of apology, penance and punishment as to strongly invite acceptance. On the other hand, dramatic failures here can lose the game as well. If an offender so overstates the crime and exaggerates the penalty that the others regard his entire performance as flippant, they may refuse his offer and even call for an account of that offer. Understatement may also indicate lack of interest in social crimes and sensibilities and thus invite rejection. But if conflict is to be avoided, or a permanent rupture in the relationship is undesirable. then even a rather unseemly offering may have to be accepted.

The terminating move of the game is an acknowledgment of gratitude by the offending party that he has been readmitted to his circle without any permanent loss. This move itself is fraught with delicate aspects that may upset the play and shift it back to the challenge-offering stage. Thus, the offender may not believe that his offer has been fully accepted and instead of ending the game continue to make offerings, adding penances and punishment and calling for further acceptance. This move may indeed have positive payoffs, since it can be taken as a sign of sincerity, a true expression of the state of mind of the contrite sinner against social conduct. A repetition of this offering, however, may also be overdone and signal insincerity, false contriteness, and a desire for social intimacy that overrides propriety. Persons who habitually apologize too much run the risk of exclusion from social circles, since their demand for face is greater than the available supply.

Once the gratitude phase is passed, the game is concluded and re-opening it constitutes a breach of the social etiquette by which it was played. Such breaches are themselves sources of loss of face which may not be granted salvage, as when, after the sign of gratitude has been given, one party continues the challenge. It is customary for the latter party to be cut off with a peremptory, "The incident is closed!" (Such a response requires retreat or apology.) The face game is thus an episode that usually interrupts ongoing social intercourse until face has been restored or one party has suffered a loss.

In addition to these elementary forms of face games, certain additional characteristics deserve comment. First, as suggested earlier, face games may be prevented by the process of *avoidance*. When one's face is likely to be challenged, one can avoid those contacts from whom a challenge is likely to arise. Delicate negotiations can be handled by go-betweens who, because of their neutrality, can conduct matters with impunity. Further, when an untoward act does occur on the part of the actor or his fellow participants, one or all can disassociate themselves from the deed, thus discounting it from the engagement.[25] Persons, moreover, who are well-known to one another count it as an index of their mutual knowledge that they know what topics to avoid and what information to keep secret; persons who are strangers employ tact and discretion until they have mapped out the safe social areas.

Second, the elementary forms of the face game do not absolutely define who will be the initiators and who the respondents. An offender may challenge himself immediately after the untoward act and thus monopolize the roles of accuser, judge, defendant, penitent, and guilty party, leaving the others to accept or reject his accusation or offering. Or other parties may assume the role of protector for the offender responding to the challenge, by explanations or apologies and also indicating gratitude when their offering

[25] The problem of managing studied non-observance of one's own violations of social rules deserves more attention. One obvious element is that studied non-observance is itself noticeable by others, and thus requires them to studiously non-observe not only the untoward deed but also the offender's studied non-observance of it, if interaction is to proceed smoothly. See the discussion of this and related phenomena in Erving Goffman, *The Presentation of Self in Everyday Life*, Garden City, N.Y.: Anchor Books, 1957, 233–237.

is accepted. The offending party, then, can be simply an object in a face game in which others have stakes in saving his face. In still another type of situation the offender or others can be subordinate allies to whomever is making the challenge or offering. In short, the face game offers unusual opportunities for an individual to employ multiple roles and role-switching as devices to secure his goals.

Finally, face games may be undertaken as part of a larger strategy of exploitation. Persons may pose a threat of loss of face to themselves to achieve certain gains that may thus be obtained. Here the goals sought are praise and favorable identifications for oneself, or the social downfall of another. The former is illustrated by the person who employs a strategy of self-derogation as a means of gaining greater acceptance; the latter, by the person who commits suicide leaving behind a note indicating that a certain party has forced him into this ultimate act and thus is irrevocably guilty.[26] In conclusion, face games may be undertaken for their own value, or for the payoffs they have in the context of wider strategies in other games.

Relationship games

In relationship games the interactants have one or two aims: to decrease or increase social distance. When one of the interactants undertakes a line of action to achieve a greater intimacy, he initiates a *positive* relationship game; when one of the interactants wishes to attenuate or terminate an over-intimate relationship, he initiates a *negative* relationship game. In either case the game consists of managing a presentation of self so as to suggest the desired outcome. Since the other player may not share the perspective of the first, this presentation is subject to checks and countermoves as well as supports.

Positive relationship games. In all societies individuals feel constrained to act more or less intimately with their fellows. Industrial societies with their emphasis on universalistic criteria and

---

[26] See Douglas, *op. cit.*, 310–319.

achievement orientations still find a place for intimacy in friendship cliques and the neolocal kinship system.[27] The problem for individuals involved in intimacy struggles is how to achieve the desired degree of social and personal proximity without suffering material or moral losses. The typical arenas of action for such games are situations of courtship, and incipient or established friendship groups, though other arenas can certainly be found.

In contrast to the face game in which actors cooperate to maintain character equilibrium and allow no one to lose face, the positive relationship game involves at least one actor seeking to maximize one aspect of character above and beyond that of mere face. That aspect has to do with the *quality* of the interpersonal relationship, a quality that he wishes to deepen and enrich to such an extent the object of his attentions will feel a sense of loss if faced with total estrangement. The ultimate sense of this deepened relationship is love, especially as that term is defined and experienced in the Western world and when prefixed by the elusive but powerful element of romanticism.[28]

Strong relationships, however, do not necessarily demand a deep sense of intimacy. As Simmel has observed,[29] modern societies have a tendency toward social differentiation that leads to the isolation of activities involving intimacy from those requiring reserve and formality. Building relationships often implicitly calls

[27] Talcott Parsons has observed that in what he calls the "universalistic-achievement pattern": "There is also room for an ecological system of diffuse affective attachments. These are exceedingly prominent in the cross-sex relationships of the 'dating' period with the attendant romantic love complex, but tend to be absorbed into the kinship unit by marriage. Intrasex friendship as diffuse attachment is much less prominent, probably because it can too readily divert from the achievement complex. Among men it tends rather to be attached as a diffuse 'penumbra' to occupational relationships in the form of an obligation in a mild way to treat one's occupational associate as a friend also." *The Social System*, Glencoe: The Free Press, 1951, 189.

[28] For relevant discussions on this point, see Ernest van den Haag, "Love or Marriage," in *The Family*, edited by Rose Laub Coser, N.Y.: St. Martin's Press, 1964, 192–202; Peter Blau, *Exchange and Power in Social Life*, N.Y.: Wiley, 1964, 76–87; and William J. Goode, "The Theoretical Importance of Love," *American Sociological Review*, 24 (1959), 38–47.

[29] Georg Simmel, "Friendship, Love and Secrecy," *American Journal of Sociology*, 11 (1906), 457–466, and reprinted in *The Substance of Sociology*, edited by Ephraim H. Mizruchi, N.Y.: Appleton-Century-Crofts, 1967, 128–134.

for an inhibition of activities and sentiments that threaten to overstep the boundaries of the limited relationship. Thus a reciprocal recognition of and respect for one another's secret areas of action and thought may be the tacit cause for and consequence of a successful relationship. Relation building may depend on a silent promise to respect those secrets one does not know in return for the receipt of intimacies one does not now have.

Relation building constitutes a mutual and deepening reciprocal escalation of trust and commitment. But in modern societies—characterized by formal arrangements, fleeting acquaintances, and fractured sociations—one finds a basic distrust of the informal and the intimate. In their everyday lives persons are on guard against unwarranted affection, excessive cordiality, and ingenuous intimacy. The American argot indicates the degree of distrust of intimacy by the numerous pejorative terms referring to its various forms: "gold digger," "lover boy," "phony," "con man," and so on. Indeed, the language of altruism and love is so susceptible to derogatory connotations that individuals and categories of persons who live in especially untrustworthy environments (e.g., Negroes and youth) find it necessary to invent new terms or redefine old ones when the formally acceptable terms have lost all but their derogatory meaning. Thus "tough" comes to mean "fine," "crazy" to mean "worthwhile," and "bad" to mean "good." Building intimate relationships in such societies requires steering a course toward affectionate mutuality while always avoiding the Scylla of privacy invasion and the Charybdis of exploitation.

Enhanced intimacy has a value that is determined in its specific sense in great measure by the interactants themselves.[30] The scale of value, however, is a function of scarcity and allocation in the relational as well as the cash nexus. In courtship, for example, a girl's attractiveness to a man is a function of the relative scarcity of salable and normatively defined feminine characteristics.[31] However, the girl herself modifies her value if she bestows emotional or sexual gratification too soon or too late. Thus, in romantic love

---

[30] See Blau, *op. cit.*, 76–85.

[31] See Kingsley Davis, "Intermarriage in Caste Societies," *American Anthropologist*, 43 (July–September, 1941), 388–395.

societies such as the United States, a girl may lose the man she desires either by giving in too quickly, or not at all, to his requests for increased intimacy. A successful courtship—and, *mutatis mutandis*, successful relation building in general—consists of a series of turns in which each interactant engages in activities vis-à-vis the other which provide some enhancement of rewards, indicate an increasing degree of commitment, and promise both further rewards and greater commitment for each response in kind. For lovers the game is over when each indicates to the other an exclusive commitment and a monopoly on sexual possession,[32] or when they break off the relationship. For friends, the game is over when each indicates to the other that he is willing to meet the obligations of friendship to the other without requiring further proof of friendship by immediate rewards in kind.

Placed in its game framework the moves in a positive relationship game consist of the *introduction*, the *invitation*, and the *acceptance*. Whenever two persons are physically copresent they become eligible for mutual social identification. Introductions in the restricted and formal sense of the word provide ready-made mechanisms for reciprocal discovery, for very often a third party who knows both persons will present each to the other providing an identity that either might accept, reject, or modify as the occasion unfolds. However it occurs—whether formal or not, by self-introduction or third parties—an identity must be provided for a relationship to ensue. The question for any set of actors who are physically copresent but unknown to one another is, Which identity to present? Since individuals possess a repertoire of identities any of which has an unknown value for a particular set of others, the introduction constitutes a test of viable identities. It is unsafe to reveal the entire set of identities at once, so actors typically present one identity—and a relatively innocuous one at that, in the very first instance—to see how acceptable it is. The choice of identity is made by taking a reading of the cues and clues given and given off by alter and determining which identity is most suitable.

---

[32] Blau, *op. cit.*, 82, provides a typical sequence of moves in such a game: "The girl lets the boy kiss her, he takes her to the 'prom,' she permits some sex play, he ceases to date others, so does she, and he ultimately gives her the ring that formalizes their relation. . . ."

The introduction consists not only of an identity disclosure, but also of an unstated request for alter to invite further disclosures. These will be forthcoming only if the identities uncovered are shown to be gratifying to and worthy of reward by alter. Ultimately, the person making the opening move would like to find out if his secret and less-conventional identities are acceptable to the other. However, precisely because these identities are potentially discrediting, no actor will intentionally introduce them first if he truly desires to build up a relationship with someone who is a stranger. The introductory move is then a tentative exploration of the other person's receptivity to one's identities. If the exploration is promising it will be continued, although tentativeness coupled with awareness will mark the relationship until enough discoveries have allayed suspicion.

In those cultures where people who do not know one another hold themselves in reserve and regard one another with suspicion, the first encounter with a stranger is likely to terminate with only a tentative degree of commitment and trust. In the United States, for example, folk wisdom about "first impressions" warns people not to take their initial reading of one another as necessarily correct. Those who seem hostile or indifferent may turn out to be warm and loving; those who are open and friendly may be concealing ulterior motives. Where impression management is cultivated as an art or science, those who would make friends and influence people are on guard against their competitors.

Thus the introduction, or first move, is likely to be repeated several times, testing different identities and seeking to determine whether the totality of identities making up the person is acceptable.[33] In each introductory move, John may seek to present for Marsha's acceptance more of the identities making up his total personality. Each identity revelation poses a dilemma. On the one hand, John risks the termination of the relationship with each new unveiling of an identity; on the other, to leave the "total self" unrevealed is discomforting since it implicitly involves a special kind of "passing"—namely, presenting oneself not as something one is

[33] The following analysis draws on George J. McCall and J. L. Simmons, *Identities and Interactions*, N.Y.: The Free Press, 1966, 185–186.

not, but rather as not being something one in fact is. Furthermore, non-disclosure risks the possibility that Marsha will unmask John without his cooperation or consent.

Following the introduction, Marsha is in a position to issue an *invitation*. The invitational move is one that indicates to John that the identity he has presented is acceptable, gratifying and worthy of reward. Moreover, it invites John to disclose more, and tentatively signifies that these future disclosures may also be accepted and rewarded. The invitational move typically includes an introduction by Marsha of herself, an introduction that presents an identity that is complementary and supportive to that presented by John.

The next move is the *acceptance*. Once Marsha has indicated some reciprocity of identification, John is placed in the position of continuing the relational development, disclosing more about himself and in turn requesting another invitation, or terminating the encounter with a sign that the degree of involvement already sustained is as much as he wishes to carry. Typically, an invitation calls for more than an introducer wishes to bring to the actual occasion. Therefore, the strategy for John is to convey a sign that he is still interested in Marsha and wishes to receive a further invitation, but not to disclose all that is requested.[34]

In relationship games each encounter involves introduction, invitations, and acceptance. There is a dialectic to these moves, since each contains elements of the other and seeks to evoke the appropriate sequential response. A relationship itself is established completely after several of these encounters, when the interactants have mutually reached the limits of their "strain toward totality" and reciprocally regard one another as persons whom they know "fully" and for whom they have sincere affection, deep trust, and broad commitment.

Negative relationship games. Society is characterized as much by the breaking as by the building of relationships. Once a relationship has been established, one or both of the parties may wish to

---

[34] Albert K. Cohen provides a similar interaction model in discussing the formation of the delinquent gang. See his *Delinquent Boys*, N.Y.: Free Press, 1955, 60–61.

reduce its intensity or end it altogether. Since intimate relationships are based upon commitment and trust, the most overt form of breaking off is denial of commitment and betrayal of trust.

A betrayal of trust indicates to the betrayed party that fundamental and intrinsic elements of the intimate relationship no longer occupy their quasi-sacred place, that any future activities with the betrayer ought to be governed by at least that degree of formality and reserve accorded to a stranger and, more likely—since there had existed a condition of trust—that the betrayer ought to be regarded with suspicion.

A very common betrayal of trust is the disclosure of secrets. Secrecy is a basic ingredient of intimacy, and indeed those aspects of life that are secretly shared by an intimate group constitute the core of the intimacy itself. This is true not only for dyadic groups, such as lovers and married couples, but also of larger intimate groups such as social fraternities and other secret societies for whom disclosure of secrets constitutes an irreparable breach.[35] Betrayal has its own fascination, as Simmel has noted, but its specific consequence is to end intimacy itself, insofar as that state of relationship is conditioned by confidence.

The "moves" in such a betrayal might be as follows: John reveals to Dick a confidence previously shared only by John and Marsha; Dick indicates to Marsha that he is aware of the once closely-guarded secret; Marsha confronts John with his betrayal; John can give no adequate account for his breach of trust; Marsha decides to break off intimate association with John. Of course there are many possible variations in this sequence. The crucial elements are John's betrayal, Marsha's discovery of John's treachery, Marsha's confrontation of John, John's inability to fend off the accusation of betrayal, and Marsha's subsequent dissociation with John.

Note that betrayal constitutes a prevalent danger precisely

---

[35] See Georg Simmel, "The Secret and the Secret Society," in *The Sociology of Georg Simmel*, edited by Kurt Wolff, Glencoe: The Free Press, 1950, 307–378, especially 324–333 and 345–349. For a discussion of the relative importance of ritual secrets to different kinds of secret societies, see Stanford M. Lyman, "Chinese Secret Societies in the Occident," *Canadian Review of Sociology and Anthropology*, 1 (1964), 79–102.

because intimates reveal secrets to one another or share clandestine activities as a mechanism by which they obtain enhanced commitment to one another. One tacit assumption of this sharing of secrets is that the hearer will not blackmail the teller. When an intimate uses the threat of revealing knowledge obtained through intimate association as a means for exacting further rewards from his confidant, the nature of the relationship is shifted onto a new plane combining the elements of exploitation and concealment. Thus one opening move in a relation-destroying game is the threat to disclose the secrets that united the intimate group. Even if the threat is idle, the others will be on their guard against the potential traitor in their midst. They might respond by closing off the sources of his information or by ostracizing him. Either is sufficient to attenuate what was once an intimate situation.

Betrayals of trust may go beyond the disclosure of secrets to include "the enclosure in involuntary institutional networks." The meaning of this phrase will now be made clear. An intimate association usually requires involvement in a wider social network than the intimates themselves.[36] For friends there are one another's friends and kin; for the married there are the "relatives." Our point here is that a betrayal of trust can be engendered by forcibly requiring extra-curricular social relations to exist as a price of the intimate ones. When this occurs as an unstated or post hoc incident of an established relationship—as when a husband requires that his wife share their home with his mother—a challenge is hurled to the original relationship. In effect one party invites the other to accept an unwarranted situation in return for continuing the relationship. The offended party is in a position to respond to the challenge directly by offering a choice: "Either me or your mother, not both." The challenger must then choose, or seek to effect a compromise.

The very presence of social networks poses a threat to intimacy and introduces jealousy as a potential element in every intimate social arrangement.[37] Incumbents of network statuses are thus eligible for accusations of trespass and subversion. Such accusations

---

[36] See Marvin B. Sussman and Lee G. Burchinal, "Kin Family Network," *Marriage and Family Living*, 24 (August, 1952), 231–240.

[37] See Kingsley Davis, *Human Society*, N.Y.: Macmillan, 175–193.

constitute an ever-present opening move in a strategy designed to cool or terminate a relationship. When friends are cast in the role of seducers, the accuser presents himself in an image not likely to invite further intimacy.

Beyond jealousy is uninvited benevolence. Thus a wife may act as the "conspiratorial" agent arranging for her husband's visit to a dentist, physician, psychiatrist, or priest. In this role, she invites distrust and derogation since such visits are often first steps in a process of pejorative labelling or a subsequent degradation ceremony.[38] Indeed, as Goffman has observed, the benevolent activities undertaken by kin or friends in behalf of health or welfare can leave the beneficiary in a state of abandonment and with a feeling of betrayal.[39] This is especially the case if treatment requires hospitalization or commitment to an asylum. Thus, an opening and often unintentional move in terminating a relationship is one that introduces the other to the possibility of a negative redefinition of himself. Persons who, however well-intentioned, invite others to participate in their own degradation ceremonies, or who arrange for them without the other's consent are likely to find that they are redefined in the process as well.

Primary relations may also be attenuated or ended by a process related to betrayal, namely, denial of commitment. Here one partner in an intimate relationship, say, a boyfriend, indicates to his girlfriend that she no longer holds the high place she once did in his affection. For those engaged in dating the simplest method is to cease "going steady" and to resume dating a number of persons. One can often indicate this shift in commitment silently and out of the audial or visual presence of the other by arranging to be reported in a situation that communicates the desired message. Thus a boy wishing to break off with his steady girl may walk hand in hand with another girl past the "steady" girl's house, or ask another girl to the "prom," or manage to commit an indiscretion in such a manner that it will be communicated and interpreted as a terminating deed.

[38] The term is borrowed from Harold Garfinkel, "Conditions of Successful Degradation Ceremonies," *American Journal of Sociology*, 61 (March, 1956), 420–424.

[39] See Erving Goffman, *Asylums*, Garden City, N.Y.: Doubleday Anchor, 1961, 136–141.

Shifting commitments need not be loaded on to another person—an object or a status may do as well. Consider the case of Gauguin who announced his termination of marriage and family life by abruptly sailing to Tahiti and devoting his life to painting. Indeed, the proper allocation of energies to wife or career is apparently a common enough dilemma to be a source for popular fiction. A husband may make the opening move in a sequence that leads to divorce by staying late at his office every night. Friendships may also be terminated by excessive zeal in one's career. In general, intimate relations are vulnerable to the re-sorting of allocative priorities on the part of the members, a re-sorting that may move the once deeply appreciated friendship to an intermittent acquaintanceship or off the agenda of activities entirely.

Viewed as an episodic occurrence, a negative relationship game has three basic moves—*the opening-terminating gambit, the supportive response,* and *the acceptance of termination.* The opening-terminating move is usually a challenge flung at an actor who has done something that the challenger defines as relation-breaking. A husband may be confronted with evidence of his philandering; a boyfriend accused of dating others; a friend's excuse for refusing an invitation proven to be false. In other words, from among the welter of life's events, one event is picked out by a challenger, interpreted as a betrayal of trust or a denial of commitment and offered to the offending party for action. The challenged in turn must ratify the challenger's interpretation, or offer an account (i.e., an excuse or justification) for the untoward deed.

The challenged party may respond with any of several tactics in response. In a cooperative effort he may undertake a line of action indicating to the challenger that he has indeed done exactly what he has been accused of doing and deserves to be treated accordingly. Such an effort may be observed when the parties have independently reached the decision to break off and are in need of a legitimating reason to do so. Thus husbands and wives in an "empty shell"[40] marriage may leap at the opportunity provided by an untoward act by one of them to end a tasteless marriage. Another

[40] William J. Goode, *The Family*, Englewood Cliffs, N.J.: Prentice Hall, 1964, 92.

common situation in which the cooperative response emerges is when a condition of "pretense awareness"[41] underlies an intimate relationship; that is, both interactants are fully aware of the reason for ending a relationship but pretend not to be. Such a situation may be found, for example, when a man discovers that the woman he loves has a terminal disease, or when lovers are unable to disentangle themselves from marriages to other persons, or when one partner's ardor has cooled, while the other's has not—in each case, the incident chosen for the challenge may provide precisely the right excuse for breaking off when the actual reason cannot be broached. A "staged" quarrel may legitimate the mutually desired break.

In some cases, however, a challenge is not forthcoming even when anticipated. A husband's careful planting of a lipstick-stained handkerchief in his lapel may go unnoticed by his wife or she may simply laugh it off; or his announcement that he loves another may be disbelieved or disattended. Untoward events may be excused in advance by the potential challenger. Preserving the relationship may be so important to the offendable party that she overlooks failings, saves her partner's face, and refuses to become perturbed when relation-negating events occur. When one party wishes to break off a relation and the other does not, the former may have to commit several acts of trust defiance or commitment withdrawal before his deeds are accepted for their relation-breaking value.

In a conflict response, the challenged party may refuse to accept the construction put upon his deed, deny it occurred, or make excuses and apologies for his behavior. Such a response, if accepted, terminates the relation-breaking game. However, a challenger need not accept the accused's interpretation; he may insist on the original interpretation, and even escalate the vehemence of the colloquy or the seriousness of the charges. Just as one party may so desire to end a relationship that he commits deeds likely to bring about challenges, so a challenger may be so interested in the rectitude of her position or the opportunity of ending the relationship that no excuse or apology is acceptable.

The acceptance move is one in which the challenger commits

[41] See Barney Glaser and Anselm Strauss, "Awareness Contexts and Social Interaction," *op. cit.*

herself to the relation-breaking interpretation put upon her original challenge and acknowledged by the offender. When a husband admits to philandering and suggests getting a divorce, a wife may respond by calling her attorney and beginning discussions of property settlements. When a boy tells his steady girlfriend that she is not his date for the prom, she may reply that she already has another date. When one room-mate accuses the other of eating more than his share of the communal food supply, the accused party may pack his belongings and move out.

Of course some challengers will be opposed to the ultimate interpretation of their original challenge. If the challenger expected apology and contriteness but not termination of the relationship, she may pull back at the last minute, begin to soften the charges, advance excuses for the other's untoward deeds, engage in a conciliatory *mea culpa*, and in other ways seek to forestall the final break. Such a situation poses a problem for the accused who wishes his untoward deed to have a terminating effect. He must put off these conciliatory moves, insist on the reprehensible (but perhaps justified) interpretation of his deeds, and not acknowledge a shared responsibility.

Exploitation games

In an exploitation game one actor or group seeks to gain compliance from another actor or group. In such a game a line of action is undertaken in order to get another to do or believe something that the would-be exploiter cannot predict in advance will follow from his request. Exploitation games occur on the brink of power relationships;[42] that is, one actor hopes to obtain "imperative control"[43] over another but is not absolutely sure he can do so. In

[42] Power here is defined in Weber's sense as "the probability that one actor within a social relationship will be in a position to carry out his own will despite resistance, regardless of the basis on which this probability rests." Max Weber, *The Theory of Social and Economic Organization*, Glencoe: The Free Press, 1947, 152.

[43] Again, following Weber, *loc. cit.*, we refer here to "the probability that a command with a given specific content will be obeyed by a given group of persons."

such a situation the actor seeking compliance from another will counteract his moves by direct and deflecting maneuvers.

An exploitation game begins with one actor attempting to establish a frame of meaning from which compliance to his wishes is a "natural" or "normal" consequence. His attempt may be countermanded by a contradictory or different frame of meaning introduced by the potential exploitee. Or the latter may accept the general structure of meaning introduced by the would-be exploiter, but redefine its specific elements, modify its "infrastructure," so to speak. The next move is that of the exploiter-to-be who must either insist on his original definition, try another that also has positive payoffs for himself, or utilize elements of his opponent's presentation for their own exploitative value. Thus, an exploitation game is often "phased." One frame of meaning is introduced but quickly thwarted; the original thrust is insisted on, or a new one is tried, and it too is thwarted; a third thrust, parry, and so on. The game is over when the would-be exploiter has triumphed over his adversary who has succumbed to the former's will; when the intended victim has avoided or evaded the compliance frame into which he might have been cast; or when there is a stand-off, a breaking up of the engagement with an apparent promise or hint that the game may be resumed later, perhaps with one or both antagonists better prepared.

The general strategies employed for such a game are variants of the reward-punishment dichotomy. A person may comply with another's wishes if he is rewarded for doing so or threatened for not so doing. The reward-punishment technique may be applied before, during, or after the desired behavior is manifested. Thus John, wishing Marsha to do "X," may reward her first and tell her that "X" is expected as a return favor in exchange; or he may reward her after a pattern of punishment. (Various other possibilities suggest themselves.) The temporal dimension of the reward-punishment mechanism is usually an interplay of three factors: the specific situation where compliance is a feature, the norms of permissibility and constraint governing that situation, and the temporal efficacy of the rewards and punishments.

The method of obtaining compliance is usually an appeal

either to situational or motivational aspects of another's identity.[44] An appeal to the situational employs references to the target person's specific "external" environment—his job, his neighborhood, his family. An appeal to the motivational employs reference to the "internal" state of the target person—his motives, commitments, and feelings. Each of these general types of appeals has reward-punishment variants which are adopted in accordance with tactics. Thus, an appeal along the situational dimension may promise to grant, say, a job promotion—a positive thrust—if compliance is forthcoming; or it may promise to withhold that promotion, or direct a demotion—a negative thrust—if it is not. In an appeal along the motivational dimension, a would-be exploiter may reward the target person by pointing up how good he will feel if he complies, or how bad he will feel if he does not.

The situational appeal has other features that turn out to be tactful weapons in any exploitative encounter. Compliance may be "explained" as necessary not because of its effects on the person asking for it, but because of its general consequence and meaning for the relationship. Thus, Marsha may point out to John that he must refrain from sexual intercourse with her because he is a cousin. In a counteractive response, however, John might indicate to Marsha that he is in an exchange relationship with her: he has paid for the theater and the dinner and therefore she owes him a debt of gratitude, which can only be paid off in bed.

Note that in this example we see several features of the exploitation game simultaneously operating. To begin with, two exploitation games are going on at the same time. In one, Marsha is seeking to get John to refrain from sexual intercourse; in the second, John is seeking to make Marsha yield. Moreover, two "situations" are available to which the respective parties may appeal. Marsha appeals to the universal aspects of their relationship; John appeals to the particular conditions of the same relationship. Most importantly, each party is engaged in the negotiation of identities suitable

[44] For the following we lean heavily on Talcott Parsons, "On the Concept of Influence," *Sociological Theory and Modern Society*, N.Y.: The Free Press, 1967, 355–382. See also the analytic treatment of Parsons' schema in Gerald Marwell and David R. Schmitt, "Dimensions of Compliance-Gaining Behavior," *Sociometry*, 30 (December, 1967), 350–364, especially 352–358.

to the play of the game: Marsha defines John as a relative and ineligible as a sexual partner; John defines their relationship as one of that between a creditor and a debtor. The moves in an exploitation game, then, reflect the underlying negotiation of identities, as well as definitions of the situation.

Further, we may note that another tactic available to a player is to shift at the right moment from a situation-oriented to an identity-oriented appeal. This tactic is employable by either or both players and may be used at just the right moment to overcome an opponent when victory appears to be in the latter's grasp. Thus, a young lady, having exhausted all situational defenses against sleeping with her hot-blooded boyfriend, may introduce her religion—a heretofore unrevealed identity—as a final bar to his demands. Religious as well as other identities, in this sense, may be kept in reserve in order to be available as a final trump card playable at precisely the right moment.[45] In this respect we may note the "softness-hardness" hierarchy of identities: those that are "soft" being new, shortlived, or situationally specific; those that are "hard" being old, permanent, and trans-situational. In general the ascribed characteristics of a person are "hard" while the achieved characteristics border on "softness." Thus, in any competitive win-lose, or zero-sum game, the invocation of a "hard" identity is likely to be a tactically effective move, since it is much more difficult to be dislodged from a permanent identity with its attendant rules and limitations than it is from a "softer" one.

To sum up then, the model play of an exploitation game in which John seeks to get Marsha to do "X" looks like this:

John will open the game by a positive or negative thrust appealing either to the situational or motivational aspects of Marsha's condition, or to both. In a positive situational thrust John will appeal to Marsha's situational needs and the advantages accruing from compliance; in a positive motivational thrust John will engage in a construction of Marsha's feelings indicating that Marsha will "feel" better, or have an integrated sense of self, or a feeling of emotional well-being if she complies. In a negative

[45] See Jessie Bernard, *The Sex Game*, Englewood Cliffs, N.J.: Prentice Hall, 1968, 194–195.

situational thrust John will warn Marsha of the threat to her status, career, or security should she refuse to comply; in a negative motivational appeal John recasts Marsh'a personal identity in such a manner that Marsha is made to feel bad, or is shown that she will feel bad should she not comply.

Marsha may frustrate John's strategy by rejecting the construction put by him on either self or situation. Marsha may switch from a situational to an identificational reply; may readjust the definition of self or situation so as to make compliance unnecessary or irrelevant; or may invoke a condition of self or situation which ranks higher in terms of moral investment or commitment.

John in turn may reply by disputing any of the constructions which Marsha has employed; he may invoke still another "ranking" construction, or insist with new argument or enhanced vehemence on his original construction of the situation

Information games [46]

Information games arise whenever one actor wishes to uncover information from another who wishes to conceal it. In one sense information games overlap all others because knowledge of others is a prerequisite to social life, and individuals rarely convey openly the kind or amount of knowledge "required" by their fellows. All men are placed in positions of information control and concealment when they present themselves on any particular social scene, for by its very nature any social scene is habitable only by a few of the identities which make up the total "personality." The unwelcome identities will have to be inhibited or hidden. This becomes a problem for the actors on the scene when one of the unpresented identities is thought to be under scrutiny by another person. Moreover, some persons and categories of persons must play information games almost all the time, or as part of their occupations. Among the former are all those possessing discreditable identities;[47] among the latter, all those charged with

---

[46] For a fuller statement on information games as well as an empirical application, see Marvin B. Scott, *The Racing Game*, Chicago: Aldine Press, 1968.
[47] Erving Goffman, *Stigma*, Englewood Cliffs, N.J.: Prentice Hall, 1963, 41–104.

keeping institutionalized secrets. Presumably those who are regular players in information games are more adept at it or conscious of the exigencies than occasional players and amateurs. Thus Negroes,[48] thoroughbred horse trainers,[49] and homosexuals[50] share in common the continued use of stratagems by which they respectively "put on" white folks, deceive race track bettors, and pass as "straight."

An information game may be said to be underway when an actor perceives that information he wishes to keep secret is being sought. Once the game has been perceived, the sequence of moves that takes place are *control* moves, *covering* moves, *uncovering* moves, and *re-covering* moves.[51] Although these moves may be planned and executed in advance as part of a total strategy to deceive the person seeking information, each move is itself modified by physical and environmental limitations, normative constraints, and personal and idiosyncratic desires. Thus gathering, managing, and concealing information are bounded by social rules and personal wishes.

In the preliminary, or control, moves, the seeker of information tries to discover the regular behavior patterns, preferred activities, normative constraints, and secret activities of the information concealer. The seeker then is in a position to judge the meaning of the concealer's acts, having gleaned clues from his seemingly non-informative behavior.

Once the concealer is aware that his actions are under scrutiny, he mobilizes informational vigilance in a series of covering moves. He will attempt to limit the information state of the seeker by sealing off certain arenas of action and information and by opening up others.

Sealing off is a process created in part by the compartmentalized arenas of action available to most social actors whereby they can secretively carry on activities that have relevance in later public displays. Backstage preparatory areas are typically closed to front

---

[48] See Richard Wright, "The Psychological Reactions of Oppressed People," in *White Man Listen!*, Garden City, N.Y.: Doubleday Anchor, 1964, 17–18.

[49] Scott, *op. cit.*, chapter 4.

[50] Gordon Westwood, *A Minority*, London: Longmans, Green and Co., 1964.

[51] For a full discussion of these terms, see Goffman, "Communications and Strategic Interaction," *op. cit.*

stage audiences. In their most direct and simple usage these backstage areas are undisguised and would reveal what actually is the case, but these areas are closed to outsiders. Thus members of the audience are not permitted in the dressing rooms before a theater performance, bettors are not permitted to prowl around the shed area and backstretch of the race track, and guests are not usually invited to the back bedrooms at a cocktail party. "Open privacy" in backstage areas provides an arena of action where possessors of secret information may relax their guard without fear of revealing that which ought to remain undisclosed. The balding actress can remove her wig without fear of embarrassment, the trainer can discuss the horse's winning chances openly with the exercise boy, and the housewife can leave the beds unmade with impunity.

However, an adroit concealer might attempt to foil a seeker by revealing information seemingly valuable but in fact irrelevant or misleading. Such a tactic may involve opening the supposedly-private backstage area to inspection but in fact contriving the situation so that a false impression is given. Thus a housewife might allow guests to wander into the back bedroom where beds and furniture are neatly arranged to give the impression of a house that is everywhere tidy. A "passing" homosexual might invite someone who suspects his true identity to his bedroom where a seemingly casual and careless display of pictures of female nudes and his baseball cap and glove convey a contradictory definition. And a suspected Communist might stock his library shelves with books in praise of capitalism and business, so that police and other snoopers "find" evidence which contradicts their suspicions.

Concealing and revealing involve more than management of ecological niches. They include what one conceals or reveals by personal behavior. Thus in controlling information an actor will attempt to manage not only the physical environment, but also expressive and idiomatic behavior. Since seekers of information are likely to be watching quite carefully for clues to what they wish to know, adroit concealers attempt to manage not only their direct actions but also their seemingly accidental and casual activities as well. When activities must be undertaken in the presence of those from whom information is to be kept, the most revealing acts might be undertaken with an air of careless abandon or casualness unrelated to their actual seriousness. To further throw a seeker off the track, actually unimportant activities may be undertaken with a stylized seriousness of purpose that exaggerates their actual importance and shifts attention away from the truly revealing. If a game player suspects that a seeker is in fact wise to the "rule of reversals"—whereby the revealing is treated unseriously and vice versa—he might reverse this once more and actually indicate seriousness to what is serious, supposing that this is just what the seeker will take as a sign of unimportance. This escalated complexity is characteristic of the next phase of the information game, namely, the one involving uncovering moves.

The uncovering phase begins when the seeker is aware that the concealer is aware of the seeker's information-gleaning activities. As a general strategy, the seeker brackets the person and situation under investigation within an assessment perspective designed to discover just what might be revealed by extraordinary scrutiny. The otherwise routine activities and taken-for-granted world are subjected to at least a mental search and seizure, so to speak. The adept seeker will focus on just those aspects of verbal expression or body idiom, which, because of inadequate control, uncover what is otherwise hidden beneath the surface. Especially significant here is the face—interpreting the movements of the eyes, nostrils, and lips, and its flushed or pale coloration.[52] Thus Chinese jade dealers are sensitive to the dilation of the pupils of the eye as a clue to the particular interest of a customer otherwise being careful not to indicate his actual preferences.[53] And some aficionados of the bull ring believe that the length of the bullfighter's beard is a clue to his anxiety state.[54]

Sometimes information can be obtained by interviewing, although answers obtained through this method, like answers obtained in clinical interviews, cannot be assumed to have great reliability—especially when the interactants are aware that they

[52] See Georg Simmel, "Sociology of the Senses," translated and adapted in R. E. Park and E. W. Burgess, *Introduction to the Science of Sociology*, Chicago: University of Chicago Press, 1924, 356–361.

[53] Reported in Eugene J. Webb, *et al.*, *Unobtrusive Measures*, Chicago: Rand McNally, 1966, 148.

[54] *Ibid.*

are both engaged in an information game. Face-to-face contact, however, provides opportunities for observing unobtrusive indicators. Furthermore, indirect questioning may have payoffs for an adroit interrogator. Some race track bettors have developed the fine art of indirectly interrogating trainers to glean clues as to a particular horse's chances.[55] Questioning a civil rights worker about the kind of clothing to be worn at a demonstration may indicate whether arrests are expected.[56] And Japanese employ a reciprocal roundaboutness in conversation, discreetly avoiding the subject of interest in order to elicit information about it.[57]

Another kind of uncovering device is spying, or observing the person when he believes he is unobserved. In addition to clandestine voyeurism, technological advances have placed all manner of "hardware" at the disposal of the seeker. Vision can be increased by the use of telescopes, and minute details may be attended to with microscopes. The ears may be assisted by a wide variety of bugging devices ranging in size from a cocktail olive to a room-size amplifier.

A third uncovering tactic is seduction in which exchange (usually but not always confined to a trade of sexual services for information) rather than espionage is employed. Certain occupational statuses are apparently frequent victims of this tactic. At least in legend, military men are thought to be particularly vulnerable to Mata Hari stratagems; and college professors are said to be prone to exchange test information for coed-comforting. Seductions are common occurrences even in such lesser known occupations as race track trainer and jockey, where innocents are forced to play information games, as hoards of information-seeking beauties utilize their sexual talents to pump the men for reliable information.[58]

When seduction fails, the seeker may employ the ultimate tactic—"coercive exchange." Here force or threat of force is used to obtain information.

[55] Scott, *op. cit.*, 166.

[56] Webb, *op. cit.*, 118.

[57] Edward T. Hall, *The Hidden Dimension*, Garden City, N.Y.: Doubleday, 1966, 141–142.

[58] Scott, *op. cit.*, 167–168.

The final phase of the information game is initiated by re-covering moves. They are undertaken by a concealer when he suspects his cover is suspected. For example, the jade buyer who is aware that his dilated pupils betray his interest may take a chemical that dilates the pupils—a re-covering strategy to be employed when he wishes to feign interest in some purchase. Thus the best evidence for the seeker to obtain in order to uncover the concealer's motives is the best "evidence" the concealer has to tamper with if he wants to re-cover information control.

Re-covering moves clearly illustrate that information games take on the behavioristic elements described when mirrors are looking into mirrors. Each actor may suspect the other suspects him and thus undertake counteractive measures. Since the most funda-mental rule of deception is that of the contradiction between appearances and reality, game players will be on guard to judge the meaning of events according to the rule of reversals. But since the reversals can be reversed again and again, the problem for the actors is to determine what state of suspicion awareness their antagonist is in.

Before concluding this discussion of information games, special note must be made of the concept of deception.

Although most codes of ethics and statements of ideals de-precate deception, the latter has its place as a regular and indeed often expected code of conduct. Forms of deception ranging from "little white lies" to tactful meretriciousness, to dissimulation are not only noticeable features of social life but even required patterns of behavior in specially designated situations. Beyond these situa-tions are those categories of persons whose very occupation pre-supposes deception as a routine procedure—magicians, spies and confidence men. And still further integrated into a deception-oriented frame of reference are those persons whose actual identities are permanently shrouded from public view, covered up by a "front" quite different from that which it conceals, best illustrated perhaps in the case of the passing homosexual.

At the outset, then, we may distinguish between the situated and occasional falsifier and the career deceiver. The former, found in nearly every walk of life, is familiar to everyone and is universally justified in his behavior by reference to the widespread belief that the end served by the deception is of a higher order of priority than candidness. Phrases like "What he doesn't know won't hurt him," "The truth hurts," and "It's better not to know" indicate that approved deception must be rooted in a moral evaluation of the situation with which others—including ultimately, the deceived person—would agree.

Career deceivers are not under the same moral constraints. They aim at different purposes: the magician presents himself as capable of superimposing his will on nature in ways that the ordinary man cannot; the espionage agent masquerades as a citizen to obtain extraordinary information; the confidence man parades at the race track in the regalia of a horseman to exploit the credulity of the betting public for private gain. For the professional deceiver the problem is not one of moral rectitude but rather of social comprehension. He must understand the seen-but-unnoticed features of everyday life. And like a stage manager, the deceiver must create the meaning of the setting in which he wishes the audience to participate and sustain that definition of the situation against alternative, contradictory and revelatory interpretations.

In essence deception is the placement of the individual or group to be deceived into one frame of meaning, while the deceiver is operating in quite another. Magic tricks provide numerous examples.[59] The magician actually creates an environment in which—given his definition of objects and activities—the events can be explained as magical. Meanwhile, he is operating in quite another environment in which certain objects and activities defined as irrelevant to the central feature of the trick in fact control the outcome. This is what is meant by the art of misdirection. Other deceivers employ a method similar to that of the magician. The race horse trainer, exposed to public view in the paddock, gives his do-or-die riding instructions to the jockey in a casual seemingly off-hand manner, while pretending to be most concerned with saddling the horse. A confidence man, employing the "pigeon drop" swindle, knows that no one will turn over their life savings to anyone but a bona fide official charged with a bonded responsibility for them; so he provides a well-credentialed confederate who

---

[59] On this point, we are indebted to Marcello Truzzi.

accompanies the "mark" to the bank and guards him against danger from thieves. The "plant," inserted by the F.B.I. into the Communist party, debates ideology and practice with the vigorous spirit that animates true believers; in the very process he obtains documents, names, and other information for use in subsequent prosecutions.

Relevant to the success of a deception is the deceiver's knowledge of just what will be taken as reliable evidence on the part of the other, so that the latter will conclude that he is in the frame that the deceiver has credited. Information must be managed so that it has the properties of coherence, validity, and naturalness. This means that the deceiver must be alive to that one false note which, when sounded, rings down the curtain on the entire performance. To succeed in his deception, the deceiver must be alive to the dramaturgic elements of routine behavior. To him furniture provides props; his clothing, a costume; his manner, a well-rehearsed, situationally appropriate performance. For the deception to go undiscovered, his self-presentation must be a coherent representation of the person whom he impersonates; and the minute details and gross features must all fit together to form, for the deceived party, an *undramatic* whole.

Deceivers also realize that the validity of their presentation is increased when confirmed by an independent party. Thus professional deceivers—such as confidence men and field anthropologists—usually employ "independent" agents to assist in the masquerade. The role of assistants in every facet of swindling is well known, including the use of a special functionary who remains after the swindle to "cool the mark out." In ethnographic investigations of exotic peoples, the anthropologist often finds it necessary to employ native assistants to validate his right to intrude on local private life. The use of native assistants tends to reduce the suspicion and hostility of the people to be investigated, while at the same time highlighting the anthropologist's trustworthy image.

Let us conclude this section by noting finally that, while mathematicians have posited a model of game behavior in which perfect information is a characteristic feature, sociologists must recognize that all social games proceed from a condition of imperfect information. In this sense every game includes an information game in which each player seeks to uncover the real identity, the actual intentions, and the secret stratagems employed by the other. The condition of imperfect information renders all social games problematic. Indeed, uncertainty of outcomes is a feature of games that provides the players with anxious concern over strategic decisions and zestful incentive for action when the game is on.

CONCLUSION

Game frameworks provide the sociologist with a useful way of ordering action in human encounters. Such encounters will almost always have prizes of honor, compliance, knowledge, and emotional ties at stake; and thus face, exploitation, information, and relationship games, respectively, will emerge as the essential procedural properties of the interaction.

Human beings vary in their adeptness at the playing of these games, and their varying skills certainly modify the outcome in any particular game. Beyond individual skills, however, are several related factors—all components of the concept of dominance—that influence which game will emerge in any encounter and what limits in game play are binding on all participants.

As pointed out, whether a game is going on and which of several possible games is being played are both functions of the specific social situation. Any game in theory and each game in practice requires a definition of the situation to be imposed on past, present, and future events. This definition or framework is itself a social product emanating from the actual conditions that prevail. Power is among the most important of these conditions, and, as a general rule, "He who has the bigger stick has the better chance of imposing his definitions of reality." [60]

Even in those cases in which the weaker party secretly plays a different game with its own risks and stakes, he must take into

[60] Peter Berger and Thomas Luckman, *The Social Construction of Reality*, Garden City, N.Y.: Doubleday, 1966, 101. See also the seminal discussion in Ralf Dahrendorf, "In Praise of Thrasymachus," *Essays in the Theory of Society*. Stanford University Press, 1968, 129–150.

account the game defined by the more powerful person and in the process mobilize his sign equipment to satisfy the requirements of the dominant game.[61] Thus, while several games may be going on in the same encounter, it is certainly relevant to inquire into the hierarchy of domination that governs the engagement and the modifications on game play imposed by this hierarchy.

Domination in games is grounded in the same source from which it arises in social life: traditional, legal, bureaucratic, and charismatic statuses.[62] Where tradition prevails the ascribed statuses of the actors may indicate who is the official defining authority in a game. Among traditional Japanese, for example, siblings deferred to one another according to age;[63] and in nearly all societies men exercise traditional authority over women.[64]

Legal statuses may freeze authority relations in accordance with juridically established hierarchies. Thus, policemen are free to define the meaning and strongly affect the outcome of their encounters with juveniles because of the widespread deference given to the former's legal status and the relatively low esteem given to the latter.[65]

Bureaucratic authority encloses relationships in the clasp of office, thus defining hierarchical rights and privileges. School principals, for example, exercise dominance in situations involving both fellow teachers and students by dint of their official position, modified of course by the manner in which they exercise it.[66]

Finally, charismatic authority arises out of the "majesty" with

[61] A telling example is the double game in which, for twenty-five cents, a Negro operator allows his white passenger to kick him—a game complex in which each obtains valued prizes while losing relatively disvalued ones. See the description in Richard Wright, *Black Boy*, N.Y.: Signet, 1951, 248–250.

[62] Max Weber, "The Three Types of Legitimate Rule," in *Complex Organizations*, edited by Amitai Etzioni, N.Y.: Holt, Rinehart, and Winston, 1961, 4–14.

[63] See Edward Norbeck, *Takashima: A Japanese Fishing Community*, Salt Lake City: University of Utah Press, 1954, 51.

[64] Bernard, *The Sex Game, op. cit.*, 59–64, refers to this as the "cichlid effect," pointing out that male dominance depends on female awe, and that it is therefore by no means an irrevocable condition.

[65] See Carl Werthman and Irving Piliavin, "Gang Members and the Police," in *The Police*, edited by David Bordua, N.Y.: Wiley, 1967, 56–98.

[66] See Howard S. Becker, "The Teacher in the Authority System of the Public School," in Etzioni, *op. cit.*, 243–252.

which an actor is cloaked by others,[67] a majesty which is compounded of awe and reverence of someone who seems to occupy a position at, or a control over, the elements at the center of life.[68] Charisma may lodge in any actor—regardless of formal status—who behaves in such a manner as to evoke its imputation.

Dominance in any game situation may be subverted. Sentiment may invade the status hierarchy. In this respect the most powerful sentiment is affection, whether it appears as romantic love or comradely friendship. While status apartheid limits affectionate contacts, interdependence makes hermetic isolation impossible. Thus formally dominant authorities—such as guards in a prison[69]—may be corrupted by frequent intimate encounters with social inferiors; and charismatic leaders—such as bandit chiefs—may be toppled by their sentimental attachments or betrayal by their amorous affairs.[70] In sum, while dominance and asymmetry are features of nearly every social relationship, and while social factors govern their allocation, no social situation is without possibility of subversion and restructuring of dominating relationships.

A final note is due on what might be called a humanistic objection to the game perspective. Some critics of the game and related frameworks have objected to what they perceive as their image of man as basically immoral and essentially opportunistic. Thus Martindale[71] contrasts what he alleges to be Goffman's model of self ("opportunist") with that of James, Cooley, and Mead ("autonomous moral agent") and seems to find the former wanting. But let us interpose an objection. It is not that game frameworks,

[67] Consider the comment by Ralph Waldo Emerson on the English nobility: "You cannot wield great agencies without lending yourself to them, and when it happens that the spirit of the earl meets his rank and duties, we have the best examples of behavior. Power of any kind readily appears in the manners; and . . . gives a majesty which cannot be concealed or resisted." Quoted in Hans Gerth and C. Wright Mills, *Character and Social Structure*, N.Y.: Harcourt, Brace and World, 1964, 196.

[68] See Edward Shils, "Charisma, Order, and Status," *American Sociological Review*, 30 (April, 1965), 199–213.

[69] See Gresham Sykes, "The Corruption of Authority and Rehabilitation," in Etzioni, *op. cit.*, 191–198.

[70] See E. J. Hobsbawm, *Social Bandits and Primitive Rebels*, Glencoe: Free Press, 1959, 13–28.

[71] Don Martindale, *American Society*, Princeton: Van Nostrand, 1960, 72.

or the earlier models of Goffman—to whom we gratefully acknowledge a debt of insight and guidance—presuppose (much less honor) a particular human morality; rather, the model of games indicates only that skill in play has advantageous payoffs. The amoral and adept opportunist is but one of several social types—for some, he is a hero to be emulated; for others, a scoundrel to be brought low. The game framework may be used to discover moral man in immoral society or vice versa.

3

Paranoia, homosexuality and game theory

Sociologists studying deviant behavior are increasingly thinking about labeled deviants,[1] but few are studying what labeled deviants are thinking.

To ask, who gets labeled and what are the fateful consequences for those so labeled has proved a fruitful question. But in pursuing this question recent investigators have neglected to study the qualities of consciousness of the deviants themselves. There are at least two reasons for this neglect. First, the very concern with states of consciousness is considered to be within the psychological rather than sociological realm of inquiry, and only of peripheral or *a priori* interest to the sociologist; second, sociological theory apparently lacks a framework within which to investigate the problem. However, we shall argue that sociological theory is both appropriate and equipped to investigate what may appear as a psychological or psychiatric concern.

Marvin B. Scott and Stanford M. Lyman, "Paranoia, Homosexuality, and Game Theory," *Journal of Health and Social Behavior*, Vol. 9, No. 3 (1968), pp. 179–187. By permission of the authors and of the American Sociological Association.
[1] Howard S. Becker, *Outsiders*, New York: The Free Press of Glencoe, 1963; John I. Kitsuse, "Societal Reaction to Deviant Behavior," in *The Other Side*, edited by Howard S. Becker, New York: The Free Press of Glencoe, 1964; Eliot Freidson, "Disability as Social Deviance," in *Sociology and Rehabilitation*, edited by Marvin B. Sussman, Publication of the American Sociological Association, n.d.; Thomas Scheff, *Being Mentally Ill*, Chicago: Aldine Press, 1966.

We hold that the model most fruitful for exploring the qualities of consciousness of deviants in general and paranoids and homosexuals in particular is that derived from recent thought in game theory.[2] First we shall present the components of a game model, then illustrate its usefulness in comprehending the behavior of normals in abnormal situations, and finally, we shall describe two deviant types—paranoids and homosexuals—and suggest that their presumed quality of consciouness might best be analyzed in terms of the game model.

THE GAME MODEL

Any encounter between two or more individuals may be analyzed as a game if the following condition holds true: at least one of the interactants is aware or capable of being made aware that, in realizing his aims in an encounter, he must take into account the others' expectations of him, also the others' expectations of what he expects of them, and vice versa.

Two problems have beset the game framework analysis of social relationships: the problem of consciousness, and the problem of goals and goal orientation, sometimes called the problem of rationality. One can easily exaggerate these problems, however. To begin with, consciousness is not in fact a problem of the model, but a potential condition of the empirical situation. True, encounters ordinarily proceed without the consciousness of the rules of the game so long as behavior follows along the lines of "the recipes for living" that "everyone knows."[3] But once an interruption or breakdown of these "recipes," or "background expectancies," occurs

[2] T. C. Schelling, *Strategy of Conflict*, New York: Galaxy Books, 1963. Credit for the idea of applying a game-like model to the analysis of certain kinds of deviance goes to Erving Goffman. His unpublished manuscript, "Communication and Strategic Interaction," consists—among other things—of an explication of Schelling's work and a brilliant application of game-theoretic notions for the analysis of a variety of diverse social structures. We are deeply indebted to Goffman's paper for many of the ideas presented here.

[3] Alfred Schutz, "The Problem of Rationality in the Social World," in *Collected Papers, Vol. II*, The Hague: Martinus Nijhoff, 1964, pp. 64–88, esp. pp. 72–76.

there arises in the minds of the interactants a heightened awareness context in which the expectations of self, others, and the scanning of reciprocal meanings becomes manifest.[4] To put it another way, the awareness of self, and the need to properly interpret the language, signs, and gestures of others becomes conscious when the situation is made problematic. We will shortly return to this point.

Similarly, the so-called problem of rationality need not be perceived as an obstacle to the adoption of a game framework for analysis. As Boulding[5] has noted, all behavior—including that of the "irrational" man—is characterized by the actor's having an image of the state of things and a preferential ordering of behavior patterns in accordance with that image. (The principal differentiation between rational and irrational behavior is that the latter is characterized by a rigid orientation, unmodified by further information, and an inconsistent and shifting order of preferences governing behavior choices.[6]) Furthermore, the game model can be employed to recognize that the goals of men are variable and not necessarily reducible to the material benefits so dear to users of the *homo economicus* model. Men may choose goals involving sacrifice, long term gains for short term losses, deferred gratifications, and so on. These are all empirical properties of encounters, and as such merely represent the raw data to which the game framework model is applied.

As these remarks suggest, one unit in which a game model may be fruitfully employed for analysis is a focused gathering or an encounter. Goffman[7] has defined this unit as existing when for the participants there is "a single visual and cognitive focus of attention; a mutual and preferential openness to verbal communication; a heightened mutual relevance of acts; an eye-to-eye ecological huddle that maximizes each participant's opportunity to perceive the other participants' monitoring of him." Such a unit may proceed on the

---

[4] Erving Goffman, "The Nature of Deference and Demeanor," *American Anthropologist* (June, 1956), pp. 473–474.

[5] Kenneth Boulding, *Conflict and Defense: A General Theory*, New York: Harper and Row Torchbook, 1963.

[6] *Ibid.*, pp. 150–151.

[7] Erving Goffman, *Encounters: Two Studies in the Sociology of Interaction*, Indianapolis: Bobbs-Merrill, 1961, p. 17.

course of interaction without any of the members becoming especially conscious of any game being involved in their own or others' behavior. But should obtrusive information, unexpected events, or untoward behavior intrude on the proceedings, a situation having all the properties of a game might then become a conscious as well as an active part of the encounter. Moreover, within any focused gathering one or more of the participants might be more or less conscious of their presentation of social selves than others. Thus, the game properties of a situation may be a greater or lesser part of the awareness contexts[8] of the actors in such a gathering.

Focused gatherings in which games may be observed are circumscribed by time, space, and boundary rules. Such gatherings have an episodic character so that the actions carried on may be observed by both actors and analysts as having a beginning and an ending. Despite their temporal boundaries, episodic events provide the occasion for the actors to reconstruct their own and others' biographies. And it is the mutually established biographies of the actors that constitute the social selves involved in a game. These include the actor's perception of the self he is presenting, alter's perception of that self, and both actor's and alter's estimation of that biographical self.

Once a game has consciously begun (that is, once at least one of the actors in the encounter realizes he has a stake in the outcome of the situation) he becomes consciously aware of rules of conduct appropriate to the situation—rules which define what and how other actors and objects are relevant to the stakes at issue,[9] and which indicate appropriate norms of conduct. These rules of relevance and rectitude constitute what for both the actor and analyst are the game parameters.

Furthermore, the goal-directed actions undertaken by an actor constitute the "moves" of the game. When an actor conceives and executes or attempts to execute a set of moves—which in context take into account the moves, including countermoves, of those with whom he is interacting—he is carrying out a strategy.

[8] Barney G. Glaser and Anselm L. Strauss, "Awareness Contexts and Social Interaction," *American Sociological Review*, 29 (1964), pp. 669–679.

[9] Goffman, *Encounters, op. cit.*, pp. 19–34.

A game may be said to be under way, then, when at least one actor in an encounter perceives a situation as problematic, estimates his own and others' construction of self and situation, and undertakes a line of action designed to achieve a goal or goals with respect to the situation.

Normal people and abnormal situations

Consider the following situation. John is a postal clerk; Marsha, a customer wishing to mail a package. The encounter proceeds. Marsha and John at once recognize each other as possessing certain identities—customer and postal clerk—and thus have a set of mutual expectations that smooth the flow of interaction. John will assume that Marsha will act as a customer and that she will act toward him as toward a postal clerk. Marsha assumes that he will act as a postal clerk and also assumes that he recognizes her as a customer and will behave accordingly.

The package and its arrival are of great importance to Marsha (say, a gift to her beloved). Now after weighing the package, announcing the postal charge and taking Marsha's money, John does not affix any stamps to the package. If the package were not of unusual importance to Marsha she might turn and leave, taking for granted that the postage will later be affixed. But because of the package's unusual importance she waits about the post office, engaging in some activity that warrants her continued presence, all the while furtively glancing at the clerk to see if her package is properly processed. As the moments pass and the act of affixing stamps is not completed, Marsha gets nervous, anxious and distraught. She analyzes the situation: he did not write the price of the postage in the corner of the package; therefore, he is not going to put the stamps on—he is going to keep the money. But no, she corrects herself: if he wanted to keep the money, the best thing he could have done was to make a point of marking the postal charge on the package, thinking that this action would allay any doubts she might have. But then another correction: he would be more interested in keeping the package than the price of postage, and a package could be taken at any time—even after postage has been affixed.

At this point Marsha might make a scene, take a tranquilizer, or at once write to the person destined to receive the package insisting that he reply immediately as to whether the package had been received. Now if a clinical investigator (a psychiatrist) were on the scene he would be observing a highly agitated woman—a woman whom he might, after brief questioning, describe as paranoid.

Let us leave John and Marsha, going now to another part of the world to investigate the interaction between Abdul and Abraham. Tensions are high between Egypt and Israel. Abdul, Egyptian military chief of staff, learns that his Israeli counterpart, Abraham, has granted massive leaves to the Israeli army, whose soldiers are filling the streets of Tel Aviv. Egypt can relax its guard; after all, if Israel were going to attack, they would not be giving leaves to the army. But Abdul reasons: If Israel were to attack, this would be the very best moment—while Egypt relaxes, having assumed that Israel has relaxed. So Abdul reports his suspicions to his head of state, who responds with: "Be quiet, Abdul; you are suspicious of everything. . . . Everyone knows that an army doesn't give leaves to its men if they are going to attack. I would send you to a psychiatrist, if they weren't all Jewish!"

Both Marsha and Abdul share a certain situated state of consciousness, a consciousness not typical in their other activities. Marsha and Abdul are both confronted by a problematic situation. For Marsha, involved in a very important relationship, a routine activity linked to that relationship turns out not to be routine. She becomes suspicious and mentally reconstructs the meaning of the activity, searching for motives and the connection between imagined motives and actual situated activity. She mentally rehearses the possible motives and strategies which would govern the seemingly unusual behavior of the postal clerk. She now regards him as an adversary, and his actions are thought to be part of an ulterior scheme. Notice that Marsha's situation has, at the moment of her agitation, the properties of a game—and the outward characteristics of paranoia.

Marsha does not exhibit the signs of "paranoia" all the time, but only when the ordinary world has abruptly become extraordinary; that is, when conditions of trust that undergird the social world have broken down.

Abdul is also suspicious: he is engaged in mentally constructing and reconstructing the relationship between actual events, alleged motives, and future events in certain situations associated with his occupation. His occupation requires suspiciousness, though his head of state does not always share his suspicion-oriented perspective. Away from staff headquarters Abdul does not exhibit the same signs of suspiciousness; elsewhere, he is just plain Abdul. But on the job he must ask himself, "What does Israel really intend? What strategies would achieve the end, but keep us off guard?" He too performs in what may be called a game frame of reference; he too exhibits signs that under clinical investigation might be labeled "paranoid."

Homosexuals and the game framework

Suspicion arises as a consequence of questioning taken-for-granted phenomena. Like Abdul, philosophers and sociologists, as part of their respective occupational concerns, transform the taken-for-granted into the problematic. And, as the incident between Marsha and John illustrates, normal men and women are occasionally confronted with problematic situations in everyday life, giving rise to suspicion, "paranoid" tendencies, and game behavior.

In addition to the irregular breakdown of conditions of trust and the occupations requiring a suspicion orientation, there are some persons who continually regard their social world as problematic, and who thus exhibit a heightened awareness. Among these are the *stigmatized*. As a result of possessing a stigma, an individual[10]

may be led into placing brackets around a spate of casual social interaction so as to examine what is contained therein for general themes. He can become "situation conscious" while normals present are spontaneously involved *within* the situation, the situation itself constituting for these normals a background of unattended matters.

This extension of consciousness on the part of the stigmatized persons is reinforced . . . by his special aliveness to the contingencies of acceptance and disclosure, contingencies to which normals will be less alive.

[10] Erving Goffman, *Stigma*, Englewood Cliffs, N.J.: Prentice-Hall Spectrum Paperback, 1963, p. 111.

Among the stigmatized a particularly significant issue is "passing," that is, concealing from others that portion of one's identity that is discreditable. Negroes who "pass" for whites, spies who pose as ordinary citizens, and homosexuals who move in heterosexual circles must take special precautions to preserve their secret identity against disclosure. Because of this danger of discovery "passers" must develop a more heightened awareness and a sharper perspective on ordinary affairs and everyday encounters than those for whom concealment is not an issue.

It is as a "passer" that the homosexual exhibits the behavior sometimes called "paranoid" by clinical investigators. The situations that are quite routine for normals become problematic for him. Thus one homosexual reports, "You know what was really hard? Watching television with my folks. I'd catch myself saying, 'There's a good-looking boy'."[11] Another homosexual reported his fear that a request to the landlord for more heat in the apartment he shared with his friend might lead to discovery and even arrest.[12]

As these cases illustrate, the "passing" homosexual must be more cognizant of all those "little things" that might give him away. Thus, his manner of dress and speech, his mobilization of gestures, especially those of the eyes, and his indications of interests and avocations are all potential clues to his "real" identity. The same is true for the heterosexual who thinks that others think he is a homosexual. The case of R.R., a young Negro man, illustrates the point nicely.[13] To all outward appearances, according to the psychiatrists that treat him, R.R. displays a masculine appearance. Yet he is troubled by doubts about his own sexuality, and by his belief that others think him to be homosexual. Therefore he calculates the impressions others get of him and behaves so as to belie the imagined identity of homosexual.

[11] George J. McCall and J. L. Simmons, *Identities and Interactions: An Examination of Human Associations in Everyday Life*, New York: The Free Press of Glencoe, 1966, p. 190.

[12] Gordon Westwood, *A Minority*, London: Longmans, Green and Co., 1960, p. 147.

[13] Abram Kardiner and Lionel Ovesey, *The Mark of Oppression*, Cleveland: Meridian Books, 1962, pp. 179–190.

I try to make myself appear to others what I really am not. If they could see into my mind, they would get a different impression than they have. . . . I just wonder what in my appearance now suggests a feminine person?[14]

Further, R.R. is alive to those events in his everyday life that suggest a homosexual identity to ordinary persons, even if his psychiatrists are not. Thus he reports about radio listening:

Yesterday I was sitting and listening to music on one radio at work. Everybody else was at another radio listening to the ball game. A person came in and said, "Get up. Let's listen to the game." I said, "I would rather listen to music." The boss came in and said, "I always thought something was wrong with you. Now, I know it." He wouldn't have said it if he didn't have something in the back of his mind."

And R.R. adopts a game strategic—or to the psychiatrists, a "paranoid"—interpretation of these events:

To him [i.e., the boss] my behavior is not usual. Maybe to him it isn't normal for a young man to prefer music to a baseball game. Evidently, people have formulated ideas and opinions that I have an unusual personality. Rather than being a strong young man interested in athletics and sports, I am more interested in light things. I must appear effeminate to them.[15]

The strategies open to R.R., once he begins to gauge the meanings his peers attach to events like listening to the radio, are many and varied. He might try to convince his fellow workers that love of music is not unmasculine. He might try to "compensate" for his one "feminine" trait by excelling in another activity that demonstrates masculinity, such as, for example, use of obscene language. He might confine his music listening to the privacy of his home, join his co-workers in listening to ball games, feigning interest in the subject, even reading up on it in private so as to be

[14] *Ibid.*, pp. 185–186.
[15] *Ibid.*, p. 186.

able to validate his meretricious interest. He might purchase a tiny transistorized portable radio outfitted with an earphone so that his taste in radio programs will be unknown to his peers, but actually tune it to the ball game so that when asked he can prove he is a "man" by handing the earphone to the interrogator. And he might —and in fact, R.R. does—avoid as much as possible any social contact with his peers. In other words, once a problem is recognized in the interaction, R.R. might carefully evaluate the seemingly innocuous items in the encounter environment for their meanings and utility. He may seek to reorganize his own image or environment in order to convey a new or different image from that which he presently suspects he is giving. He may correctly or incorrectly implement his strategy, make wise or inept tactical moves, succeed or fail to achieve his objective. He might, indeed, play a game.

"Passing" poses another kind of problem for the homosexual, namely, communicating the secret identity he is trying to conceal in order to make contact with a fellow homosexual "passer." The successful homosexual "passer" must be able to mobilize his sign equipment so that a double identity is available—a normal one for "straight" people, and a homosexual one for those seeking his sexual services. However, the indicators of homosexuality must be capable of withdrawal or redefinition should he have to revert to the "pure" version of the passing identity. The elements of this situation amount to a special kind of information game in which A, a homosexual, seeks to outwardly manifest a heterosexual identity to B, a suspected homosexual, but provide the latter with the necessary information to suggest A's identity as a homosexual and thus invite B to disclose his own homosexual identity. Of course should B turn out to be "straight," A is left with the problem of managing the clues already given off to his own true identity so as not to give himself away. Ideally the situation amounts to a reciprocally escalating presentation of relevant information by which each actor enhances the risk of revealing himself in order to ascertain the definite and unambiguous identity of the other. The game is concluded either when both actors recognize one another as homosexuals and drop all pretense as heterosexuals, or when one actor concludes that the other is "straight" and determines upon a strategy to salvage his own "passing" identity.

To repeat the important point: the exigencies of "passing" necessitate that the real or suspected homosexual take as problematic what others take for granted. He must take into account the nuances of verbal meaning, the symbolic definitions of objects, and the fact that others are (or may be) taking into account his taking them into account. He operates in a context of "suspicion awareness,"[16] asking: Do they know? How are they reacting to me? When can I stop observing them observe me observing them? This is the orientation of professional spies, the manifest symptoms of paranoia, an orientation not employed in everyday life, except perhaps as a background expectancy.

The awareness contexts of the interactants may vary; consequently, the strategies may vary in accordance with them. Thus homosexuals may encounter one another or "straights" when each is openly aware of the other's identity and aware that the other knows his identity; when one is unaware of the other's identity and also unaware of the other's knowledge of his own identity; when one or both suspects the true identity of the other and that the other suspects his own; and when each is aware of the other's identity but pretending ignorance of it.[17] Homosexuals must ascertain which awareness context they are in (or if they are in multiple contexts simultaneously), and then mobilize the sign equipment appropriate to the context. Thus, unlike many straights in the same situation, passing homosexuals or ambivalent males must be more game aware.

The game-theoretic perspective is a model of strategic man playing with hyper-consciousness of the opponent's moves. It is a normative model in the sense of what a thinking actor must do to defeat an opponent and not an empirical model of how people in fact typically experience their social world. However, in the case of the passing homosexual or the ambivalent heterosexual, it approaches an empirical model.

[16] Glaser and Strauss, *op. cit.*
[17] *Ibid.*

Paranoids and the game framework

What we have said about homosexuals in particular applies to paranoids and paranoid-like states in general. Certain individuals —especially but not exclusively persons with something to hide, or bearers of discrediting stigmas—may come to see all or part of their world in terms of a conspiracy in which they must constantly be on guard against physical or financial harm, exploitation, or loss of status. Unlike normals, "paranoids" are more aware of social realities, more alive to contingencies and nuances, more strategic in their responses.

Until recently a paranoid was regarded as a person who had fashioned and come to inhabit a "pseudo-community" directed against himself; a person who aroused the concern of the actual community only after having struck out at it in his vengeful reaction to the unreal world in which he lived.[18] The researches of Lemert[19] suggest that this definition and sequence is questionable, if not wholly wrong. Lemert's study of paranoids points out that the allegedly paranoid state of mind grows out of the context of a *real* community of suspicion, hostility and exclusion in which the "paranoid" finds himself actually alone, under suspicion, and the object of secret conversations, closed-door sessions, and extra-curricular plans. The incidents reported by Lemert indicate the kind of events that make up this dynamic exclusionary process. An office research team used huddles around the water cooler to discuss an unwanted associate; a researcher's interview schedule was changed at a conference arranged without him; office rules against extraneous conversation were introduced with the connivance of superiors in order to isolate an unwanted worker. Plans may be made that affect the after-hours situation of the excluded person. In one instance, reported by Lemert, fellow workers considered the possibility of placing an all night watch in front of their perceived malefactor's home. The conspiracy said to be imagined by the

[18] Norman Cameron, "The Paranoid Pseudo-Community Revisited," *American Journal of Sociology*, 65 (1959), pp. 52–58.
[19] Edwin Lemert, "Paranoia and the Dynamics of Exclusion," *Human Deviance, Social Problems and Social Control*, Englewood Cliffs, N.J.: Prentice-Hall, 1967, pp. 197–211.

paranoid may not then be due originally to a malfunction in his interior mental processes, but rather it may arise out of an actual conspiratorial setting.

Kitsuse's[20] study of the grounds for which a person is designated "homosexual" provides further evidence of the dynamics of the conspiratorial and exclusionist process. Among the incidents respondents recalled as indicating to them that a person was a sex deviant were that an officer "spent more time with the enlisted men than is expected of an officer"; that a tennis coach offered to give a back rub to the guest invited for dinner; that a stranger in a bar expressed interest in the fact that the person sitting next to him was studying psychology. Following their interpretation of these events as signs of homosexuality, the "normals" either watched the person closely, or withdrew hastily from the encounter. Thus the labeled deviant was given an indication of a problem in his interaction with others, an indication that might make him react with game-awareness responses.

Once a person establishes for himself that he is in a conspiratorial setting, it is likely that he will begin to be suspiciously aware of just those items and events that "everyone else" takes for granted. Thus, R.R., suspecting that his fellow workers harbor doubts about his masculinity, watches closely the events that follow a conversation:

I feel that people when they are in groups are talking about me. Especially if a person I have just been talking to goes over to another and they laugh. I feel they are talking about me.[21]

The paranoid is suspicious of objects in his social environment. For him, the taken-for-granted world is placed under suspicion. The strategic concerns and hyper-awareness of alternative meanings routinely manifested by the theorist in a game of conflict is found among the paranoid, except now the entire social environment is the opponent. Like an intelligence officer continually engaged in doping out the opponent's real intentions, the paranoid is hyper-conscious of others' motives. Note that in the literature of paranoid

---

[20] Kitsuse, *op. cit.*, pp. 92–93.
[21] Kardiner and Ovesey, *op. cit.*, p. 186.

schizophrenia, we find a recurrent theme depicting the paranoid as possessing a "mysterious intuition,"[22] as engaging in a kind of "emotional eaves-dropping,"[23] as being "diffusely vigilant."[24] The paranoid, as Cameron describes him, "watches everything uneasily; he listens alertly for clues; he looks everywhere for hidden meanings." Jackson[25] nicely illustrates the point:

A therapist and his patient had inadvertently occupied another doctor's office. When the owner of the office appeared at the door, the therapist apologized. The second physician remarked it was "perfectly all right" and retired. The patient immediately told his therapist, "Gosh, Dr. X was angry." The therapist had not detected such a reaction in his colleague, but on checking later he discovered that the patient was correct. Indeed, therapists are sometimes a little frightened and disconcerted to learn that their schizophrenic patients have an uncanny way of nosing out things about their personalities which they have unconsciously tried to cover up.

The paranoid explores, in game-theoretic fashion, the possibilities of all encounters. To illustrate, in one case reported by Laing and Esterson[26] a girl feared her father was going to kill her; and so when she was given a sedative, she believed it was poison, for if her father were indeed out to kill her, he could—from her viewpoint— do no better than attempt to poison her while presumably offering her a sedative. Like a good game theorist, the paranoid ascribes to the opponent just the kind of rationality necessary to make the best strategic move.[27]

The paranoid—again, like a good intelligence officer—becomes attuned to concealment and detection. The pathological component develops from the shift in interest in "what really is going on" to the

[22] Alfred H. Stanton and Morris S. Schwartz, *The Mental Hospital*, New York: Basic Books, 1964, p. 200.

[23] Frieda Fromm-Reichmann, *Principles of Intensive Psychotherapy*, Chicago: University of Chicago Press, 1950.

[24] Cameron, *op. cit.*, p. 54.

[25] Don D. Jackson, "Psychotherapy for Schizophrenia," *Scientific American* (January, 1953), p. 5.

[26] R. D. Laing and A. Esterson, *Sanity, Madness, and the Family*, Vol. I., London: Tavistock Publications, 1964.

[27] *Ibid.*, p. 16f.

conviction that "something is going on behind my back."[28] Thus:

> Patients maintained delusional misinterpretations by continually overemphasizing an inferred, implied, concealed meaning (the "real" meaning) and discarding the obvious or superficial content of a statement or action of a staff member.[29]

Otherwise put, the paranoid schizophrenic is routinely engaged in interpreting the world in terms of a game-theoretic model.

Now if we ask, how is it that some people routinely put together their world in these terms, we are approaching the etiology of paranoia. And in this regard, the work of Bateson and his associates[30] is highly suggestive. Consider this illustration:

> For example, if mother begins to feel hostile (or affectionate) toward her child and also feels compelled to withdraw from him, she might say, "Go to bed, you're very tired and I want you to get your sleep." This overtly loving statement is intended to deny a feeling which could be verbalized as "Get out of my sight because I'm sick of you." If the child correctly discriminates her meta-communicative signals, he would have to face the fact that she both doesn't want him and is deceiving him by her loving behavior. He would be "punished" for learning to discriminate orders of messages accurately. He therefore would tend to accept the idea that he is tired rather than recognize his mother's deception. This means that he must deceive himself about his own internal state in order to support mother in her deception. To survive with her he must falsely discriminate his own internal message as well as falsely discriminate the messages of others.

Laing's work on family and schizophrenia is a rich source of examples illustrating the "double bind" hypothesis of Bateson and associates. His main point of emphasis is the family's negation of the child's perceived reality. Only one example, the case of Maya, need be mentioned here:[31]

---

[28] Stanton and Schwartz, *op. cit.*, p. 203.

[29] *Ibid.*

[30] Gregory Bateson, et al., "Toward a Theory of Schizophrenia," *Behavioral Science*, 1 (October, 1956), pp. 251–264.

[31] Laing, *op. cit.*, p. 26.

She was frightened that her parents knew that she had sexual thoughts about them. She tried to tell them about this, but they told her *she did not have any thoughts of that kind.* She told them she masturbated *and they told her that she did not.* What happened then is of course inferred, but *when she told her parents in the presence of the interviewer that she still masturbated, her parents simply told her she did not!*

Of course the family is not the only group of significant others having a consequential impact in the etiology of the paranoid interpretive framework. Lemert's[32] study of the onset of paranoia focuses on the conspiratorial denial of reality that emerges in the small, informal groups embedded in the bureaucratic milieu.

The empirical investigations of Bateson[33], Laing[34] and Lemert[35] converge on this point: The constellation of significant others that systematically negates reality for an individual is engaged in producing persons who routinely place their world under suspicion. Whether the product of such a constellation will be identified as "ill" will depend on "career contingencies,"[36] a discussion of which would take us beyond our immediate interests.

CONCLUSION

The game-theoretic model provides a framework whereby the quality of consciousness of many who would clinically occupy the categories of homosexual and paranoid is made sociologically intelligible. The game framework is a model of behavior of man under consciously problematic situations trying to make sense of and plans for that and future situations of a similar nature. The model suggests the contextual establishment of identities, the situation-oriented aliveness to objects and events, and the calculation of strategies.

The game model may not be suited to the analyses of all

[32] Lemert, *op. cit.*
[33] Bateson, *op. cit.*
[34] Laing, *op. cit.*
[35] Lemert, *op. cit.*
[36] Erving Goffman, *Asylums*, Garden City, N.Y.: Anchor Paperback, 1961, 134 ff.

behavior, but rather to those situations having the properties of games—namely, imagination of the interactant's identities, motives, and strategies, and the development of counter-strategies, contingency tactics, and rescue operations.

While all persons are cast into game-potential situations whenever an interruption in ordinary activities occurs, certain persons are in them as routine matters of their everyday lives. Homosexuals, who have sometimes been treated as clinically paranoid, can be seen as persons embedded in a permanently problematic environment so long as they inhabit heterosexually oriented societies. Their allegedly paranoid behavior—indicated by a heightened suspiciousness, conspiratorial interpretation of events, and strategies of deviance disavowal or concealment—can be seen as behavior oriented to their peculiar problematic status. The game framework, a model of a thinking man in a win-lose-draw situation, not only provides the model for distinguishing the elements of the homosexual's behavior, but also by inference suggests the "normal" nature of this behavior.

Paranoids, typically treated as inhabitants of an unreal world, may manifest their unusual behavior pattern because of the dynamics of exclusion and conspiracy which constitute their actual environment. Like homosexuals, their behavior, especially in its early stages, may be analyzed in terms of that of a game player. The persistence of a game environment in their actual lives may be the factor that brings about the clinically diagnosed symptoms of paranoia.

Homosexuals and paranoids have a heightened awareness. Beyond this, their awareness is patterned in accordance with their perception of the nature, rules, and problems of the "game" in which they find themselves. Future research should focus on the classification of such games, the linkage of game-types to particular environments and groups, and the rules governing games.

Finally, our paper suggests that problematic environments are stable features of life for certain groups in society. In addition to homosexuals and paranoids, minority groups, physically disabled persons, the blind and the deaf are some that might be suggested. It may be that these groups are more sensitized to game situations than others and more subject to being labeled as mentally ill when they exhibit their awareness of the game aspects of life. Future research might focus on the game properties of stigmatized behavior, the dynamics of exclusion and conspiracy that originate it, and the non-pathological aspects of this "paranoia."

4

Territoriality:
A neglected sociological dimension

All living organisms observe some sense of territoriality,[1] that is, some sense—whether learned or instinctive to their species—in which control over space is deemed central for survival.[2] Although man's domination over space is potentially unlimited, in contemporary society it appears that men acknowledge increasingly fewer *free* territories for themselves.[3]

Free territory is carved out of space and affords opportunities for idiosyncracy and identity. Central to the manifestation of these opportunities are boundary creation and enclosure. This is so

Stanford M. Lyman and Marvin B. Scott, "Territoriality: A Neglected Sociological Dimension," *Social Problems*, Vol. 15, No. 2 (1967), pp. 236–248. By permission of The Society for the Study of Social Problems.

[1] The concept of territoriality was introduced into sociological analysis in the twenties under the label of "the ecological school." For an early statement see Robert E. Park, Ernest W. Burgess and R. D. McKenzie, *The City*, Chicago: University of Chicago Press, 1925. For a summary and bibliography of the school see Milla Aissa Alihan, *Social Ecology*, N.Y.: Columbia University Press, 1938. An updated version of this school is found in James A. Quinn, *Human Ecology*, N.Y.: Prentice-Hall, 1950, and Amos H. Hawley, *Human Ecology, A Theory of Community Structures*, N.Y.: The Ronald Press, 1950.

Originating in animal studies, "territoriality" still looms large as an organizing concept in ethology. For a summary statement see C. R. Carpenter, "Territoriality: A Review of Concepts and Problems," in A. Roe and G. Simpson, editors, *Behavior and Evolution*, New Haven: Yale University Press, 1958, pp. 224–50.

because activities that run counter to expected norms need seclusion or invisibility to permit unsanctioned performance, and because peculiar identities are sometimes impossible to realize in the absence of an appropriate setting.[4] Thus the opportunities for freedom of action—with respect to normatively discrepant behavior and maintenance of specific identities—are intimately connected with the ability to attach boundaries to space and command access to or exclusion from territories.

In American society where territorial encroachment affects nearly all members of society, certain segments of the population are particularly deprived, namely, Negroes, women, youth, and inmates of various kinds. With these categories in mind, this paper re-introduces a neglected dimension of social analysis important to understanding deprived groups.

Our strategy is twofold: first, to bring together under a new set of organizing concepts the notions of types of territory, types of territorial encroachment and types of responses to encroachment; and second, to specify the reactions of spatially deprived groups.

THE TYPES OF TERRITORIES

We can distinguish four kinds of territories, namely, *public territories*, *home territories*, *interactional territories* and *body territories*.

For a challenging argument that sociological investigation can fruitfully employ the techniques of comparative ethology—especially to such subjects as territoriality—see Lionel Tiger and Robin Fox, "The Zoological Perspective in Social Science," *Man*, I, 1, (March, 1966), esp. p. 80.

Only very recently have sociologists revived ecological thinking to include a truly *interactional* dimension. The outstanding contributor is, of course, Edward T. Hall. See his *The Silent Language*, Garden City, N.Y.: Doubleday and Co., 1959, and *The Hidden Dimension*, Garden City, N.Y.: Doubleday and Co., 1966. For a masterful application of the concept of territoriality in interactional terms see Erving Goffman, *Asylums*, Garden City, N.Y.: Doubleday and Co., Anchor Books, 1961, pp. 227–248. In a slightly different vein see the interesting efforts of Robert Sommer, "Studies in Personal Space," *Sociometry*, 22 (September, 1959), pp. 247–60, and the writings of Roger Barker, especially his "Roles, Ecological Niches, and the Psychology of the Absent Organism," paper presented to the conference on the Propositional Structure of Role Theory, University of Missouri, 1962.

Public territories

Public territories are those areas where the individual has freedom of access, but not necessarily of action, by virtue of his claim to citizenship.[5] These territories are officially open to all, but certain images and expectations of appropriate behavior and of the categories of individuals who are normally perceived as using these territories modify freedom. First, it is commonly expected that illegal activities and impermissible behavior will not take place in public places. Since public territories are vulnerable to violation in both respects, however, policemen are charged with the task of removing lawbreakers from the scene of their activities and restricting behavior in public places.[6]

Second, certain categories of persons are accorded only limited access to and restricted activity in public places. It is expected, for instance, that children will not be playing in public playgrounds after midnight; that lower class citizens will not live—although they might work—in areas of middle class residence; and that Negroes will not be found leisurely strolling on the sidewalks, though they might be found laying the sewer pipe under the streets of white neighborhoods.

Since the rights of such discrepant groups to use these territories as citizens sometimes contradicts the privileges accorded them as persons, such territories are not infrequently the testing grounds of challenges to authority. The wave of sit-ins, wade-ins, and demonstrations in racially segregated restaurants, public beaches, and schools constitute an outstanding recent example. Informal

[2] For the argument that human territoriality is a natural rather than a cultural phenomenon see Robert Ardrey, *The Territorial Imperative*, New York: Athenum, 1966, pp. 3–41.

[3] The idea of "free territory" is derived from Goffman, *loc. cit.*

[4] See Erving Goffman, *The Presentation of Self in Everyday Life*, Garden City, N.Y.: Doubleday Anchor Books, 1959, p. 22.

[5] The term "citizenship" is used in a sense similar to that employed by T.H.Marshall in *Class, Citizenship and Social Development*, Garden City, N.Y.: Doubleday Anchor Books, 1965, esp. pp. 71–134.

[6] See Harvey Sacks, "Methods in Use for the Production of a Social Order: A Method for Warrantably Informing Moral Character," Center for the Study of Law and Society, University of California, Berkeley, 1962; and Aaron Cicourel, *The Social Organization of Juvenile Justice*, New York: John Wiley, 1968.

restrictions on access to public territories often violate unenforced or as yet untested rights of citizens. Since the informal delineation of some of these territories implies the absence of certain persons, their presence stands out. Policemen frequently become allies of locals in restricting citizenship rights when they remove unseemly persons from territories which they do not regularly habituate, or when they restrict certain categories of persons to specific areas.[7]

Public territories are thus ambiguous with respect to accorded freedoms. First, the official rights of access may be regularly violated by local custom. Second, status discrepancy may modify activity and entrance rights. For example, the ambiguity in the distinction between minors and adults is a source of confusion and concern in the regulation of temporal and access rights to those whose status is unclear. Finally, activities once forbidden in public may be declared permissible, thus enlarging the freedom of the territory; or activities once licit may be proscribed thus restricting it. Hence display of female breasts is now permitted in San Francisco night-clubs, but not on the streets or before children. Nude swimming enjoys police protection at certain designated beaches, but watching nude swimmers at these same beaches is forbidden to those who are attired.

Home territories

Home territories are areas where the regular participants have a relative freedom of behavior and a sense of intimacy and control over the area. Examples include makeshift club houses of children, hobo jungles, and homosexual bars. Home and public territories may be easily confused. In fact "the areas of public places and the areas of home territories are not always clearly differentiated in the social world and what may be defined and used as a public place by some may be defined and used as a home territory by others."[8] Thus, a home territory that also may be used as a public

---

[7] See Jerome Skolnick, *Justice Without Trial*, New York: John Wiley, 1966, pp. 96–111 *et passim*; and Sacks, *op. cit.*

[8] Sherri Cavan, "Interaction in Home Territories," *Berkeley Journal of Sociology*, 8 (1963) p. 18.

one is defined by its regular use by specific persons or categories of persons and by the particular "territorial stakes" or "identity pegs" that are found in such places. The style of dress and language among the patrons at a bar may immediately communicate to a homosexual that he has arrived in home territory, while a hetero-sexual passerby who pauses for a drink may be astonished or out-raged when he is accosted for sexual favors from the stranger seated next to him. Large-scale clandestine brotherhoods indoctrinate their members in secret codes of dress and demeanor so that regardless of their later travels they can unobtrusively communicate their fraternal identity and ask for assistance from one another in other-wise public places. Home territories sometimes enjoy a proactive status, beyond the presence of their inhabitants, in the form of reserved chairs, drinking mugs, signs or memorabilia that serve to indicate special and reserved distinctions.

Home territories may be established by "sponsorship" or "colonization." An example of the former is found in the merchant emigrants from China who established caravansaries in certain quarters of Occidental cities which served as public trading estab-lishments but also as living quarters, employment agencies, meeting places, and courts for their *Landsmänner*.[9] Colonization occurs when a person or group lays claim to a formally free territory by virtue of discovery, regular usage, or peculiar relationship. Thus certain restaurants become home territories to those who are impressed with their first meal there; to those who eat there on specific occasions, such as luncheons, birthdays, or after sporting events; and to those who are intimate with the waitress.

Loss of home status may be occasioned by the death or resigna-tion of a sponsor, by violation of the previously established usages, by rejection, or by conquest. Erstwhile "regulars" at a bar may discover they are no longer warmly greeted nor eligible for a free drink when the proprietor dies or when their patronage becomes irregular. Homosexuals may desert a "queer bar" when it becomes a place which heterosexuals frequent to observe deviant behavior.

It is precisely because of their officially open condition that

[9] See Stanford M. Lyman, *The Structure of Chinese Society in Nineteenth Century America*, unpublished, Ph.D. dissertation, Berkeley: University of California, 1961.

public areas are vulnerable to conversion into home territories. The rules of openness are sufficiently broad and ambiguous so that restrictions on time, place, and manner are difficult to promulgate and nearly impossible to enforce. Armed with a piece of chalk children can change the public sidewalk into a gameboard blocking pedestrian traffic. Despite building codes and parental admonitions youngsters convert abandoned buildings or newly begun sites into forts, clubs, and hideaways.[10]

But children are not the only colonizers on the public lands. Beggars and hawkers will stake out a "territory" on the sidewalks or among the blocks and occupy it sometimes to the exclusion of all others similarly employed. The idle and unemployed will loiter on certain streetcorners, monopolizing the space, and frightening off certain respectable types with their loud, boisterous, or obscene language, cruel jests, and suggestive leers. Members of racial and ethnic groups colonize a portion of the city and adorn it with their peculiar institutions, language, and rules of conduct.[11] Ethnic enclaves, like certain notorious homosexual bars and prisons on open-house day, are often "on display" to non-ethnics who thus grant legitimacy to the colony's claim for territorial identity.

Among the most interesting examples of colonizing on the public lands are those attempts by youths to stake out streets as home territories open only to members of their own clique and defended against invasion by rival groups. Subject always to official harassment by police and interference by other adults who

[10] Indeed, children are among the most regular and innovative creators of home territories from the space and material available to the public in general. Speaking of their peculiar tendency to violate the rules governing trespass, William Prosser has aptly observed, "Children, as is well known to anyone who has ever been a child, are by nature unreliable and irresponsible people, who are quite likely to do almost anything. In particular, they have a deplorable tendency to stray upon land which does not belong to them, and to meddle with what they find there." "Trespassing Children," *California Law Review* (August, 1959), p. 427.

[11] Ethnic Groups in the process of assimilation sometimes discover to their astonishment that the isolated slum wherein they have traditionally and unwillingly dwelt is in fact a home territory possessed of cherished values and irreplaceable sentiments. A militant Negro thus writes: "For as my son, Chuck, wrote me after exposure to the Negro community of Washington: 'I suddenly realized that the Negro ghetto is not a ghetto. It is home.'" John Oliver Killens, *Black Man's Burden*, New York: Trident Press, 1965, p. 94.

claim the streets as public territories, youths resolve the dilemma by redefining adults as non-persons whose seemingly violative presence on the youth's "turf" does not challenge the latter's proprietorship. Streets are most vulnerable to colonizing in this manner and indeed, as the early studies of the Chicago sociologists illustrated so well, streets and knots of juxtaposed streets become unofficial home areas to all those groups who require relatively secluded yet open space in which to pursue their interests or maintain their identities.[12]

Interactional territories

Interactional territories refer to any area where a social gathering may occur. Surrounding any interaction is an invisible boundary, a kind of social membrane.[13] A party is an interactional territory, as are the several knots of people who form clusters at parties. Every interactional territory implicitly makes a claim of boundary maintenance for the duration of the interaction. Thus access and egress are governed by rules understood, though not officially promulgated, by the members.

Interactional territories are characteristically mobile and fragile. Participants in a conversation may remain in one place, stroll along, or move periodically or erratically. They may interrupt the interaction only to resume it at a later time without permanently breaking the boundary or disintegrating the group. Even where "settings" are required for the interaction, mobility need not be dysfunctional if the items appropriate to the setting are movable. Thus chemists may not be able to complete a discussion without the assistance of a laboratory, but chess players may assemble or disassemble the game quite readily and in the most cramped quarters. Similarly, so long as Negroes were chattel slaves slaveholders might move them anywhere where their services or appearance were needed.

The fragility of interactional territories is constantly being

[12] Harvey W. Zorbaugh, *The Gold Coast and the Slum*, Chicago: University of Chicago Press, 1929. See also Jane Jacobs, *The Death and Life of Great American Cities*, N.Y.: Vintage Books, 1961, pp. 29–142.

[13] See Erving Goffman, *Behavior in Public Places*, N.Y.: The Free Press of Glencoe, 1963, pp. 151–165 *et passim*.

tested by parvenus and newcomers. The latter, even when they possess credentials entitling them to entrance into the interactional circle, break down ongoing interaction and threaten it by requiring all to start over again, end it instead and begin a new subject of common interest, or disintegrate.[14] Parvenus are a greater threat since their presence breaks the boundaries of the interaction and challenges the exclusiveness of the group. They may be repulsed, or accepted fully, though the latter is less likely than the granting of a "temporary visa," i.e., rights to interact for the instant occasion with no promise of equal rights in the future.

Body territories

Finally, there are body territories, which include the space encompassed by the human body and the anatomical space of the body. The latter is, at least theoretically, the most private and inviolate of territories belonging to an individual. The rights to view and touch the body are of a sacred nature, subject to great restriction. For instance, a person's rights to his own body space are restricted where norms govern masturbation, or the appearance and decoration of skin. Moreover, rights of others to touch one's body are everywhere regulated, though perhaps modern societies impose greater restrictions than others.[15]

Body territory is also convertible into home territory. The most common method is marriage in a monogamous society in which sexual access to the female is deemed the exclusive right of the husband so long as he exercises propriety with respect to his status. Ownership, however, is not necessarily or always coterminous with possession, so that sexual rivalry might continue illegitimately after

[14] An excellent illustration of the several facets of this process and attendant issues in social gatherings is found in David Riesman, et al., "The Vanishing Host," *Human Organization* (Spring, 1960), pp. 17–27.

[15] Talcott Parsons notes that "the very fact that affectionate bodily contact is almost completely taboo among men in American Society is probably indicative of [the limited nature of intra-sex friendship] since it strongly limits affective attachment." *The Social System*, Glencoe: Free Press, 1951, p. 189. For an empirical study and analysis of touching relations see Erving Goffman, "The Nature of Deference and Demeanor," *American Anthropologist*, 58 (June, 1956), pp. 473–502.

a marital choice has been made and erupt in trespass on to the husband's sexual property.[16] Under situations where women are scarce, such as nineteenth-century overseas Chinese communities in the United States, sexual property was institutionalized through organized prostitution, and the few Chinese wives among the homeless men were carefully secluded.[17]

Body space is, however, subject to creative innovation, idio-syncracy, and destruction. First, the body may be marked or marred by scars, cuts, burns, and tattoos. In addition, certain of its parts may be inhibited or removed without its complete loss of function. These markings have a meaning beyond the purely anatomical. They are among the indicators of status or stigma. They can be signs of bravado as was the dueling scar among German students, or of criminality as is a similar scar on Italians and Negroes in America. Loss of an eye may prevent one's entrance into dental school, but at least one clothing manufacturer regards one-eyed men as status symbols for starched shirts. Tatoos may memorialize one's mother or sweetheart as well as indicate one's seafaring occupation.

The human organism exercises extraterritorial rights over both internal and external space. In the latter instance the space immediately surrounding a person is also inviolate.[18] Thus conversations

[16] See Kingsley Davis, *Human Society*, New York: MacMillan, 1948, pp. 189-193.

[17] Lyman, *op. cit.*, pp. 97-111.

[18] The perceptions of Simmel on this subject surpass all others and we are indebted to his work. Thus Simmel has noted: "In regard to the 'significant' [i.e., "great"] man, there is an inner compulsion which tells one to keep at a distance and which does not disappear even in intimate relations with him. The only type for whom such distance does not exist is the individual who has no organ for perceiving distance . . . The individual who fails to keep his distance from a great person does not esteem him highly, much less too highly (as might superficially appear to be the case); but, on the contrary, his importune behavior reveals lack of proper respect . . . The same sort of circle which surrounds a man—although it is value-accentuated in a very different sense—is filled out by his affairs and by his characteristics. To penetrate this circle by taking notice, constitutes a violation of personality. Just as material property is, so to speak, an extension of the ego, there is also an intellectual private property, whose violation effects a lesion of the ego in its very center." Georg Simmel, "Secrecy and Group Communication," reprinted in T. Parsons, *et al.*, *Theories of Society*, New York: The Free Press of Glencoe, 1961, p. 320. For an updated statement of Simmel's point see Goffman, *Behavior in Public Places, op. cit.*

among friends are ecologically distinguishable from those between acquaintances or strangers. A person who persists in violating the extraterritorial space of another of the same sex may be
accused of tactlessness and suspected of homosexuality, while uninvited intersex invasion may indicate unwarranted familiarity.[19]
Moreover, eye contact and visual persistence can be a measure of
external space. Thus two strangers may look one another over at
the proper distance but as they near one another propriety requires
that they treat one another as non-persons unless a direct contact
is going to be made.[20]

Control over "inner space" is the quintessence of individuality
and freedom. Violations of "inner space" are carried out by
domination, ranging in intensity from perception of more than is
voluntarily revealed to persuasion and ultimately hypnosis.[21]
Demonstration of idiosyncracy with respect to "inner space" is
exemplified by the modifications possible in the presentation of self
through the uses of the several stimulants and depressants.

TERRITORIAL ENCROACHMENT

We can distinguish three forms of territorial encroachment:
violation, invasion, and contamination.

Violation of a territory is unwarranted use of it. Violators are

[19] An interesting dilemma in this respect arises for the deaf and myopic. In
attempting to appear as "normals" they may overstep another's territorial space
and thus call attention to the very stigma they wish to conceal. On the problems
of those who are stigmatized see Goffman, *Stigma*, Englewood Cliffs, New Jersey:
Prentice-Hall, 1963.

[20] Goffman refers to this as "civil inattention." See *Behavior in Public Places*,
op. cit.

[21] Compare the remarks by Simmel, *op. cit.*, p. 321. "In the interest of interaction and social cohesion, the individual *must* know certain things about the other
person. Nor does the other have the right to oppose this knowledge from a moral
standpoint, by demanding the discretion of the first: he cannot claim the entirely
undisturbed possession of his own being and consciousness, since this discretion
might harm the interests of his society . . . But even in subtler and less unambiguous forms, in fragmentary beginnings and unexpressed notions, all of
human intercourse rests on the fact that everybody knows somewhat more about

those who have repulsed or circumvented those who would deny them access. Violators are also by virtue of their acts claimants in some sense to the territory they have violated. Their claim, however, may vary in scope, intensity, and objective. Children may violate the graves of the dead by digging "for treasure" in the cemetery, but unlike ghouls, they are not seeking to remove the bodies for illicit purposes. Some territories may be violated, however, merely by unwarranted entrance into them. Among these are all those territories commonly restricted to categorical groups such as toilets, harems, nunneries, and public baths—areas commonly restricted according to sex. Other territories may not be necessarily violated by presence but only by innovative or prohibited use. Thus some parents regard family-wide nudity as permissible but hold that sexual interest or intercourse among any but the married pair is forbidden. Interactional territories are violated when one or more of the legitimate interactants behaves out of character.[22]

Invasion of a territory occurs when those not entitled to entrance or use nevertheless cross the boundaries and interrupt, halt, take over, or change the social meaning of the territory. Such invasions, then, may be temporary or enduring.

Contamination of a territory requires that it be rendered impure with respect to its definition and usage. Cholera may require that a portion of the city be quarantined. In a racial caste society the sidewalks may be contaminated by low caste persons walking upon them. Home territories may be contaminated by pollution or destruction of the "home symbols". Orthodox Jews may destroy their dinnerware when an unwary maid has accidentally mixed the milk and meat dishes. Heterosexuals who regularly congregate at a bar sometimes discontinue their patronage when known homosexuals begin frequenting the bar. (This example illustrates a continuum in

---

the other than the other voluntarily reveals to him; and those things he knows are frequently matters whose knowledge the other person (were he aware of it) would find undesirable." See also Goffman, *The Presentation Of Self in Everyday Life, op. cit.,* pp. 1–16.

[22] The structural properties and parameters of interactional territories in unserious gatherings have been admirably presented by Georg Simmel. See his "The Sociology of Sociability," *American Journal of Sociology,* (November, 1949), pp. 254–261. Reprinted in Parsons, *et al., Theories of Society, op. cit.,* pp. 157–163.

the process of territorial encroachment from invasion to contamination.) Interactional territories may be contaminated by
sudden odors, especially if they emanate from one of the interactants,
or by indiscreet language, e.g., obscenity, among those for whom
identification with such language constitutes a loss of face or a
reduction in status.[23]

Contamination of bodily territories occurs whenever the immediate space of or around the body is polluted. The removal by
bathing of material involuntarily attached to the skin constitutes a
ritualized purification rite of considerable importance in industrial
societies.[24] However, body space may be contaminated in many
ways, by smell, look, touch, and by proximity to contaminated
persons or things. The sensitivity with respect to touch illustrates
the complex nature of this contamination and also its peculiarly
social character. The rules regarding touch are highly developed in
American society and are clear indicators of social distance between
individuals and groups.[25] Typically older people can touch younger
ones, but suspicions of sexual immorality modify such contacts.
Women who are friends or relatives may greet one another with a
light kiss (commonly called a "peck") on the cheek, but not on the
lips. Men who are long absent may be greeted by male friends and
relatives with a hearty embrace and a touching of the cheeks, but
the embrace must not be overlong or tender. Indeed, "rough-
housing," mock-fighting, and pseudo-hostility are commonly employed in masculine affective relationships. Touch which would
otherwise be contaminating is exempt from such designation
when it takes place in situations of intense social action, e.g., on

[23] Here perhaps it is worth noting that language has a "tactile" dimension,
in the sense that to be "touched" audially by certain terms is to be elevated or
reduced in status. For Southern Negroes to be publicly addressed as "Mr.,"
"Miss," and "Mrs.," and by last names is considered so relevant for removal of
caste barriers that legal action to require these usages has been undertaken. We
may also note that genteel persons are polluted by audial contact with slang,
obscenity, and, on occasion, idiomatic expression.

[24] See Horace Miner, "Body Ritual Among the Nacirema," *American Anthropologist*, 55, No. 3, (1956).

[25] Note such phrases as "I wouldn't touch him with a ten-foot pole"; "she's
under my skin"; "he's a pain in the neck," and "Look, but don't touch." For the
rules regarding touch see Erving Goffman, "The Nature of Deference and
Demeanor," *op. cit.*

a dance floor, or in situations when the actors are not privileged to interact, e.g., crowded buses. At other times bodies contaminated by impermissible contacts are restored to their pure state by apologies.

Body space may be contaminated by a kind of negative charismatic contact whereby objects which, though neutral in themselves, carry contaminating effect when transferred directly to the body. Thus a comb or toothbrush may not be lent or borrowed in certain circles since to use someone else's tools of personal hygiene is to contaminate oneself. Typically when clothing, especially clothing that will directly touch the skin, is lent, it is proper for the lender to assure the borrower that the apparel is clean, and that it has not been worn by anyone since its last cleaning.[26] A more striking example involves the rule of some shops forbidding Negroes from trying on clothes—their skin being regarded as a source of pollution. Similarly, drinking from the same glass as another is discouraged as a matter of hygiene among the middle class and as a source of pollution if it occurs among persons of different races or castes.

REACTION TO ENCROACHMENT

We have already suggested that something of a reciprocal relation exists between the territorial types. For example, a public swimming pool—while officially open to all persons—might be conceived by certain regular users as an exclusive area. Strangers seeking access by virtue of their diffuse civic rights might be challenged by those whose sense of peculiar propriety is thus violated. Such a confrontation (sometimes called "when push meets shove") could result in retreat on the part of the party seeking admittance, flight on the part of those favoring denial, or strategy and tactics on the part of the contending parties to expand the area

[26] Robin Williams has shown that one test of social distance among the races in America is their unwillingness to try on clothing at an apparel shop when they have witnessed that clothing tried on and rejected by members of another—and supposedly inferior—race. Robin Williams, *Strangers Next Door*, Englewood Cliffs: Prentice-Hall, 1964, pp. 125–130.

of legitimate access on the one hand, and withhold entirely or restrict the meaning of entry on the other.

Of course, the occupants of a territory may extend its use to others whose presence is not regarded as a threat. The most common situation is that in which common usage will not destroy or alter the value of the territory.[27] When public territories have been colonized by users who do not fully monopolize the space, who embroider it by their presence or whose occupancy still allows for other public and colonizing usages, the colonists will not be seriously opposed. Delinquent gangs who often define the streets of a neighborhood as a home territory do not usually regard the presence of local adults and children as an encroachment on their own occupancy. Unwarranted intrusion on interactional territories may be countenanced if the unwelcome guest indicates his willingness to be present on this occasion alone with no future rights of reentry, or to listen only and not to interrupt the proceedings. Bodies usually invulnerable to feel and probe by strangers may be violated if the act is defined as physically safe, socially irrelevant, or emotionally neutral. Thus female nurses may massage their male patients with mutual impunity, and striptease dancers may perform unclothed upon a raised stage out of reach of the audience.[28] However, all such contacts will tend to be defined as territorial encroachment when the claimants threaten obliteration, monopoly, or fundamental alteration of a territory. Under these conditions, the holders of territory are likely to react to unwelcomed claimants in terms of *turf defense, insulation,* or *linguistic collusion.*

---

[27] Our usage is similar to that employed in describing the relationships in plant-communities. "The majority of individuals of a plant-community are linked by bonds other than those mentioned—bonds that are best described as *commensal.* The term commensalism is due to Van Beneden, who wrote 'Le commensal est simplement un compagnon de table'; but we employ it in a somewhat different sense to denote the relationship subsisting between species which share with one another the supply of food-material contained in soil and air, and thus feed at the same table." Robert E. Park and Ernest W. Burgess, *Introduction to the Science of Sociology,* Chicago: University of Chicago Press, 1921, p. 175. (Adapted from Eugenius Warming, *Oecology of Plants,* London: Oxford University Press, 1909, pp. 12–13, 91–95.)

[28] Ann Terry D'Andre, "An Occupational Study of the Strip-Dancer Career," paper delivered at the annual meetings of the Pacific Sociological Association, Salt Lake City, Utah, 1965.

Turf defense

Turf defense is a response necessitated when the intruder cannot be tolerated. The animal world provides a multitude of examples which are instructive with respect to the human situation.[29] Here we may be content, however, to confine ourselves to the human scene. When Chinese merchants sought "colonizing" rights among the urban merchants of San Francisco, they were welcomed and honored. A few years later, however, the appearance of Chinese miners in the white Americans' cherished gold fields called forth violent altercations and forced removals.[30] In contemporary American cities delinquent gangs arm themselves with rocks, knives, tire irons, and zip guns to repel invaders from other streets.[31] Among the "primitive" Kagoro the choice of weapons is escalated in accordance with the social distance of the combatants; poison spears and strategems are employed exclusively against hostile strangers and invaders.[32]

Turf defense is an ultimate response, however. Other more subtle repulsions or restrictions are available to proprietors wishing to maintain territorial control.

Insulation

Insulation is the placement of some sort of barrier between the occupants of a territory and potential invaders. The narrow streets, steep staircases, and regularized use of Cantonese dialects in Chinatowns serve notice on tourists that they may look over the

[29] See Ardrey, *op. cit.*, p. 210, who writes: "Biology as a whole asks but one question of a territory: is it defended? Defense defines it. Variability becomes the final description." See also Konrad Lorenz, *On Aggression*, New York: Harcourt, Brace and World, 1966, pp. 33–38 *et passim*.

[30] See Mary Coolidge, *Chinese Immigration*, New York: Henry Holt, 1909, pp. 15–26, 255–56.

[31] See Lewis Yablonsky, *The Violent Gang*, New York: MacMillan, 1962, pp. 29–100 for a good ethnography of urban gangs. For an analytical treatment see Frederic M. Thrasher, *The Gang*, Chicago: University of Chicago Press, 1927, pp. 97–100, 116–129.

[32] See M. G. Smith, "Kagoro Political Development," *Human Organization* (Fall, 1960), pp. 137–149.

external trappings of Chinese life in the Occidental city but not easily penetrate its inner workings. Distinct uniforms distinguishing status, rights, and prerogatives serve to protect military officers from the importunities of enlisted men, professors from students, and doctors from patients.[33] Bodily insulation characteristically takes the form of civil inattention and may be occasioned by a subordinate's inability to repel invasion directly. Another common form of insulation involves use of body and facial idiom to indicate impenetrability. It may be affected by the use of sunglasses,[34] or attained accidentally, by dint of culturally distinct perceptions of facial gestures, as, for example, often happens to orientals in Western settings.[35] It can also be attained by conscious efforts in the management and control of the mouth, nostrils, and especially the eyes.[36]

Linguistic collusion

Linguistic collusion involves a complex set of processes by which the territorial integrity of the group is reaffirmed and the intruder is labeled as an outsider. For example, the defending interactants may engage one another in conversation and gestures designed to so confuse the invader that he responds in a manner automatically labeling him eligible for either exclusion from the group or shameful status diminution. In one typical strategy the

[33] It is now a commonplace of sociological irony that persons thus insulated are vulnerable once the insulating material is removed or ubiquitously available. Thus non-coms will insult officers in clubs when both are out of uniform, psychiatrists will be mistaken for patients at dances held in the recreation room of an insane asylum, and students will adopt an inappropriate familiarity with professors not wearing a coat and tie.

[34] See Goffman, *Behavior in Public Places*, *op. cit.*, p. 85 for a succinct account of the elements of this process as a form of civil inattention.

[35] Kathleen Tamagawa, *Holy Prayers in a Horse's Ear*, New York: Long, Smith, Inc., 1932, pp. 144–151 *et passim*. Andre M.Tao-Kim-Hai, "Orientals are Stoic," in F.C.Macgregor, *Social Science in Nursing*, New York: Russell Sage, 1960, pp. 313–326.

[36] See Georg Simmel, "The Aesthetic Significance of the Face," in Kurt H. Wolff, editor, *Georg Simmel 1858–1918*, Columbus: Ohio State University Press, 1959, pp. 280–281.

defending interactants will speak to one another in a language unfamiliar to the invader. Ethnic enclaves provide numerous examples. Jewish and Chinese storekeepers will speak Yiddish and Cantonese respectively to their clerks when discussing prices, bargaining rights, and product quality in the presence of alien customers. Negroes may engage one another in a game of "the dozens" in the presence of intruding whites, causing the latter considerable consternation and mystification.[37] And teenagers develop a peer group argot (frequently borrowed from Negro and jazz musician usages) which sets them apart from both children and adults, and which, incidentally, is most frequently cited as proof for the claim that a distinctive youth culture does exist in the United States.

In another recognizable strategy, the participants continue to engage in the same behavior but in a more exaggerated and "staged" manner. Mood and tone of the voice are sometimes regulated to achieve this effect. Thus persons engaged in conversation may intensify their tone and include more intra-group gestures when an outsider enters the area. Professors may escalate the use of jargon and "academese" in conversations in the presence of uninvited students or other "inferiors." Homosexuals engaged in flirtations in a "gay" bar may exaggerate their femininity when heterosexuals enter the establishment. Such staged displays call attention to the exclusive culture of the interactants and suggest to the outsider that he is bereft of the cards of identity necessary to participate.

REACTION TO THE ABSENCE OF FREE SPACE

There are some segments of society that are systematically denied free territories. One outstanding example is that of lower-class urban Negro youth. Their homes are small, cramped, and

---

[37] The usual situation is quite the reverse, however. The "dozens" and other verbal contest forms are most frequently used by Negroes within the ethnic enclave out of earshot and view of whites. See Roger D. Abrahams, *Deep Down in the Jungle*, Hatboro, Penn.: Folklore Associates, 1964, esp. pp. 41–64.

cluttered and also serve as specialized areas of action for adults; their meeting places are constantly under surveillance by the agents of law enforcement and social workers; and, when in clusters on the street, they are often stopped for questioning and booked "on suspicion" by the seemingly ever-present police.[38]

What is the condition of Negro youth in particular appears to be an exaggerated instance of the trend with respect to denial of freedom among youth in general. Thus it has been suggested that youth are adrift somewhere between humanism and fatalism, i.e., between situations in which they feel they have control over their destinies and those in which such control is in the hands of forces outside youth's individual direction and influence.[39] In such a situation one response is to seek to maximize the area of freedom, the situations in which one can exercise liberty and license, the times one can be cause rather than effect. Among lower-class youth the carving of home territories out of the space provided as public ones is common and has already been noted. Note also, however, the frequency with which youth-created home territories are subject to invasion, violation, and contamination and the relative vulnerability of youth home territories to such encroachments.

Exercising freedom over body territory provides a more fruitful approach to those for whom public territories are denied and home territories difficult or impossible to maintain. The body and its attendant inner and external space have an aura of ownership and control about them that is impressed upon the incumbent. The hypothesis we wish to suggest here is that as other forms of free territory are perceived to be foreclosed by certain segments of the society, these segments, or at least those elements of the segments not constrained by other compelling forces, will utilize more frequently and intensively the area of body space as a free territory. Three forms of such utilization are prominent: *manipulation*, *adornment*, and *penetration*.

Manipulation rests upon the fact that the body is adjustable in a greater number of ways than are positively sanctioned and that

---

[38] See Carl Werthman, *Delinquency and Authority*, M.A. Thesis, University of California, Berkeley, 1964.

[39] David Matza, *Delinquency and Drift*, New York: John Wiley, 1964.

by modifying the appearance of the self one can establish identity, and flaunt convention with both ease and relative impunity. Thus children, separated from one another for being naughty and enjoined from conversation, may sit and "make faces" at one another, conforming to the letter of their punishment but violating its principle. Teenagers, denied approval for the very sexual activity for which they are biologically prepared and also enclosed more and more from private usage of public territories for such purposes, have developed dance forms which involve little or no body contact but are nevertheless suggestive of the most intimate and forbidden forms of erotic interaction. Further, male youth—enjoined from verbal scatalogical forms by customs and by rules of propriety— have developed a gesture language by which they can communicate the desired obscenity without uttering it.

Adornment of the body is another response.[40] By covering, uncovering, marking, and disfiguring the body individuals can at least partly overcome whatever loss of freedom they suffer from other encroachments. Both the French "bohemians" of the nineteenth century and the disaffected American Negro youths of the twentieth have exhibited themselves as "dandies,"[41] while the ascetic Doukhobors of British Columbia disrobe entirely and in public when challenged by authority.[42] Body space may also be attended by filling in the apertures in nose, mouth and ears by rings, bones, and other emblematic artifacts; by marking upon the skin with inks and tattoos; and by disfigurements, scars, and severance of non-vital members. An alternative mode of adornment, that appears to be directed definitely against elements of the core culture, is the refusal to use instruments of personal hygiene. We have already noted how these instruments acquire a peculiar aspect of the personal charisma of the user so that people do not customarily borrow the comb, toothbrush, and razor of another

---

[40] Many suggestive essays on this subject can be found in *Dress, Adornment, and the Social Order*, ed. by M. E. Roach and J. B. Eicher, N.Y.: John Wiley, 1965.

[41] See Cesar Grana, *Bohemian vs. Bourgeois*, New York: Basic Books, 1964, and Harold Finestone, "Cats, Kicks, and Color," *Social Problems*, V. 5, 1 (1957), pp. 3–13.

[42] See Harry B. Hawthorn, editor, *The Doukhobors of British Columbia*, Vancouver, B.C.: The University of British Columbia and Dent & Sons, 1955.

unless the contamination that occurs thereby is neutralized. Here, however, adornment occurs by simply *not* washing, combing, shaving, cutting the hair, etc. Like public nudity this form of assertiveness and reaction to oppression has the advantage of inhibiting a like response among those who are offended by the appearance created thereby, but, unlike stripping in public, the added advantage of being legal.

Penetration refers to the exploitation and modification of inner space in the search for free territory. One might hypothesize that the greater the sense of unfreedom, the greater the exercise of body liberty so that penetration is an escalated aspect of manipulation and adornment. There is, as it were, a series of increasing gradations of body space. The ultimate effort is to gain freedom by changing one's internal environment. The simplest form of this is cultivating a vicarious sense of being away, of transporting the self out of its existential environment by musing, daydreaming, or relapsing into a reverie.[43] However, voluntary reorganization of the inner environment can be assisted by alcohol and drugs. Contemporary college youth sometimes partake of hallucinogenic and psychedelic drugs in order to make an inner migration (or "take a trip" as the popular idiom has it).

CONCLUSION

The concept of territoriality offers a fruitful approach for the analysis of freedom and situated action. Although the early school of ecology in American sociology provided a possible avenue for this kind of exploration, its practitioners appear to have eschewed the interactionist and phenomenological aspects of the subject in favor of the economic and the biotic. Nevertheless, much of their work needs to be examined afresh for the clues it provides for understanding the nature and function of space and the organization of territories. Similarly the work done by the students of non-human animal association provides clues to concept formation and

---

[43] Goffman, *Behavior in Public Places, op. cit.*, pp. 69–75.

suggestions for research. Here we may mention several potentially fruitful areas. The first involves cross-cultural studies of territoriality. Such studies would attempt to describe in greater specificity the constituent features of types of territoriality, the ways in which they vary, and their interrelationships. Using a cross-cultural perspective would also serve to specify generic forms of reactions to territorial encroachment and to establish how certain contexts predispose one type of response rather than another. A second area of research would focus on a variety of deviant behaviors (e.g., crime, juvenile delinquency, drug addition) with the purpose of understanding the part the territorial variable plays in the etiology of such behaviors. Finally, we may suggest that micro-sociological studies of .territoriality—which are perhaps more amenable to rigorous research design—may be extrapolated to an analysis of macro-sociological inquiries, especially in the realm of international affairs.

5

Accounts

From time to time sociologists might well pause from their ongoing pursuits to inquire whether their research interests contribute in any way to the fundamental question of sociology, namely, the Hobbesian question: How is society possible? Answers addressed to this question might well serve to unite a discipline that may not yet have forgotten its founders, but nevertheless may have forgotten why it was founded.

Our purpose here is not to review the various answers to the Hobbesian question,[1] but rather to suggest that an answer to this macro-sociological problem might be fruitfully explored in the analysis of the slightest of interpersonal rituals and the very stuff of which most of those rituals are composed—talk.

Talk, we hold, is the fundamental material of human relations. And though sociologists have not entirely neglected the subject,[2] the

Marvin B. Scott and Stanford M. Lyman, "Accounts," *American Sociological Review*, Vol. 33, No. 1 (1968), pp. 46–62. By permission of the authors and of The American Sociological Association.

[1] For a now classic statement and analysis of the Hobbesian question, see the discussion by Talcott Parsons, *The Structure of Social Action*, Glencoe, Ill.: The Free Press, 1949, pp. 89–94.

[2] See, for instance, William Soskin and Vera John, "The Study of Spontaneous Talk," in *The Stream of Behavior*, edited by Roger Barker, N.Y.: Appleton-Century-Crofts, 1963, pp. 228–282. Much suggestive material and complete bibliography can be found in Joyce O. Hertzler, *A Sociology of Language*, N.Y.: Random House, 1965.

sociology of talk has scarcely been developed. Our concern here is with one feature of talk: its ability to shore up the timbers of fractured sociation, its ability to throw bridges between the promised and the performed, its ability to repair the broken and restore the estranged.

This feature of talk involves the giving and receiving of what we shall call *accounts*.

An account is a linguistic device employed whenever an action is subjected to valuative inquiry.[3] Such devices are a crucial element in the social order since they prevent conflicts from arising by verbally bridging the gap between action and expectation.[4] Moreover, accounts are "situated" according to the statuses of the interactants, and are standardized within cultures so that certain accounts are terminologically stabilized and routinely expected when activity falls outside the domain of expectations.

By an account, then, we refer to a statement made by a social actor to explain unanticipated or untoward behavior—whether that behavior is his own or that of others, and whether the proximate cause for the statement arises from the actor himself or someone else.[5] An account is not called for when people engage in routine, common-sense behavior in a cultural environment that recognizes that behavior as such. Thus, in American society we do not ordinarily ask why married people engage in sexual intercourse, or why they

---

[3] An account has a family resemblance to the verbal component of a "motive" in Weber's sense of the term. Weber defined a motive as "a complex of subjective meaning which seems to the actor himself or to the observer as an adequate ground for the conduct in question." Max Weber, *Theory of Social and Economic Organization*, translated by Talcott Parsons and A. M. Hendersen, Glencoe: The Free Press, 1947, pp. 98–99. Following Weber's definition and building on G. H. Mead's social psychology and the work of Kenneth Burke, C. Wright Mills was among the first to employ the notion of accounts in his much neglected essay, "Situated Action and the Vocabulary of Motives," *American Sociological Review*, V. 6 (December, 1940), pp. 904–913. Contemporary British philosophy, following the leads of Ludwig Wittgenstein, has (apparently) independently advanced the idea of a "vocabulary of motives." An exemplary case is R. S. Peters' *The Concept of Motivation*, London: Routledge and Kegan Paul, 1958.

[4] The point is nicely illustrated by Jackson Toby in "Some Variables in Role Conflict Analysis," *Social Forces*, V. 30 (March, 1952), pp. 323–327.

[5] Thus, by an account we include also those non-vocalized but lingual explanations that arise in an actor's "mind" when he questions his own behavior. However, our concern is with vocalized accounts and especially those that are given in face-to-face relations.

maintain a home with their children, though the latter question might well be asked if such behavior occurred among the Nayars of Malabar.[6] These questions are not asked because they have been settled in advance in our culture and are indicated by the language itself. We learn the meaning of a "married couple" by indicating that they are two people of opposite sex who have the legitimate right to engage in sexual intercourse and maintain their own children in their own household. When such taken-for-granted phenomena are called into question, the inquirer (if a member of the same culture group) is regarded as "just fooling around," or perhaps as being "sick."[7]

To specify our concerns more sharply we should at this point distinguish accounts from the related phenomena of "explanations." The latter refers to statements about events where untoward action is not an issue and does not have critical implications for a relationship. Much of what is true about accounts will also hold for explanations, but our concern is primarily with linguistic forms that are offered for untoward action. Qualifying our concern in this way, we may now specify further the nature and types of accounts.

TYPES OF ACCOUNTS

There are in general two types of accounts: *excuses* and *justifications*.[8] Either or both are likely to be invoked when a person is accused of having done something that is "bad, wrong, inept, unwelcome, or in some other of the numerous possible ways,

---

[6] William J. Goode, *World Revolution and Family Pattern*, New York: The Free Press of Glencoe, 1963, pp. 254–256.

[7] Moreover, common-sense understandings that violate widespread cognitive knowledge, such as are asserted in statements like "the sun rises every morning and sets every night," or avowed in perceptions that a straight stick immersed in water appears bent, are expected to be maintained. Persons who always insist on the astronomically exact statement about the earth's relation to the sun might be considered officious or didactic, while those who "see" a straight stick in a pool might be credited with faulty eyesight. For a relevant discussion of social reactions to inquiries about taken-for-granted phenomena see Harold Garfinkel, "Studies of the Routine Grounds of Everyday Activities," *Social Problems*, V. 11 (Winter,

untoward."[9] Justifications are accounts in which one accepts responsibility for the act in question, but denies the pejorative quality associated with it. Thus a soldier in combat may admit that he has killed other men, but deny that he did an immoral act since those he killed were members of an enemy group and hence "deserved" their fate. Excuses are accounts in which one admits that the act in question is bad, wrong, or inappropriate but denies full responsibility. Thus our combat soldier could admit the wrongfulness of killing but claim that his acts are not entirely undertaken by volition: he is "under orders" and must obey. With these introductory remarks, we now turn our focus to a more detailed examination of types of justifications and excuses.

Excuses are socially approved vocabularies for mitigating or relieving responsibility when conduct is questioned. We may distinguish initially four model forms by which excuses are typically formulated:[10] *appeal to accidents, appeal to defeasibility, appeal to biological drives,* and *scapegoating.*

Excuses claiming *accident* as the source of conduct or its consequences mitigate (if not relieve) responsibility by pointing to the generally recognized hazards in the environment, the understandable inefficiency of the body, and the human incapacity to control all motor responses. The excuse of accident is acceptable precisely because of the irregularity and infrequency of accidents occurring to any single actor. Thus while hazards are numerous and ubiquitous, a particular person is not expected ordinarily to experience the same accident often. In other words social actors employ a lay version of statistical curves whereby they interpret certain acts as occurring or not occurring by chance alone. When a person conducts himself so that the same type of accident befalls him frequently, he is apt to earn a label—such as "clumsy"—which will operate to stigmatize him and to warn others not to put him and

---

1964), pp. 225–250, and "A Conception of and Experiments with 'Trust' as a Condition of Concerted Action" in *Motivation and Social Interaction*, edited by O. J. Harvey, N.Y.: Ronald Press, 1963, pp. 187–238.

[8] We have taken this formulation from J. L. Austin. See his *Philosophical Papers*, London: Oxford University Press, 1961, pp. 123–152.

[9] *Ibid.*, p. 124.

[10] These types of excuses are to be taken as illustrative rather than as an exhaustive listing.

themselves or their property in jeopardy by creating the environment in which he regularly has accidents. When the excuse is rooted in an accident that is unobservable or unable to be investigated—such as blaming one's lateness to work on the heaviness of traffic—frequent pleas of it are likely to be discredited. Excuses based on accidents are thus most likely to be honored precisely because they do not occur all the time or for the most part to the actor in question.[11]

Appeals to *defeasibility*[12] are available as a form of excuse because of the widespread agreement that all actions contain some "mental element." The components of the mental element are "knowledge" and "will." One defense against an accusation is that a person was not fully informed or that his "will" was not completely "free." Thus an individual might excuse himself from responsibility by claiming that certain information was not available to him, which if it had been would have altered his behavior. Further, an individual might claim to have acted in a certain way because of misinformation arising from intentional or innocent misrepresentation of the facts by others. An excuse based on interference in the "free will" of an individual might invoke duress or undue influence. Finally, both will and knowledge can be impaired under certain conditions, the invocation of which ordinarily constitutes an adequate mitigation of responsibility—intoxication (whether from alcohol or drugs) and lunacy (whether temporary or permanent) being examples.

In ordinary affairs and in law a person's actions are usually

---

[11] Only where nothing is left to chance—as among the Azande where particular misfortunes are accounted for by a ubiquitous witchcraft—is the excuse by accident not likely to occur. Zande do not assert witchcraft to be the sole cause of phenomena; they have a "practical" and "realistic" approach to events which would enjoy consensual support from Occidental observers. However, Zande account for what Occidentals would call "chance" or "coincidence" by reference to witchcraft. E. E. Evans-Pritchard writes: "We have no explanation of why the two chains of causation [resulting in a catastrophe] intersected at a certain time and in a certain place, for there is no interdependence between them. Zande philosophy can supply the missing link. . . . It is due to witchcraft. . . . Witchcraft explains the coincidence of these two happenings." *Witchcraft, Oracles and Magic Among the Azande*, London: Oxford University Press, 1937, p. 70.

[12] Defeasibility, or the capacity of being voided, is a concept developed by H. L. A. Hart. This section leans heavily on Hart's essay, "The Ascription of Responsibility and Rights," in *Logic and Language, First Series*, edited by Antony Flew, Oxford: Basil Blackwell, 1960, pp. 145–166.

distinguished according to their intent. Further, a person's intentions are distinguished from the consequences of his actions. Under a situation where an action is questioned an actor may claim a lack of intent or a failure to foresee the consequences of his act, or both. If the action in question involves a motor response—such as knocking over a vase—the situation is not very different from that subsumed under the term accident. When actions going beyond motor responses are at issue, the actor's intentions and foresight can be questioned. "Why did you make her cry?" asks the accuser. The presentational strategies in reply to this question allow several modes of defeating the central claim implied in the question, namely, that the actor intended with full knowledge to make the lady weep. The accused may simply deny any intention on his part to have caused the admittedly unfortunate consequence. However, men ordinarily impute to one another some measure of foresight for their actions so that a simple denial of intent may not be believed if it appears that the consequence of the action in question was indeed what another person might expect and, therefore, what the actor intended.

In addition to his denial of intent an actor may also deny his knowledge of the consequence. The simplest denial is the cognitive disclaimer: "I did not *know* that I would make her cry by what I did." But this complete denial of cognition is often not honored, especially when the interactants know one another well and are expected to have a more complete image of the consequences of their acts to guide them. A more complex denial—the gravity disclaimer—includes admitting to the possibility of the outcome in question but suggesting that its probability was incalculable: "I knew matters were serious, but I did not know that telling her would make her weep."

Still another type of excuse invokes *biological* drives. This invocation is part of a larger category of "fatalistic" forces which in various cultures are deemed in greater or lesser degree to be controlling of some or all events. Cultures dominated by universalist-achievement orientations[13] tend to give scant and ambiguous

[13] For a general discussion of cultures in terms of their "fatalistic" orientations or universalist-achievement orientations, see Talcott Parsons, "A Revised Analytical Approach to the Theory of Social Stratification," in *Essays in Sociological Theory*, Glencoe: The Free Press, 1954, pp. 386–439. See also Parsons, *The Social System*, Glencoe: The Free Press, 1951.

support to fatalistic interpretations of events, but rarely disavow them entirely. To account for the whole of one's life in such terms, or to account for events which are conceived by others to be controlled by the actor's conscience, will, and abilities is to lay oneself open to the charge of mental illness or personality disorganization.[14] On the other hand, recent studies have emphasized the situational element in predisposing certain persons and groups in American society to what might be regarded as a "normalized" fatalistic view of their condition. Thus, for example, Negroes[15] and adolescent delinquents[16] are regarded and tend to regard themselves as less in control of the forces that shape their lives than caucasians or middle-class adults.

Among the fatalistic items most likely to be invoked as an excuse are the biological drives. Despite the emphasis in Occidental culture since the late nineteenth century on personality and social environment as causal elements in human action, there is still a popular belief in and varied commitment to the efficacy of the body and biological factors in determining human behavior. Such commonplaces as "men are like that" are short-hand phrases invoking belief in sex-linked traits that allegedly govern behavior beyond the will of the actor. Precisely because the body and its biological apparatus are always present but not always accounted for in science or society, invocation of the body and its processes is available as an excuse. The body and its inner workings enjoy

[14] Thus, in the most famous study of the psychodynamics of prejudice, one of the characteristics of the intolerant or "authoritarian" personality is "externalization," i.e., the attribution of causality of events believed to be within the actor's power or rational comprehension to uncontrollable forces beyond his influence or understanding. See T. W. Adorno, *et al.*, *The Authoritarian Personality*, N.Y.: Harper and Row, 1950, pp. 474-475. See also Gordon W. Allport, *The Nature of Prejudice*, Garden City: Doubleday Anchor, 1958, p. 379. In a recent study an intermittently employed cab driver's insistence that there would inevitably be a revolution after which the world would be taken over by Negroes and Jews is recalled as one of several early warning cues that he is mentally ill. Marion Radke Yarrow, *et al.*, "The Psychological Meaning of Mental Illness in the Family," in Thomas J. Scheff, *Mental Illness and Social Process*, N.Y.: Harper and Row, 1967, p. 35.

[15] See Horace R. Cayton, "The Psychology of the Negro Under Discrimination," in Arnold Rose, editor, *Race Prejudice and Discrimination*, N.Y.: Alfred Knopf, 1953, pp. 276-290; and Bertram P. Karon, *The Negro Personality*, N.Y.: Springer, 1958, pp. 8-53, 140-160.

[16] David Matza, *Delinquency and Drift*, N.Y.: Wiley, 1964, pp. 88-90, 188-191.

something of the status of the sociological stranger as conceived by Simmel, namely, they are ever with us but mysterious. Hence, biological drives may be credited with influencing or causing at least some of the behavior for which actors wish to relieve themselves of full responsibility.

The invocation of biological drives is most commonly an appeal to natural but uncontrollable sexual appetite. Among first and second generation Italians in America the recognition and fear of biologically induced sexual intercourse serves men as both an excuse for pre- and extra-marital sex relations and a justification for not being alone with women ineligible for coitus. Thus, one student of Italian-American culture observes:

> What the men fear is their own ability at self-control. This attitude, strongest among young unmarried people, often carries over into adulthood. The traditional Italian belief—that sexual intercourse is unavoidable when a man and a woman are by themselves—is maintained intact among second-generation [Italians], and continues even when sexual interest itself is on the wane. For example, I was told of an older woman whose apartment was adjacent to that of an unmarried male relative. Although they had lived in the same building for almost twenty years and saw each other almost every day, she had never once been in his apartment because of this belief.[17]

Biological drive may be an expected excuse in some cultures so that the failure to invoke it and the use of some other excuse constitutes an improper account when the appropriate one is available. Oscar Lewis provides such an example in his ethnography of a Mexican family. A cuckolded wife angrily rejects her wayward husband's explanation that the red stains on his shirt are due to paint rubbed off during the course of his work. She strongly suggests, in her retelling of the incident, that she would have accepted an excuse appealing to her husband's basic sex drives:

> And he had me almost believing it was red paint! It was not that I am

---

[17] Herbert J. Gans, *The Urban Villagers*, N.Y.: The Free Press, 1962, p. 49. According to another student of Italian-American life, slum-dwelling members of this subculture believe that "a man's health requires sexual intercourse at certain intervals." William F. Whyte, "A Slum Sex Code," *American Journal of Sociology*, V. 49 (July, 1943), p. 26.

jealous. I realize a man can never be satisfied with just one woman, but I cannot stand being made a fool of.[18]

Homosexuals, too, frequently account for their deviant sexual desires by invoking the principle of basic biological nature. As one homosexual put it:

It's part of nature. You can't alter it, no matter how many injections and pills they give you.[19]

Another of the biological elements that can be utilized as an excuse is the shape of the body itself. Body types are not only defined in purely anatomical terms, but also, and perhaps more importantly, in terms of their shared social meanings. Hence, fat people can excuse their excessive laughter by appealing to the widely accepted proverb that fat men are jolly. Similarly, persons bearing features considered to be stereotypically "criminal"[20] may be exonerated for their impoliteness or small larcenies on the grounds that their looks proved their intentions and, thus, their victims ought to have been on guard. The phrase, "he looks crooked to me," serves as a warning to others to carefully appraise the character and intentions of the person so designated since his features bespeak an illegal intent.

The final type of excuse we shall mention is scapegoating. Scapegoating is derived from another form of fatalistic reasoning. Using this form a person will allege that his questioned behavior is a response to the behavior or attitudes of another. Certain psychological theory treats this phenomenon as indicative of personality disorder, and if found in conjunction with certain other characteristic traits, a signal of authoritarian personality.[21] Our treatment

---

[18] Oscar Lewis, *The Children of Sanchez*, N.Y.: Random House, 1961, p. 475.

[19] Gordon Westwood, *A Minority*, London: Longmans, Green and Co., 1960, p. 46.

[20] For an interesting study showing that criminals believe that a fellow criminal's physical attractiveness will vary with type of crime—robbers are the most attractive, murderers the least; rapists are more attractive than pedophiles, etc.—see Raymond J. Corsini, "Appearance and Criminality," *American Journal of Sociology*, V. 65 (July, 1959), pp. 49–51.

[21] Adorno, *op. cit.*, pp. 233, 485; Allport, *op. cit.*, pp. 235–249, suggests the historicity and uniqueness of each instance of scapegoating.

bypasses such clinical and pathological concerns in order to deal with the "normal" situation in which individuals slough off the burden of responsibility for their actions and shift it on to another. In Mexican working-class society, for example, women hold a distinct secondary position relative to men, marriage causes a loss of status to the latter, and sexual intercourse is regarded ambivalently as healthy, natural, and yet also as a necessary evil.[22] Such a set of orientations predisposes both men and women to attribute many of their shortcomings to women. An example is found in the autobiography of a Mexican girl:

> I was always getting into fights because some girls are vipers; they get jealous, tell lies about each other, and start trouble.[23]

Similarly, a Mexican youth who tried unsuccessfully to meet a girl by showing off on a bicycle explains:

> She got me into trouble with my father by lying about me. She said I tried to run her down with my bike and that all I did was hang around spying on her.[24]

In another instance the same youth attributes his waywardness to the fact that the girl truly loved was his half-sister and thus unavailable to him for coitus or marriage:

> So, because of Antonia, I began to stay away from home. It was one of the main reasons I started to go on the bum, looking for trouble.[25]

Like excuses, *justifications* are socially approved vocabularies that neutralize an act or its consequences when one or both are called into question. But here is the crucial difference: to *justify* an act is to assert its positive value in the face of a claim to the contrary. Justifications recognize a general sense in which the act in question

[22] Arturo de Hoyos and Genevieve de Hoyos, "The Amigo System and Alienation of the Wife in the Conjugal Mexican Family," in Bernard Farber, editor, *Kinship and Family Organization*, N.Y.: Wiley, 1966, pp. 102–115, esp., pp. 103–107.

[23] Lewis, *op. cit.*, p. 143.

[24] *Ibid.*, p. 202.

[25] *Ibid.*, p. 86.

is impermissible, but claim that the particular occasion permits or requires the very act. The laws governing taking of life are a case in point. American and English jurisprudence are by no means united on definitions or even the nature of the acts in question, but in general a man may justify taking the life of another by claiming that he acted in self-defense, defense of others' lives or property, or in action against a declared enemy of the state.

For a tentative list of types of justifications we may turn to what has been called "techniques of neutralization."[26] Although these techniques have been discussed with respect to accounts offered by juvenile delinquents for untoward action, their wider use has yet to be explored. Relevant to our discussion of justification are the techniques of "denial of injury," "denial of victim," "condemnation of condemners," and "appeal to loyalties."[27]

In *denial of injury* the actor acknowledges that he did a particular act but asserts that it was permissible to do that act since no one was injured by it; or since no one about whom the community need be concerned with was involved; or, finally, since the act resulted in consequences that were trifling. Note that this justification device can be invoked with respect to both persons and objects. The denial of injury to *persons* suggests that they be viewed as "deserving" in a special sense: that they are oversupplied with the valued things of the world, or that they are "private" persons ("my friends," "my enemies") who have no standing to claim injury in the public, or to be noticed as injured. Denial of injury to *objects* involves redefining the act as not injurious to it but only using it (e.g., car "borrowing" is not theft).

In *denial of the victim* the actor expresses that the action was permissible since the victim deserved the injury. Four categories of persons are frequently perceived as deserving injury. First, there are proximate foes (i.e., those who have directly injured the actor); second, incumbents of normatively discrepant roles (e.g., homosexuals, whores, pimps); third, groups with tribal stigmas (e.g.,

---

[26] Gresham M. Sykes and David Matza, "Techniques of Neutralization," *American Sociological Review*, V. 22 (December, 1957), pp. 667–669.

[27] One other neutralization technique mentioned by Sykes and Matza, "denial of responsibility," is subsumed in our schema under "appeal to defeasibility."

racial and ethnic minorities); and finally, distant foes, that is, incumbents of roles held to be dubious or hurtful (e.g., "whitey," the "reds," "politicians"). Besides categories of persons, there are categories of objects perceived as deserving of injury. To begin with, the property of any of the above mentioned categories of persons may become a focus of attack, especially if that property is symbolic of the attacked person's status. Thus the clothing of the whore is torn, the gavel of the politician is smashed, and so on. Secondly, there are objects that have a neutral or ambiguous identity with respect to ownership (e.g., a park bench). A final focus of attacked objects are those having a low or polluted value (e.g., junk, or kitsch).

Using the device of *condemnation of the condemners*, the actor admits performing an untoward act but asserts its irrelevancy because others commit these and worse acts—and these others are either not caught, not punished, not condemned, unnoticed, or even praised.

Still another neutralization technique is *appeal to loyalties*. Here the actor asserts that his action was permissible or even right since it served the interests of another to whom he owes an unbreakable allegiance or affection.[28]

Besides these "techniques of neutralization," two other sorts of justifications may be mentioned: "sad tales," and "self-fulfillment." The *sad tale* is a selected (often distorted) arrangement of facts that highlight an extremely dismal past that "explains" the individual's present state.[29] For example, a mental patient relates:

[28] Note that appeal to loyalties could be an *excuse* if the argument runs that X did do A under the influence of Y's domination or love, or under the coercive influence of Y's injury to him were he not to act (e.g., loss of love, blackmail, etc.). In other words, appeal to loyalties is an excuse if X admits it was bad to do A but refuses to monopolize responsibility for A in himself.

[29] Erving Goffman, *Asylums*, Garden City: Doubleday Anchor, 1961, pp. 150–151. The sad tale involves the most dramatic instance of the general process of reconstructing personal biography whereby—for example—a husband may account for his present divorce by reconstructing the history of earlier events in an ascending scale leading up to the final dissolution. The idea of a reconstruction of biography is a continual theme in the writings of Alfred Schutz. See his *Collected Papers*, Vol. I, edited by Maurice Natanson, The Hague: Martinus Nijhoff, 1962. A short clear summary of Schutz's contribution on the reconstruction of biography is found in Peter L. Berger, *Invitation to Sociology*, Garden City: Doubleday Anchor,

I was going to night school to get a M.A. degree, and holding down a job in addition, and the load got too much for me.[30]

And a homosexual accounts for his present deviance with this sad tale:

I was in a very sophisticated queer circle at the university. It was queer in the sense that we all camped like mad with "my dear" at the beginning of every sentence, but there was practically no sex, and in my case there was none at all. The break came when I went to a party and flirted with a merchant seaman who took me seriously and cornered me in a bedroom. There was I, the great sophisticate, who, when it came to the point, was quite raw, completely inexperienced; and I might tell you that seaman gave me quite a shock. I can't say I enjoyed it very much but it wasn't long after before I started to dive into bed with anyone.[31]

Finally, we may mention a peculiarly modern type of justification, namely, *self-fulfillment*. Interviewing LSD users and homosexuals in the Haight-Ashbury district of San Francisco, we are struck by the prominence of self-fulfillment as the grounds for these activities. Thus, an "acid head" relates:

The whole purpose in taking the stuff is self-development. Acid expands consciousness. Mine eyes have seen the glory—can you say that? I never knew what capacities I had until I went on acid.[32]

And a lesbian:

Everyone has the right to happiness and love. I was married once. It was hell. But now I feel I have fulfilled myself as a person and as a woman.[33]

1963, pp. 54–65. Drawing on Schutz, Garfinkel details the concept of reconstruction of biography in a series of experiments on the "retrospective reading" of social action. See his "Common Sense Knowledge of Social Structures," in *Theories of the Mind*, edited by Jordon M. Scher, Glencoe: The Free Press, 1962, pp. 689–712. The empirical use of the concept of retrospective reading of action is nicely illustrated by John I. Kitsuse, "Societal Reaction to Deviant Behavior," in *The Other Side*, edited by Howard S. Becker, N.Y.: The Free Press of Glencoe, 1964, pp. 87–102.

[30] Goffman, *op. cit.*, p. 152.
[31] Westwood, *op. cit.*, p. 32.
[32] Tape recorded interview, May, 1967.
[33] Tape recorded interview, June, 1967.

We might also note that the drug users and homosexuals interviewed (in San Francisco) who invoked the justification of self-fulfillment did not appear to find anything "wrong" with their behavior. They indicated either a desire to be left alone or to enlighten what they considered to be the unenlightened establishment.

HONORING ACCOUNTS AND BACKGROUND EXPECTANCIES

Accounts may be honored or not honored. If an account is honored, we may say that it was efficacious and equilibrium is thereby restored in a relationship. The most common situation in which accounts are routinely honored is encounters interrupted by "incidents"—slips, boners, or gaffes which introduce information deleterious to the otherwise smooth conduct of the interactants.[34] Often a simple excuse will suffice, or the other interactants will employ covering devices to restore the *status quo ante*. A related situation is that in which an individual senses that some incident or event has cast doubt on that image of himself which he seeks to present. "At such times," the major student of impression management writes, "the individual is likely to try to integrate the incongruous events by means of apologies, little excuses for self, and disclaimers; through the same acts, incidentally, he also tries to save his face."[35]

One variable governing the honoring of an account is the character of the social circle in which it is introduced. As we pointed out earlier, vocabularies of accounts are likely to be routinized within cultures, subcultures, and groups, and some are likely to be exclusive to the circle in which they are employed. A drug addict may be able to justify his conduct to a bohemian world, but not to the courts. Similarly, kin and friends may accept excuses in situations in which strangers would refuse to do so. Finally, note that while ignorance of the consequences of an act or of its prohibition may exculpate an individual in many different circles, the law

---

[34] Erving Goffman, *Encounters*, Indianapolis: Bobbs-Merrill, 1961, pp. 45–48.
[35] *Ibid.*, p. 51.

explicitly rejects this notion: "Ignorance of the law excuses no man; not that all men know the law but because 'tis an excuse every man will plead, and no man can tell how to confute him."[36]

Both the account offered by ego and the honoring or non-honoring of the account on the part of alter will ultimately depend on the *background expectancies* of the interactants. By background expectancies we refer to those sets of taken-for-granted ideas that permit the interactants to interpret remarks as accounts in the first place.[37] Asked why he is listless and depressed, a person may reply, "I have family troubles." The remark will be taken as an account, and indeed an account that will probably be honored, because "everyone knows" that "family problems" are a cause of depression.

This last illustration suggests that certain accounts can fit a variety of situations. Thus, in response to a wide range of questions— why don't you get married? why are you in a fit of depression? why are you drinking so heavily?—the individual can respond with "I'm having family problems." The person offering such an account may not himself regard it as a true one, but invoking it has certain interactional payoffs: since people cannot say they don't understand it—they are accounts that are part of out socially distributed knowledge of what "everyone knows"—the inquiry can be cut short.

Clearly, then, a single account will stand for a wide collection of events; and the efficacy of such accounts depends upon a set of shared background expectations.

In interacting with others, the socialized person learns a repertoire of background expectancies that are appropriate for a variety of others. Hence the "normal" individual will change his account for different role others. A wife may respond sympathetically to her depressed husband because his favorite football team lost a championship game, but such an account for depression will

[36] John Selden, *Table Talk*, 1696, quoted in Harry Johnson, *Sociology*, New York: Harcourt, Brace and Co., 1960, p. 552n.

[37] The term is borrowed from Harold Garfinkel. Besides the footnote references to Garfinkel already cited, see his *Studies in Ethnomethodology*, Englewood Cliffs, N.J.: Prentice-Hall, 1968. For an original discussion on how the meaning of an account depends upon background expectancies and a methodology for its study, see Harvey Sacks, *The Search for Help*, unpublished doctoral dissertation, University of California, Berkeley, 1966.

appear bizarre when offered to one's inquiring boss. Thus background expectancies are the means not only for the honoring, but also for the non-honoring of accounts. When the millionaire accounts for his depression by saying he is a failure, others will be puzzled since "everyone knows" that millionaires are not failures. The incapacity to invoke situationally appropriate accounts—i.e., accounts that are anchored to the background expectancies of the situation—will often be taken as a sign of mental illness.[38] There are grounds then for conceptualizing normal individuals as "not stupid" rather than "not ill."[39] The person who is labeled ill has been behaving "stupidly" in terms of his culture and society: he offers accounts not situationally appropriate according to culturally defined background expectancies.[40]

Often an account can be discredited by the appearances of the person offering the account. And so when a girl accounts for her late return from a date by saying the movie was overlong—that no untoward event occurred and that she still retains virgin status—her mother may discredit the account by noting the daughter's flushed appearance. Since individuals are aware that appearances may serve to credit or discredit accounts, efforts are understandably made to control these appearances through a vast repertoire of "impression management" activities.[41]

[38] On how background expectancies are used to determine whether a person is judged criminal or sick see the neglected essay by Vilhelm Aubert and Sheldon L. Messinger, "The Criminal and the Sick," *Inquiry*, V. 1 (Autumn, 1958), pp. 137–160.

[39] This formulation is persistently (and we believe rightly) argued in the various writings of Ernest Becker. See especially *The Revolution in Psychiatry*, N.Y.: The Free Press of Glencoe, 1964; and his essay "Mills' Social Psychology and the Great Historical Convergence on the Problem of Alienation," in *The New Sociology*, edited by Irving L. Horowitz, N.Y.: Oxford University Press, 1964, pp. 108–133.

[40] In the case of schizophrenics, it has been noted that they are individuals who construct overly elaborate accounts—i.e., accounts that are perceived as being elaborately constructed. These accounts, it appears, take the form of "building up" the possibilities of a situation that others find improbable. Thus, the paranoid husband accounts for his frenzied state by relating that his wife went shopping—and, to him, going shopping constitutes the most opportune occasion to secretly rendezvous with a lover. In response to the inquirer, the paranoid asks: "If you wanted to meet a lover wouldn't you tell your spouse you're going shopping?" For a general discussion, see Becker, *The Revolution in Psychiatry, op. cit.*

[41] Erving Goffman, *Presentation of Self in Everyday Life*, Edinburgh: University of Edinburgh, 1956.

When an account is not honored it will be regarded as either *illegitimate* or *unreasonable*. An account is treated as *illegitimate* when the gravity of the event exceeds that of the account or when it is offered in a circle where its vocabulary of motives is unacceptable. As illustration of the first instance we may note that accidentally allowing a pet turtle to drown may be forgiven, but accidentally allowing the baby to drown with the same degree of oversight may not so easily be excused. In illustration of the second instance we may note that male prostitutes may successfully demonstrate their masculinity within the subculture of persons who regularly resort to homosexual acts by insisting that they are never fellators, but such a defense is not likely to lift the label of "queer" from them in heterosexual circles.[42]

An account is deemed *unreasonable* when the stated grounds for action cannot be "normalized" in terms of the background expectancies of what "everybody knows." Hence, when a secretary explained that she placed her arm in a lighted oven because voices had commanded her to do so in punishment for her evil nature, the account was held to be grounds for commitment to an asylum.[43] In general, those who persist in giving unreasonable accounts for questioned actions are likely to be labeled as mentally ill. Or, to put this point another way, unreasonable accounts are one of the sure indices by which the mentally ill are apprehended. Conversely, those persons labeled as mentally ill may relieve themselves of the worst consequences of that label by recognizing before their psychiatrists the truth value of the label, by reconstructing their past to explain how they came to deviate from normal patterns, and by gradually coming to give acceptable accounts for their behavior.[44]

Beyond illegitimacy and unreasonableness are special types of situations in which accounts may not be acceptable. One such type involves the incorrect invocation of "commitment" or

[42] Albert J. Reiss, Jr., "The Social Integration of Queers and Peers," in *The Other Side, op. cit.*, pp. 181–210.

[43] Marguerite Sechehaye, *Autobiography of a Schizophrenic Girl*, New York: Grune and Stratton, 1951.

[44] See Thomas Scheff, *Being Mentally Ill*, Chicago: Aldine Press, 1966. See also Erving Goffman, *Asylums, op. cit.*

"attachment"[45] in account situations where one or the other, but only the correct one, is permitted. By commitment we refer to that role orientation in which one has through investiture become liable and responsible for certain actions. By attachment we refer to the sense of vesting one's feelings and identity in a role. Certain statuses, especially those dealing with distasteful activities or acts that are condemned except when performed by licensed practitioners, are typically expected to invest their incumbents with only commitment and not with attachment. Hangmen who, when questioned about their occupation, profess to be emotionally attracted to killing, are not likely to have their account honored. Indeed, distasteful tasks are often imputed to have a clandestine but impermissible allure, and so those who regularly perform them are often on their guard to assert their commitment, but not their attachment to the task.

It should be mentioned here that organizations systematically provide accounts for their members in a variety of situations. The rules of bureaucracy, for instance, make available accounts for actions taken toward clients—actions which, from the viewpoint of the client, are untoward.[46] Again, these accounts "work" because of a set of background expectancies. Thus, when people say they must perform a particular action because it is a rule of the organization, the account is regarded as at least reasonable, since "everyone knows" that people follow rules. Of course, the gravity of the event may discredit such accounts, as the trials of Nazi war criminals dramatically illustrate.[47]

Under certain situations behavior that would ordinarily require an account is normalized without interruption or any call for an account. Typically such situations are social conversations in which the values to be obtained by the total encounter supersede those

---

[45] These terms are adapted from Erving Goffman, *Behavior in Public Places*, N.Y.: The Free Press of Glencoe, 1963, p. 36n, and *Encounters, op. cit.*, pp. 105ff.

[46] The theme is widely explored in the literature on formal organizations. For an early—and perhaps still the clearest statement of the theme—see Robert K. Merton's widely reprinted "Bureaucratic Structure and Personality," available in *Complex Organizations*, edited by Amitai Etzioni, New York: Holt, Rinehart and Winston, 1962, pp. 48–60.

[47] For a literary illustration, see the play by Peter Weiss, *The Investigation*, N.Y.: Atheneum Books, 1967.

which would otherwise require excuses or justifications. Two values that may override the requirement of accounts are *sociability* and *information*.

In the case of *sociability* the desire that the interactional circle be uninterrupted by an event that might break it calls for each interactant to weigh carefully whether or not the calling for an account might disrupt the entire engagement. When the gathering is a convivial one not dedicated to significant matters—that is, matters that have a proactive life beyond the engagement itself— the participants may overlook errors, inept statements, lies, or discrepancies in the statements of others. Parties often call for such behavior but are vulnerable to disruption by one who violates the unwritten rule of not questioning another too closely. In social and unserious situations in which strangers are privileged to interact as a primary group without future rights of similar interaction—such as in bars—the interactants may construct elaborate and self-contradictory biographies without fear of being called to account.[48]

In some engagements the interactants seek to obtain *information* from the speaker which is incidental to his main point but which might be withheld if any of the speaker's statements were called into account. Among the Japanese, for example, the significant item in a conversation may be circumscribed by a verbal wall of trivia and superfluous speech. To interrupt a speaker by calling for an account might halt the conversation altogether or detour the speaker away from disclosing the particularly valued pieces of information.[49] Among adolescent boys in American society engaged in a "bull session" it is usually inappropriate to challenge a speaker describing his sexual exploits since, no matter how embellished and exaggerated the account might be, it permits the hearers to glean knowledge about sex—ordinarily withheld from them in the regular channels of education—with impunity. Calling for an account in the midst of such disclosures, especially when the account would require a discussion of the speaker's morality, might cut off the hearers from

[48] See Sherri Cavan, *Liquor License*, Chicago: Aldine Press, 1966, pp. 79–87.
[49] Edward T. Hall, *The Hidden Dimension*, Garden City: Doubleday, 1966, pp. 139–144.

obtaining precisely that kind of information which is in no other way available to them.[50]

So far we have discussed accounts in terms of their content. But it should be pointed out that accounts also differ in form or style. Indeed, as we will now suggest, the style of an account will have bearing on its honoring or dishonoring.

LINGUISTIC STYLES AND ACCOUNTS

We may distinguish five linguistic styles that frame the manner in which an account will be given and often indicate the social circle in which it will be most appropriately employed. These five styles, which in practice often shade into one another and are not unambiguously separated in ordinary life, are the *intimate*, *casual, consultative, formal*, and *frozen* styles.[51] These styles, as we shall see, are ordered on a scale of decreasing social intimacy.[52]

The *intimate* style is the socially sanctioned lingual form employed between persons who share a deep, intense, and personal relationship. The group within which it is employed is usually a dyad——lovers, a married pair, or very close friends. The group can be larger but not much larger, and when it reaches four or five it is strained to its limits. The verbal style employs single sounds or words and jargon to communicate whole ideas. An account given in this form may be illustrated by the situation in which a husband, lying beside his wife in bed, caresses her but receives no endearing response. His wife utters the single word, "Pooped." By this term

[50] When a boy is interrupted by a call for an account in the midst of his own recounting of sexual exploits he may simply relapse into uncommunicative silence, change the subject, or withdraw from the group. To prevent any of these, and to aid in the continuity of the original story, the other members of the audience may urge the speaker to continue as before, assure him of their interest and support, and sharply reprove or perhaps ostracize from the group the person who called for the account.

[51] We have adapted these styles from Martin Joos, *The Five Clocks*, N.Y.: Harbinger Books, 1961.

[52] Each of these linguistic styles is associated with distinctive physical distances between the interactants. For a discussion of this point see Hall, *op. cit.*, pp. 116–122.

the husband understands that the account given in response to his unverbalized question, "Why won't you make love to me? After all, I am your husband. You have wifely duties!" is "I realize that under ordinary circumstances I should and indeed would respond to your love making, but tonight I am too exhausted for that kind of activity. Do not take it to mean that I have lost affection for you, or that I take my wifely duties lightly."

The *casual* style is used among peers, in-group members and insiders. It is different from that of intimates in that it is a style employed by those for whom the social distance is greater than that among intimates but still within the boundaries of a primary relationship. Typically it employs ellipses (i.e., omissions) and slang. In casual style certain background information is taken for granted among the interactants and may be merely alluded to in order to give an account. Thus, among those who are regular users of hallucinogenic drugs, the question "Why were you running about naked in the park?" might be answered, "I was 'on.'" The hearer will then know that the speaker was under the influence of a familiar drug and was engaged in an activity that is common in response to taking that drug.

While each style differs from that to which it is juxtaposed by degree, the difference between any two styles—skipping an interval on the afore-mentioned social intimacy scale—is one of kind. Thus, intimate and casual style differs only in degree from one another and suggest a slight but significant difference in social distance among the interactants, but *consultative* style differs in kind from intimate. Consultative style is that verbal form ordinarily employed when the amount of knowledge available to one of the interactants is unknown or problematic to the others. Typically in such an interaction the speaker supplies background information which he is unsure the hearer possesses, and the hearer continuously participates by means of lingual signs and gestures that indicate he understands what is said or that he requires more background information. In offering accounts in this form there is a definite element of "objectivity," i.e., of non-subjective and technical terms. The individual giving an account relies on reference to things and ideas outside the intimate and personal realm. In response to the question, "Why are you smoking marijuana? Don't you know that it's dangerous?" The individual might reply, "I smoke marijuana because everybody who's read the Laguardia Report knows that it's not habit forming." But a casual response could be simply, "Don't be square."

Formal style is employed when the group is too large for informal co-participation to be a continuous part of the interaction. Typically, it is suited to occasions when an actor addresses an audience greater than six. Listeners must then wait their turn to respond, or if they interject comments know that this will be an untoward event, requiring some kind of re-structuring of the situation. Speaker and audience are in an active and passive role, respectively, and, if the group is large enough, may be obligated to speak or remain silent according to pre-established codes of procedure. Formal style may also be employed when speaker and auditor are in rigidly defined statuses. Such situations occur in bureaucratic organizations between persons in hierarchically differentiated statuses or in the court room in the interaction between judge and defendant.

Frozen style is an extreme form of formal style employed among those who are simultaneously required to interact and yet remain social strangers. Typically, interaction in the frozen style occurs among those between whom an irremovable barrier exists. The barrier may be of a material or social nature, or both. Thus, pilots communicate to air scanners in a control tower in the same lingual style as prisoners of war to their captors or telephone operators to angered clients. Often the frozen accounts offered are tutored, memorized or written down in advance, and they may be applicable to a variety of situations. Thus, the prisoner of war reiterates his name, rank and serial number to all questions and refers his interrogators to the Geneva convention. The pilot replies to anonymous control tower questions about his aberrant flight pattern by a smooth flow of technical jargon quoted from his handbook on flying. The telephone operator refuses to become flustered or angered by the outraged demands and accusations of the caller unable to reach his party, and quotes from memory the rules of telephone conduct required of the situation.

In summary, then, accounts are presented in a variety of idioms. The idiomatic form of an account is expected to be socially suited to the circle into which it is introduced according to norms of culture, subculture, and situation. The acceptance or refusal of an offered account in part depends on the appropriateness of the idiom employed. Failure to employ the proper lingual style often results in a dishonoring of the account or further calls for accounts. Sometimes the situation results in requirements of compound accounting wherein an individual having failed to employ idiomatic propriety in his first account is required not only to re-account for his original untoward act but also to present an account for the unacceptable language of his first account. Note also that idiomatic errors on the part of a person giving an account provide an unusual opportunity for the hearer to dishonor or punish the speaker if he so wishes. Thus, even if the content of the tendered account is such as to excuse or justify the act, a hearer who wishes to discredit the speaker may "trip him up" by shifting the subject away from the matter originally at hand and onto the form of the account given. Typical situations of this kind arise when persons of inferior status provide substantially acceptable accounts for their allegedly untoward behavior to their inquiring superiors but employ idiomatically unacceptable or condemnable form. Thus, school children who excuse their fighting with others by not only reporting that they were acting in self-defense but also, and in the process, by using profanity still may be punished for lingual impropriety, even if they are let off for their original defalcation.[53]

STRATEGIES FOR AVOIDING ACCOUNTS

The vulnerability of actors to questions concerning their conduct varies with the situation and the status of the actors. Where hierarchies of authority govern the social situation institutionalized office may eliminate the necessity of an account, or even prevent the question from arising. Military officers are thus shielded from

[53] Besides the five linguistic styles discussed, we may note that accounts may be usefully distinguished in the manner of their delivery. For a cogent typology see Robert E. Pitenger, *et al.*, *The First Five Minutes*, Ithaca, N.Y.: Paul Martineau, 1960, p. 255.

accountability to their subordinates. Where culture distance and hierarchy are combined—as in the case of slaveholders vis-à-vis their new imported slaves—those enjoying the superior status are privileged to leave their subordinates in a perplexed and frightened state.[54]

Besides the invulnerability to giving accounts arising from the status and position of the actors are the strategies that can prevent their announcement. We may refer to these strategies as meta-accounts. Three such strategies are prominent: *mystification, referral,* and *identity switching.*[55]

When the strategy of *mystification* is employed an actor admits that he is not meeting the expectations of another, but follows this by pointing out that although there are reasons for his unexpected actions he cannot tell the inquirer what they are. In its simplest sense the actor says "It's a long story," and leaves it at that. Such accounts are most likely to be honored where the circumstances of the situation would normally hinder an elaborate account, as when students have a chance meeting while rushing off to scheduled classes.

More complicated versions of mystification are those that suggest that alter is not aware of certain facts—facts that are secret—which, if known, would explain the untoward action. Typically this is the response of the charismatic leader to his followers or the expert to his naive assistant. Thus, does Jesus sometimes mystify his disciples and Sherlock Holmes his Dr. Watson. Finally, as already mentioned, certain statuses suggest mystification: in addition to charismatic leaders and experts at occult or little understood arts are all those status characterized by specialized information including (but not limited to) doctors, lawyers, and spies.

Using the strategy of *referral* the individual says, "I know I'm not meeting your expectations but if you wish to know why please see . . ." Typically referral is a strategy available to the sick and the subordinate. Illness, especially mental illness, allows the sick

[54] Another kind of invulnerability arises in those situations in which physical presence is tantamount to task performance. Students in a classroom, parishioners in a church, and soldiers at a drill may be counted as "present"—their very visibility being all that is required for routine performance—although they might be "away" in the vicarious sense of daydreaming, musing on other matters, or relaxing into a reverie.

[55] For these terms, in the context of strategies for avoiding accounts, we are indebted to Gregory Stone.

person to refer inquiries about his behavior to his doctor or psychiatrist. Subordinates may avoid giving accounts by designating superiors as the appropriate persons to be questioned. A special example of group referral is that which arises when accounts for the behavior of a whole people are avoided by sending the interrogator to the experts. Thus, juvenile delinquents can refer inquiries to social workers, Hopi Indians to anthropologists, and unwed Negro mothers to the Moynihan report.

In *identity switching* ego indicates to alter that he is not playing the role that alter believes he is playing. This is a way of saying to alter, "You do not know who I am." This technique is readily available since all individuals possess a multiplicity of identities. Consider the following example.[56] A working-class Mexican husband comes home from an evening of philandering. His wife suspects this and she says, "Where were you?" He responds with: "None of your business, you're a wife." Here the husband is assuming that it is not the wife's job to pry into the affairs of her husband. She replies, "What kind of a father are you?" What the woman does here is to suggest that she is not a wife, but a mother—who is looking out for the welfare of the children. To this the husband replies: "I'm a man—and you're a woman." In other words, he is suggesting that in his status as a man, there are things that a woman just doesn't understand. We note in this example that the status of persons not only affects the honoring and non-honoring of accounts, but also determines who can call for an account and who can avoid it. Again, it should be pointed out that the normal features of such interaction depend upon the actors sharing a common set of background expectancies.

NEGOTIATING IDENTITIES AND ACCOUNTS

As our discussion of identity switching emphasizes, accounts always occur between persons in roles—between husband and wife,

---

[56] For this illustration we are again indebted to Gregory Stone. The illustration itself is derived from Oscar Lewis' *The Children of Sanchez, op. cit.*

doctor and patient, teacher and student, and so on. A normative structure governs the nature and types of communication between the interactants including whether and in what manner accounts may be required and given, honored or discredited.

Accounts, as suggested, presuppose an identifiable speaker and audience. The particular identities of the interactants must often be established as part of the encounter in which the account is presented.[57] In other words, people generate role identities for one another in social situations. In an account-giving situation it is necessary to cast alter into a particular kind of account, the kind suitable to the role identity conferred and assumed for at least the period of the account. To assume an identity is to don the mantle appropriate to the account to be offered. Identity assumption and "altercasting"[58] are prerequisites to the presentation of accounts since the identities thus established interactionally "set" the social stage on which the drama of the account is to be played out.

The identities of speaker and audience will be negotiated as part of the encounter. Each of the interactants has a stake in the negotiations since the outcomes of the engagement will often depend on these pre-established identities. In competitive or bargaining situations[59] the interactants will each seek to maximize gains or minimize losses, and part of the strategy involved will be to assume and accept advantageous identities, refusing those roles that are disadvantageous to the situation. *Every account is a manifestation of the underlying negotiation of identities.*[60]

The most elementary form of identification is that of human and fellow human negotiated by the immediate perceptions of strangers who engage in abrupt and involuntary engagements.

[57] For an excellent discussion of this point as well as an insightful analysis of the concept of identity, see Anselm L. Strauss, *Mirrors and Masks*, Glencoe: The Free Press.

[58] The concept of "altercasting" is developed by Eugene A. Weinstein and Paul Deutschberger, "Tasks, Bargains, and Identities in Social Interaction," *Social Forces*, V. 42 (May, 1964), pp. 451–456.

[59] See the brilliant discussion by Thomas C. Schelling, *The Strategy of Conflict*, N.Y.: Galaxy Books, 1963, pp. 21–52.

[60] The terms "identities" and "roles" may be used as synonyms in that roles are identities mobilized in a specific situation; whereas role is always situationally specific, identities are trans-situational.

Thus, once two objects on a street collide with one another and mutually perceive one another to be humans, an apology in the form of an excuse or mutually paired excuses will suffice. Those persons not privileged with full or accurate perception—the blind, myopic, or blindfolded—are not in a position to ascertain immediately whether the object with which they have collided is eligible to call for an account and to deserve an apology. In overcompensating for their inability to negotiate immediately such elementary identities, the persons so handicapped may indiscriminately offer apologies to everyone and everything with which they collide— doormen and doors, street walkers and street signs.

Some objects are ambiguously defined with respect to their deserving of accounts. Animals are an example. House pets, especially dogs and cats are sometimes imputed to possess human attributes and thus are eligible for apologies and excuses when they are trod upon by their masters. But insects and large beasts—ants and elephants, for example—do not appear to be normally eligible for accounts even when they are trod upon by unwary (Occidental) humans.

However, there are instances wherein the anthropomorphosis of the human self is more difficult to negotiate than that of a dog. Racial minorities in caste societies often insist to no avail on the priority of their identity as "human beings" over their identification as members of a racial group.[61] Indeed the "Negro-human being" role choice dilemma is but one instance of a particular form of strategy in the negotiation of identities. The strategy involves the competition between ego and alter over particularist versus universal role identities. In any encounter in which a disagreement is potential or has already occurred, or in any situation in which an account is to be offered, the particularistic or universal identity of the

---

[61] "An unconscious desire to be white, coupled with feelings of revulsion toward the Negro masses, may produce an assimilationist pattern of behavior at the purely personal level. Assimilationism is in this sense a means of escape, a form of flight from 'the problem.' It involves a denial of one's racial identity which may be disguised by such sentiments as 'I'm not a Negro but a human being'— as if the two were mutually exclusive. This denial is accompanied by a contrived absence of race consciousness and a belittling of caste barriers. By minimizing the color line, the assimilationist loses touch with the realities of Negro life." Robert A. Bone, *The Negro Novel in America*, New Haven: Yale University Press, 1965, p. 4.

interactants might dictate the manner and outcome of the account situation. Each participant will strive for the advantageous identity. A Negro psychoanalyst with considerable experience in Europe and North Africa has shown how the form of address—either consultative or deprecatingly casual—and the tone used are opening moves in the doctor's designation of his patient as European or Negro:

> Twenty European patients, one after another, came in: "Please sit down . . . Why do you wish to consult me?" Then comes a Negro or an Arab: "Sit there, boy . . ."[62]

And, as the psychoanalyst points out, the identity imputed to the patient might be accepted or rejected. To reject the particularist identity in favor of a universal one, the Negro patient might reply, "I am in no sense your boy, Monsieur" and the negotiations for identities begin again or get detoured in an argument.[63]

In an account situation there is a further complication. Once identities have been established and an account offered, the individual has committed himself to an identity and thus seemingly assumed the assets and liabilities of that role for the duration of the encounter. If he accepts the identity as permanent and unchangeable, however, he may have limited his range of subsequent accounts. And if one wishes to shift accounts to one appropriate to another identity he may also need to account for the switch in identities. Thus, in the face of a pejorative particularistic identity, a Negro might wish to establish his claim to a positive universal one devoid of the pejorative contents of the imputed one. However, once this new universal identity has been established, the Negro might wish to shift back to the particularist one, if there are positive qualities to be gained thereby, qualities utterly lost by an unqualified acceptance of the universal identity.[64] But the switch might require an account itself.

[62] Frantz Fanon, *Black Skin, White Masks*, N.Y.: Grove Press, 1967, p. 32.
[63] *Ibid.*, p. 33.
[64] Fanon, *ibid.*, provides one of the most graphic examples of this phenomenon. For a socio-literary treatment, see St. Clair Drake, "Hide My Face?—On Pan-Africanism and Negritude," in Herbert Hill, editor, *Soon One Morning*, N.Y.: Alfred Knopf, 1963, pp. 77–105.

Identity switching has retroactive dangers, since it casts doubt on the attachment the claimant had to his prior identity, and his attachment may have been a crucial element in the acceptability of his first account. On the other hand, the hearer of an account may have a vested interest in accepting the entire range of accounts and may thus accommodate or even facilitate the switch in identities. Thus, the hearer might "rationalize" the prior commitment, or reinterpret its meaning so that the speaker may carry off subsequent accounts.[65] Another strategy available to a hearer is to engage in altercasting for purposes of facilitating or frustrating an account. The fact that individuals have multiple identities makes them both capable of strategic identity change and vulnerable to involuntary identity imputations.

In ordinary life accounts are usually "phased."[66] One account generates the question giving rise to another; the new account requires re-negotiation of identities; the identities necessitate excuses or justifications, improvisation and altercasting; another account is given; another question arises, and so on. The following interview between a Soviet social worker and his client, a young woman, nicely illustrates this phenomenon.[67]

A girl about nineteen years of age enters the social worker's office and sits down sighing audibly. The interview begins on a note of *mystification* which ends abruptly when the girl establishes her identity—abandoned wife.

"What are you sighing so sadly for?" I asked. "Are you in trouble?" Lyuba raised her prim little head with a jerk, sighed pianissimo and smiled piteously.

"No . . . it's nothing much. I *was* in trouble, but it's all over now. . . ."

"All over, and you are still sighing about it?" I questioned further. Lyuba gave a little shiver and looked at me. A flame of interest had leaped into her earnest brown eyes.

"Would you like me to tell you all about it?"

---

[65] Schelling, *op. cit.*, p. 34.

[66] For a discussion on the "phasing" of encounters, see Strauss, *op. cit.*, p. 44ff.

[67] The following is from A. S. Makarenko, *The Collective Family*, Garden City: Doubleday Anchor, 1967, pp. 230–232.

"Yes, do."
"It's a long story."
"Never mind. . . ."
"My husband has left me."

The interview carries on in what must be regarded as an unsuccessful approach by the social worker. He establishes that Lyuba still loves her wayward husband, has lost faith in men, and is unwilling to take his advice to forget her first husband and remarry. The abandoned wife turns out to be an identity with which the worker has difficulty coping. He, therefore, attempts to altercast in the following manner.

"Tell me, Lyuba, are your parents alive?"
"Yes, they are. Daddy and Mummy! They keep on telling me off for having got married."
"Quite right too."
"No, it's not. What's right about it?"
"Of course, they're right. You're still a child and already married and divorced."
"Well . . . what about it! What's that got to do with them?"
"Aren't you living with them?"
"I have a room of my own. My husband left me and went to live with his . . . and the room is mine now. And I earn two hundred rubels. And I'm not a child! How can you call me a child?"

Note that little bits of information provide the cues for altercasting, so that Lyuba's volunteering the fact of her parents' disapproval of her first marriage provides the grounds for the social worker's recasting her into the child role. However, this new identity is rejected by Lyuba by further evidentiary assertions: she supports herself and maintains her own residence. The child role has been miscast. Even the social worker gives up his attempt at switching Lyuba out from her role as abandoned wife. He writes: "Lyuba looked at me in angry surprise and I saw that she was quite serious about this game she played in life." Thus, negotiations for identities—as in financial transactions—usually end with both parties coming to an agreeable settlement.

CONCLUSION

The sociologist has been slow to take as a serious subject of investigation what is perhaps the most distinctive feature of humans —talk. Here we are suggesting a concern with one type of talk: the study of what constitutes "acceptable utterances"[68] for untoward action. The sociological study of communications has relegated linguistic utterances largely to linguists and has generally mapped out non-verbal behavior as its distinctive domain. We are suggesting that a greater effort is needed to formulate theory that will integrate both verbal and non-verbal behavior.[69]

Perhaps the most immediate task for research in this area is to specify the background expectancies that determine the range of alternative accounts that are deemed culturally appropriate to a variety of recurrent situations. We want to know how the actors take bits and pieces of words and appearances and put them together to produce a perceivedly normal (or abnormal) state of affairs. This kind of inquiry crucially involves a study of background expectancies.[70] On the basis of such investigations the analyst should be able to provide a set of instructions on "how to give an account" that would be taken by other actors as "normal."[71]

[68] The term is borrowed from Noam Chomsky, *Aspects of a Theory of Syntax*, Cambridge, Mass: MIT Press, 1965, p. 10.

[69] To our knowledge the most persuasive argument for this need is made by Kenneth L. Pike, *Language in Relation to a Unified Theory of the Structure of Human Behavior*, Glendale: Summer Institute of Linguistics, 1954. A short, clear programmatic statement is found in Dell Hymes' "The Ethnography of Speaking," in Thomas Gladwin and William C. Sturtevant, editors, *Anthropology and Human Behavior*, Washington, D.C.: Anthropological Society of Washington, 1962, pp. 72–85. For an argument that stresses the analytic separation of the content of talk from the forms of talk, see the brief but lucid statement by Erving Goffman, "The Neglected Situation," in *The Ethnography of Communications*, edited by John Gumperz and Dell Hymes, *American Anthropologist*, V. 66 (December, 1964), Part 2, pp. 133–136.

[70] For the methodology of such studies sociologists may well investigate the anthropological technique of componential analysis (i.e., the study of contrast sets). The clearest statement of the method of componential analysis is that of Charles O. Frake, "The Ethnographic Study of Cognitive Systems," in *Anthropology and Human Behavior*, *op. cit.*, pp. 72–85. A related methodology is developed by Sacks in *The Search for Help*, *op. cit.*

[71] See Charles O. Frake, "How to Ask for a Drink in Subanun," in *The Ethnography of Communications*, *op. cit.*, pp. 127–132.

These instructions would specify how different categories of statuses affect the honoring of an account, and what categories of statuses can use what kinds of accounts.

Future research on accounts may fruitfully take as a unit of analysis the *speech community*.[72] This unit is composed of human aggregates in frequent and regular interaction. By dint of their association sharers of a distinct body of verbal signs are set off from other speech communities. Speech communities define for their members the appropriate lingual forms to be used amongst themselves. Such communities are located in the social structure of any society. They mark off segments of society from one another, and also distinguish different kinds of activities. Thus, the everyday language of lower-class teenage gangs differs sharply from that of the social workers who interview them, and the language by which a science teacher demonstrates to his students how to combine hydrogen and oxygen in order to produce water differs from the language employed by the same teacher to tell his inquisitive six-year-old son how babies are created. The types of accounts appropriate to each speech community differ in form and in content. The usage of particular speech norms in giving an account has consequences for the speaker depending upon the relationship between the form used and the speech community into which it is introduced.

A single individual may belong to several speech communities at the same time, or in the course of a lifetime. Some lingual devices (such as teenage argot) are appropriate only to certain age groups and are discarded as one passes into another age grouping; others, such as the lingual forms used by lawyers in the presence of judges, are appropriate to certain status sets and are consecutively employed and discarded as the individual moves into and out of interactions with his various status partners. Some individuals are dwellers in but a single speech community; they move in circles in which all employ the same verbal forms. The aged and enfeebled members of

[72] The idea of a "speech community" is usefully developed by John J. Gumperz in "Speech Variation and the Study of Indian Civilization," in *Language in Culture and Society*, edited by Dell Hymes, N.Y.: Harper and Row, 1964, pp. 416–423; and "Linguistic and Social Interaction in Two Communities," in *Ethnography of Communications, op. cit.*, pp. 137–153.

class or ethnic ghettoes are an obvious example. Others are constant movers through differing speech communities adeptly employing language forms suitable to the time and place they occupy. Social workers who face teenage delinquents, fellow workers, lawyers, judges, their own wives and children all in one day are an example.

In concluding we may note that, since it is with respect to deviant behavior that we call for accounts, the study of deviance and the study of accounts are intrinsically related, and a clarification of accounts will constitute a clarification of deviant phenomena—to the extent that deviance is considered in an interactional framework.[73]

[73] We refer to the approach to deviance clearly summarized by Howard S. Becker, *The Outsiders*, N.Y.: The Free Press of Glencoe, 1963, esp. pp. 1–18.

6

Coolness in everyday life

"Don't lose your cool!"

A common enough phrase and one easily recognized in contemporary urban America. But, sociologically speaking, what does this new moral imperative mean? What does one lose when he loses his cool? Our task is to answer these questions by analyzing the social arrangements whereby coolness gained and coolness lost are readily observable features in everyday life.[1]

Coolness is exhibited (and defined) as poise under pressure. By pressure we mean simply situations of considerable emotion or risk, or both. *Coolness, then, refers to the capacity to execute physical acts, including conversation, in a concerted, smooth, self-controlled fashion in risky situations, or to maintain affective detachment during the course of encounters involving considerable emotion.*[2]

We may distinguish three types of risk under which an individual might display coolness. First there is *physical risk* to the person in the form of danger to life and limb. The moral worth of many

Stanford M. Lyman and Marvin B. Scott, "Coolness in Everyday Life," from Marcello Truzzi, editor, *Sociology and Everyday Life*, © 1968. Reprinted by permission of Prentice-Hall, Inc., Englewood Cliffs, New Jersey.

[1] This paper explores a theoretical avenue opened up by Erving Goffman. Our orientation and some of the conceptual categories used here are derived from the various writings of this seminal thinker.

[2] This definition closely follows the one suggested by Goffman in "Where the Action Is," Unpublished Manuscript, University of California, Berkeley, p. 29.

of the heroes of the Western world is displayed in their willingness and ability to undergo trials of pain and potential death with stylized equanimity and expert control of relevant motor skills. Modern fictional heroes, such as James Bond and Matt Dillon, for example, face death constantly in the form of armed and desperate killers; yet they seem never to lose their nerve or skill. It is not merely their altruistic service in the cause of law and country that makes them attractive, but also, and perhaps more importantly, their smooth skill—verbal and physical—that never deserts them in times of risk.

Secondly, there is *financial* risk. Financial risk entails not only the possible loss of income and status, but also the loss of character associated with the venture. Captains of industry, professional gamblers, and those who play the stock market are supposed to withstand the losses sometimes occasioned in the process with calmness, detachment, even cavalier abandon.

Finally, the most crucial for our concerns, there is *social* risk. Social risks may arise whenever there is an encounter. In every social encounter a person brings a "face" or "mask"—which constitutes the value he claims for himself.[3] Given that an individual stakes this value in every encounter, it follows that encounters are morally serious occasions fraught with great risks where one puts on the line a public face. This is the most serious of risks, for in risking it—he risks his very self-hood. When the interactants are *aware* that each is putting on a public face, they will look for cues to glean some "real self" presumably lurking beneath the mask.[4] The

---

[3] Goffman, "On Face Work," *Psychiatry*, 18 (August, 1955), pp. 213–231.

[4] The hazards of social encounters are not universally recognized with the same degree of seriousness. Thus, in Japanese culture the face engagements of individuals are always regarded as character tests. Individuals are expected to be aware at all times of the proprieties. Loss of face can occur at any time. On the other hand, in American culture it would appear that social risks are not recognized as an ingredient of every encounter, but only of those that have a retro- or pro-active effect on the participants. For an analysis of the Japanese as veritable models of poise under pressure, see Nyozekan Hasegawa, *The Japanese Character*, Tokyo: Kodansha International, 1966, esp. pp. 29–34 and 90–94. See also George De Vos, "A Comparison of the Personality Differences in Two Generations of Japanese Americans By Means of the Rorschach Test," *Nagoya Journal of Medical Science*, (August, 1954), pp. 164–165, 252–261; and William Caudill, "Japanese American Personality and Acculturation," *Genetic Psychology Monographs*, 45 (1952), pp. 3–102.

capacity to maintain face in such situations constitutes a display of coolness.

As suggested, encounters are hazardous because of the ever present possibility that identity and status will be disconfirmed or damaged by behavior. Whenever an individual or a group has to stage an encounter before a particular audience in order to establish a distinctive identity and meaning, the management of the staging becomes crucial to the endeavour. The effort can fail not simply because of the inadequacies or the conflict of the presented material, but also, and perhaps more importantly, because of the failure to maintain expressive identity and control. Thus individuals and teams—for a successful performance—must not only manage what they have planned, but also carry off the presentation smoothly in the face of interruptions, intrusions, and prop failures.

Smoothness of performance can be seriously interrupted by "prop" failure. Some engagements involve the maintenance in good order of a particular setting. Included here at the minimum is the apparel of the actor. A professor lecturing before his class might be completely discomfited if he discovers his fly is unzipped; and he is indeed hard pressed to re-establish his seriousness of purpose if he is unable to repair the situation with discretion. Professional stage actors must immediately and smoothly construct dialogue to suit a situation in which the stage sets unexpectedly collapse.

Smooth performance can also be challenged by interruption or intrusion. In certain societies—England, for example—public political speeches are traditionally interrupted by hecklers, and on some occasions, objects are flung at the speaker. English politicians try to develop a style that prepares them for responding to such interruptions by having in readiness a repertoire of clever remarks. Interruption can also be occasioned by a sudden and unexpected event that would normally upset the average man. During the Second World War many actors and concert performers earned reputations for coolness under extreme situations when they continued to play out their performances after an air raid had begun.

Interruptions, intrusions and prop failures are of two sorts with respect to coolness. The first type requires deft and casual repair of self or self-possessions in order for coolness to be displayed. The professor who, aware that the class perceives his unzipped fly, casually zips it up without interrupting the flow or tone of his lecture is likely to be recognized as cool. Similarly, the Walter Mitty-like flyer who sets the broken bone of his arm while maneuvering his plane to a safe landing under hazardous conditions will be known for his coolness.

The second type of intrusion, interruption or prop failure involves those situations that require immediate action because the entire situation has been altered by their presence. Fires in theaters, air raids, tornadoes, assassinations of presidents and other major calamities are illustrations. Those who maintain presence of mind in the face of the disastrous event, and especially those who by their own example prevent others from riotous or panicky behavior, place a stamp of moral worth upon themselves.

The exhibition of coolness under situations of potential panic can be a source of leadership. Formal leaders may be thrust from their posts because they panic, and unknown persons raised to political heights because of their publicly displayed ability to remain calm. Much popular folk-lore perceives calamitous situations as those providing just the right opportunity for a person otherwise unqualified to assume a dominant position. Indeed, if his acts are sufficiently skillful and smooth, the displayer of coolness may be rewarded with future rights of charismatic authority. A doctor who performs delicate surgery in the midst of an earthquake may by that act establish rights to administer the hospital in which he works. And a teacher who manfully but non-violently prevents a gang of hoodlums from taking over a school may by his performance take over the school himself.

Embarrassment is one of the chief nemeses of coolness. Any encounter is likely to be suddenly punctured by a potentially embarrassing event—a gaffe, a boner, or uncontrollable motor response—that casts new and unfavorable light upon the actor's performance. In some instances, the audience will save the actor from needless embarrassment by studiously overlooking the event; however, this tactful inattention may itself cause embarrassment as each person in the engagement manfully seeks to overlook the obvious. In other instances, the actor himself will be on his mettle to attend or disattend to the disturbance in such a manner that it does not detract from his performance. A skillful self-rescue from a potentially embarrassing situation can win the actor more than he intended, since he may gain not only his directly intended objective but also a boost in his moral worth as well.

Thus, coolness is both a quality to be lost and a prize to be gained in any engagement. That is, coolness may be lost or gained by qualities exhibited in the behavior. A failure to maintain expressive control, a giving way to emotionalism, flooding out, paleness, sweatiness, weeping, or violent expressions of anger or fear are definite signs of loss of cool.[5] On the other hand, displays of *savoir faire*, aplomb, *sang-froid*, and especially displays of stylized affective neutrality in hazardous situations are likely to gain one the plaudits associated with coolness.

Coolness does not, therefore, refer to routine performance in a role. However, an affectively manifest departure from a role can disconfirm the presence of an actor's coolness just as a remarkable exhibition of *sang-froid* can gain for one the reputation of having it. To be cool, then, is to exhibit a definite form of expressive control during the performance of a role. Thus, we can distinguish three kinds of role performance: cool role behavior, routinized role behavior, and role behavior that indicates loss of cool.

Card playing is one type of social gathering in which all three kinds of role behavior might be exhibited. The "cool player" may push the deed to his family home into the pile of money in the center of the table with the stylized casualness of a Mississippi gambler, neither his smooth, softly smiling face nor his calm, unshaking hands indicating that he is holding only a pair of deuces. The "routine player" may take his bet with a grimace indicating seriousness of purpose and awareness of risk, but not entirely losing composure or calling undue attention to himself. The "uncool player" may become ashen, burst into tears, shriek obscenities, or suddenly accuse his opponents of cheating when his prized and final bet is raised beyond his ability to respond. The card game, like the battlefield, is a moral testing ground.

While the display of coolness is a potential in all encounters,

---

[5] The loss of cool is not everywhere a stigma. Among Shtetl Jews, for example, displays of overt emotionalism are culturally approved. See Mark Zborowski and Elizabeth Herzog, *Life is With People: The Culture of the Shtetl*, N.Y.: Schocken Books, 1962, p. 335.

there are certain typical situations where such a display is a social expectation. These involve situations in which the risks are patently obvious—e.g., bullfighting, automobile racing, and war. Literature dealing with these subjects typically portrays characterological coolness and invests it with honor and virtue. Indeed, if one wishes to find examples and evidence of coolness one need but look in the literature about activities considered risky.

Two other types of situations calling for the display of coolness are the *innovative* and the *anomic*. Innovative situations include activities associated with the rites of passage—all those "first times" in the life cycle in which one has to be poised in the face of the as yet unexperienced event. Examples include the wedding night for virgins, first days in school, and the first witnessing of death. Anomic situations are those in which at least one of the actors does not know the rules of conduct and must carry off an engagement in the face of those who do. Typically immigrants, newcomers, and parvenus find themselves in such situations—situations in which poise is at a premium.[6]

A display of coolness is often a prerequisite to entrance into or maintenance of membership in certain social circles. Since in nearly all societies coolness is taken to be part of the character syndrome of elites, we may expect to find a universal condition and a variety of forms of character testing of the elite. European nobility were expected to acquire adeptness at coquetry and repartee; the stylized insult and the witty return were highly prized and regularly tested.[7] Among would-be samurai in Japan, the martial skills were highly prized but even more highly prized was presence of mind. A samurai in training was constantly subjected to contrived sudden dangers, but if he exercised little cathectic control over his skill and strength

[6] In some instances the fears and apprehensions among newcomers are so great that not even ordinary calmness can prevail until special restorative measures are employed. For a most dramatic illustration of the point see *Equiano's Travels: The Interesting Narrative of the Life of Olaudah Equiano or Gustavus Vassa the African*, edited by Paul Edwards, N.Y.: Praeger, 1967 (originally published in 1789), pp. 30–31.

[7] Repartee and other word games apparently came into full bloom in courtly circles after women and intellectuals were admitted to participate. See Florian Znaniecki, *Social Relations and Social Roles*, San Francisco: Chandler, 1965, pp. 175–76.

he would be severely reproved by his zen master.[8] Another coolness test for membership—one involving sexual self-control—is a commonplace of college fraternity initiations. A "stag" film will be shown, and immediately upon its completion, the lights will be flashed on and the initiates ordered to stand up. Those who have "lost their cool" are then observable.

Tests of coolness among peers usually take the form of some contest relation. Teenage Italian-American slumdwellers engage in "a series of competitive encounters intended to assert the superiority and skillfulness of one individual over the other, which take the form of card games, short physical scuffles, and endless verbal duels."[9] And American ghetto-dwelling Negroes have developed a highly stylized dialogue of insult which reaches its quintessential manifestation in "sounding" or the game known as "the dozens."[10]

To successfully pass coolness tests one must mobilize and control a sizable and complex retinue of material and moral forces. First one must master all those elements of self and situation whose unmastered presence constitutes the condition of embarrassment. These include spaces, props, equipment, clothing, and body.[11]

[8] Hasegawa, op. cit., p. 88.

[9] Herbert J.Gans, The Urban Villagers, N.Y.: The Free Press of Glencoe, 1962, p. 81.

[10] See John Dollard, "The Dozens: Dialectic of Insult," The American Imago, Vol. I, (November, 1939), pp. 3–25; Rolph E.Berdie, "Playing the Dozens," Journal of Abnormal and Social Psychology, V. 42 (January, 1947), pp. 120–121; Corneleus L.Golightly and Israel Scheffler, "Playing the Dozens: A Research Note," Journal of Abnormal and Social Psychology, V. 43 (January, 1948), pp. 104–105; Roger D.Abrahams, Deep Down in the Jungle, Hatboro, Penn.: Folklore Associates, 1964, pp. 41–65, 89–98, 259–262. Abrahams (p. 50) describes sounding as follows: "Sounding occurs only in crowds of boys. One insults a member of another's family; others in the group make disapproving sounds to spur on the coming exchange. The one who has been insulted feels at this point that he must reply with a slur on the protagonist's family which is clever enough to defend his honor (and therefore that of his family). This, of course, leads the other (once again, due more to pressure from the crowd than actual insult) to make further jabs. This can proceed until everyone is bored with the whole affair, until one hits the other (fairly rare), or until some other subject comes up that interrupts the proceedings (the usual state of affairs)."

[11] Edward Gross and Gregory P.Stone, "Embarrassment and the Analysis of Role Requirements," American Journal of Sociology, 70 (July, 1964), pp. 6–10. See also Erving Goffman, "Embarrassment and Social Organization," American Journal of Sociology, 62 (November, 1956), pp. 264–71.

Maladroit usage of these often constitutes a definite sign of loss of coolness, while deft and skillful management of any intrusive action by these can signify the presence of coolness.

Coolness tests also require one to control all those elements of self which, if evidenced, constitute the sign of emotional incapacity. In addition to the body—and here we refer to its carriage, litheness, deftness and grace—there is the special case of the face, perhaps the most vulnerable agent of, as well as the most valuable instrument for, poise under pressure.[12] The eyes, nostrils, and lips are all communicators of one's mental ease and personal control. Failures here—such as a look of fear in the eyes, a flare of the nostrils, or quivering lips—communicate characterological faults that deny coolness. Finally, the color of the face must be kept neutral if coolness is to be confirmed. Those who blush or pale quickly are hard put to overcome the outward physical sign that they are not poised.

Among the most significant instruments for coolness is the voice. Both form and content are relevant here, and each must be coordinated in the service of *savoir-faire* if that character trait is to be confirmed. In institutionalized verbal contests—such as the Negro game of the "dozens"—vocal controls are the principal element of style. For these games as for other verbal artistic endeavours "style is nothing if it is not an overtly conscious striving for design on the part of the artist."[13] To engage expertly in "the dozens," and other Negro word games, one has to employ "noncasual utterances"—i.e., use of language for restricted purposes— in subculturally prescribed but seemingly effortless syntactic constructions and specified elements of diction. Of course voice control as an element of the establishment and maintenance of poise under pressure has its place in circles beyond that of the ghetto Negro. In parlor repartee, covert exchanges of hostility among colleagues, joking relations, and teasing, not only the content but also the tone and timbre count for much.

[12] See Georg Simmel, "The Aesthetic Significance of the Face," in Kurt Wolff, editor, *Georg Simmel, 1858–1918*, Columbus: Ohio State University Press, 1959, pp. 276–281. Also Goffman, "On Face Work," *op. cit.*
[13] Charles T. Scott, *A Linguistic Study of Persian and Arabic Riddles: A Language-Centered Approach to Genre Definition*, unpublished Ph.D. dissertation, University of Texas, 1963, p. 12.

Courtship and dating are perhaps the most widespread institutions in which poise is expected and thus they require mobilization of those material, anatomical, physiological, and moral forces which together, under coordinated control, constitute the armamentarium by which the coolness game may be won.[14] Activities which require for their execution a mobilization of passions—e.g., sexual intercourse—are sometimes regarded as peculiarly valuable for testing poise through affective detachment. Italian-American men admire a person "who is able to attract a good-looking woman and to conquer her without becoming involved."[15] Chinese clan rules warn husbands about the dangers created by emotional expression in sexual relations with their wives.[16] And youthful male prostitutes count it as a proof of their strong character that they do not become emotionally excited during professional acts of sexual intercourse.[17]

Where coolness is considered a positive trait, attempts will be made to demonstrate it. However, there are those statuses and situations that typically are thought to be devoid of risk and whose incumbents must therefore search out or create situations in which coolness can be demonstrated if that trait is desired. For some, then, coolness must be staged. Since, as we have said, coolness is imputed to individuals only insofar as the person's actions are seen to occur in risk-taking situations, those who strive after a reputation for coolness will seek out risky situations wherein it can be manifested. Thus, children often attempt to show emotional poise by "risky" riding on merry-go-round horses.[18] Adolescents escalate both the nature of the risk and the poise required in games of "chicken." Not surprisingly we find that slum-dwelling adolescents—who highly prize the character attribute of coolness—distinguish time in terms

---

[14] For a piquant instance in which these forces were unexpectedly tested by a Kikuyu youth studying in America see R. Mugo Gatheru, *Child of Two Worlds: A Kikuyu's Story*, Garden City: Doubleday-Anchor, 1965, pp. 153–154.

[15] Gans, *op. cit.*, p. 190.

[16] Hui-chen Wang Liu, *The Traditional Chinese Clan Rules*, Locust Valley, N.Y.: J. J. Augustin, 1959, pp. 60–93.

[17] Albert J. Reiss, "The Social Integration of Queers and Peers," in Howard S. Becker, ed., *The Other Side*, N.Y.: The Free Press of Glencoe, 1964, pp. 181–210.

[18] For a discussion of the behavioristic elements in riding a merry-go-round and other games of equipoise see Erving Goffman, "Role Distance," in *Encounters*, Indianapolis: Bobbs-Merrill, 1961, pp. 105–110.

of its potential for action (and by inference, for displays of character),
"Dead" time is time devoid of such potential.[19]

CONCLUSIONS

Although the term "coolness" is of recent vintage, the
phenomenon or trait to which it refers is universal, appearing under
a variety of rubrics: nonchalance, sophistication, savoir-faire, "blase
character," and so on. For Simmel, coolness—or blase character,
as he called it—was a trait of urbanized man.[20] Although Simmel
attributes this blase character to the preponderance of a money
economy, the rapidity of change, and the interdependence of roles
in cities, it would seem that these are but major sources of risk that
generate the conditions for displaying the character trait of coolness. These sources of risk may be matched by other types of risk
and thus other forms of coolness and character development appropriate to them may be found in non-urban settings.[21]

Coolness is often associated with nobility and wealth; indeed,
it is from among the ranks of the risk-taking rich that savoir-faire
and finesse are usually noted and often expected, but it is not
exclusively so. Bandits and burglars exhibit many of the traits
associated with coolness and sometimes explicitly link these up to
aspirations toward or identification with the nobility. Thus Robin
Hood is portrayed as a wronged lord who, although forced to flee
into the forest and adopt the outlaw life, remains noble, courageous,
temperate, and capable of considerable finesse.[22]

[19] Gans, op. cit., pp. 27–32; Jules Henry, "White People's Time, Colored
People's Time," Trans-Action, (March–April, 1965), pp. 31–34; John Horton,
"Time and Cool People," Trans-Action (April, 1967), pp. 5–12.
    [20] Georg Simmel, "The Metropolis and Mental Life," in Sociology of Georg
Simmel, N.Y.: The Free Press, 1950, pp. 413–414.
    [21] One such setting is the chivalric ideal of the fifteenth century. See Diaz de
Gamez, "The Chivalric Ideal," in James B. Ross and Mary M. McLaughlin, eds.,
The Portable Medieval Reader, N.Y.: Viking Press, 1949, esp. pp. 91–92.
    [22] See Maurice Keen, The Outlaws of Medieval Legend, London: Routledge and
Kegan Paul, 1961. For further evidence of the generalized character of bandits
and outlaws see Eric J. Hobsbawm, Social Bandits and Primitive Rebels, Glencoe:

Note, too, that coolness is not only associated with those of high rank but also among those who are so low in the social order that the most prized possession they have is personal character—a personal status that can be acknowledged or disconfirmed in everyday encounters and demonstrated particularly in the skill and finesse with which word games are played. Such people, Negroes in America are an outstanding example, develop considerable verbal ability, a pervasive pride in their own individuality, and—because of the permanent danger of character as well as physical assassination—skill in social and personal defense. And it is among quite ordinary American Negroes and persons similarly situated that we find the creative imagination developed toward posturing and prevarication and characterological coolness.[23]

On the contemporary American scene, however, the trait of coolness is not limited to any one segment of the social order. David Riesman and others have suggested that the era of moral absolutism, accompanied by the trait of inner-directedness, has declined, and among the concomitant changes is a shift in the concept of strong character.[24] In the era of inner-directedness moral character was summed up in the admonition to do one's duty. Today, such a seemingly simplistic moral model has been exchanged for the chameleon-like, radar-attuned actor who keeps pace with the rapid changes in form, content, and style. Although poise under pressure was an issue in the era of rugged individualism and unfettered capitalism, the nature of the risks involved was both different in content and differentially distributed. Modern society has changed the issue in risk and democratized it.[25] Keeping cool is now a problem for everyone.

Free Press, 1959, pp. 1–29. For a characterological analysis of the modern day fictional Robin Hood, namely, Raffles, see George Orwell, "Raffles and Miss Blandish," in *Dickens, Dali and Others*, N.Y.: Reynal and Co., 1946, pp. 202–221. These legendary bandits—Robin Hood, Raffles, etc.—are characterized by taking extra risks in the name of sportsmanship, or aesthetic reasons, and in so doing amply display strong character.

[23] See Richard Wright, "The Psychological Reactions of Oppressed People," in *White Man, Listen!*, Garden City: Doubleday Anchor, 1957, pp. 17–18.

[24] David Riesman, Nathan Glazer, Reuel Denny, *The Lonely Crowd*, Garden City: Doubleday-Anchor, 1950, 1953.

[25] See Talcott Parsons and Winston White, "The Link Between Character and Society," in S. M. Lipset and L. Lowenthal, editors, *Culture and Social Character*, N.Y.: The Free Press of Glencoe, 1961, pp. 89–135.

In the place of the earlier isolated individuality accompanied by morally clear doctrines of guilt and shame, there has arisen the coordinated group accompanied by loneliness and affected by a ubiquitous sense of anxiety. The fictional heroes of the eras reflect these changes. The Lone Ranger—perhaps the last fully developed prototype of morally correct inner direction—was a silent, skillful devotee of law and order. He traveled the uncharted trails of the frontier West accompanied only by an Indian, both in but not of their society. He spoke seldom and then in short, clipped, direct statements. He seemed to have no needs; neither women, wealth, nor power attracted or wounded him. The problems he solved were simple in form; they were *only* dangerous to life and limb: a gang of evil-doers threatened the town. Only their removal from the scene would restore the unquestionably desirable *status quo ante*.

By contrast Maverick is the prototype hero of the modern age. He is a gambler and, like Riesman's other-directed man, a cosmopolitan. For Maverick, the problems are not simple. His interest is to get through life with the maximum of pleasure, the minimum of pain. He recognizes no moral absolutes except physical and characterological survival. For him the only weapon is his wits; the only skill, verbal repartee. Only if he loses his cool will he lose to his more powerful and often ill-defined and impersonal opponents. The moral lesson implied in Maverick is quite clear. The modern age is one of permanent complex problems. They neither lend themselves to direct solution nor do they gradually disappear.[26] It is rather that the hazardous nature of life becomes ordinary, the impermanence of things and relationships becomes fixed, and to survive man must adopt the character associated with the routinization of anxiety. Its most salient feature is what we call coolness. Its manifestations are the recognition of danger in the *presentation* of self in everyday life, the risk in *attachment* to things or people, and the positive value of what Goffman calls "role distance."[27]

Despite the ubiquity of coolness in the modern world, its study may be enhanced if we look at the form and content of life for those

[26] For an analysis of the modern world in these terms see Robert Nisbet, *Community and Power*, N.Y.: Oxford Galaxy, 1962.

[27] Goffman, "Role Distance," *Encounters, op. cit.*

who are relatively permanent outsiders in society. Career deviants must manifest a considerable display of *savoir-faire* if they are to survive and especially—if like abortionists[28]—they deal with a clientele who are only situationally deviant. Minorities whose status is both anomalous and precarious have evidenced a remarkable ability to build a subculture resting in large part on the artful development of coolness forms. Here, then, are the strategic research sites.

The study of coolness—its meaning, manifestations, and metamorphosis—is surely a topic deserving further investigation, for all men in society are subject to the problems of personal risk and the preservation of poise under pressure.

[28] See Donald Ball, "An Abortion Clinic Ethnography," *Social Problems*, V. 14 (Winter, 1967), pp. 203–301.

7

Stage fright and the problem of identity

"All the world's a stage" has become a sociological as much as a Shakespearean observation for describing the nature of social life. And yet, curiously, the dramatic stage is virtually unique as the one area of social life where the potentially treacherous task of sustaining a reality is a conscious concern, and where the dangers of failure are so omnipresent that the participants continually suffer from acute anxiety. If in fact all the world were a stage, it would be a tale told by an idiot—a world of Hobbesian disorder.

Consider a world where the following experiences were permanent features of everyday life. Referring to his own performance anxiety, violinist Mischa Elman describes stage fright as "a consciousness of one's own limitations, at a moment when limitations of any sort place a barrier between what one wants to do and what one can do."[1] And actress Gertrude Lawrence reported on her own stage fright by noting: "These attacks of nerves seem to grow worse with the passing years. It's inexplicable and horrible and something you'd think you'd grow out of rather than into."[2]

Stage fright is manifested in forms familiar to the ordinary man

[1] Rose Heylbut, "How to Abolish Fear Before Audiences," *Etude*, 57 (January, 1939), p. 12.
[2] Lewis Funke, "Always in the Wings—the Shakes," *New York Times Magazine*, May 17, 1964, p. 20.

as well as the actor in terms of motor and emotional disturbance.[3] Goffman provides a fairly complete inventory of the phenomenon in his discussion of embarrassment:

> Blushing, fumbling, stuttering, an unusually low or high-pitched voice, quavering speech or breaking of the voice, sweating, blanching, blinking, tremor of the hand, hesitating, or vacillating movement, absentmindedness and malaproprisms . . . here are also symptoms of a subjective kind: constriction of the diaphragm, a feeling of wobbliness, consciousness of strained and unnatural gestures, a dazed sensation, dryness of the mouth, and tenseness of the muscles.[4]

Although embarrassment and stage fright are closely related as to the physical symptoms each produces, they differ analytically. Embarrassment occurs spontaneously when an individual's identity claims unexpectedly come under attack.[5] Stage fright, on the other hand, is generated in one of two ways: knowing in advance that a situation will open one to total inspection of self, or anticipating that a slip or flaw will suddenly thrust one into a position that invites challenges to a claimed identity, or both.

The phenomenon of stage fright highlights a fundamental problem of ordinary social interaction, namely, the problem of sustaining an identity.[6] And the dramatic stage provides the paradigm case of this problem.

---

[3] The symptoms, causes and prevention of stage fright, while neglected by sociologists, has received some attention in the psychological literature. See, for example, C.W.Lomas, "The Psychology of Stage Fright," *Quarterly Journal of Speech*, 23 (1937), pp. 35–44; M.Dickens, "An Experimental Study of Certain Physiological, Introspective and Rating Scale Techniques for the Measurement of Stage Fright", *Speech Monographs*, 18 (1951), pp. 251–259; T.Clevenger, Jr., "A Synthesis of Experimental Research in Stage Fright," *Quarterly Journal of Speech*, pp. 134–145. For an overview see Jon Eisenson, *et al.*, *The Psychology of Communications*, N.Y.: Appleton-Century-Crofts, 1963, chapter 18, pp. 320–327.

[4] Erving Goffman, "Embarrassment and Social Organization," *American Journal of Sociology*, 62 (November 1956), p. 264.

[5] *Ibid.*; see also Edward Gross and Gregory Stone, "Embarrassment and the Analysis of Role Requirements," *American Journal of Sociology*, 69 (July, 1964), pp. 1–15.

[6] This is the central problem examined in Erving Goffman's *Presentation of Self in Everyday Life*, Garden City, N.Y.: Anchor, 1959. Sheldon L.Messinger and associates, "Life as Theater" in *Sociology and Everyday Life*, edited by Marcello Truzzi, Englewood Cliffs, N.J.: Prentice-Hall, 1968), have charged Goffman with

Onstage, an actor may portray Winston Churchill, Jesus or Abraham Lincoln. Although the audience is aware that such a portrayal is "only" an impersonation, the spectators sharpen rather than relax their critical faculties and the smallest discrepancy between the ideal and the actual presentation is evaluated negatively. Below the surface of the audience's manifest consciousness, there seemingly bubbles a deep-seated resentment at the sight of a person claiming to be someone else. If this claim is going to be made, the audience seems to be saying, then the claimant had better be beyond reproach in his representation. And this attitude is prevalent not only with respect to the dramatic stage but also in everyday life.

In everyday life people frequently make claims (or are thought to be making claims) of being certain kinds of persons. In a typical case, the individual succeeds in carrying the burden of proof to substantiate his claim. But if a challenge to one's identity claims is anticipated, the condition for stage fright is activated. Thus, fellow interactants often constitute an audience possessed of powers of scrutiny and judgment, powers that might be applied to a person's identity claims with damaging results.

In everyday life a system of rules governs the operation of social interaction. These rules are understood by ordinary persons as the "recipes-for-living" that "everyone knows."[7] Among these rules are those of rectitude and relevance which indicate just what is proper and officially noticeable during the course of any interaction and just what is improper and irrelevant. One such rule involves norms of tact. Thus, when an individual makes a slip or commits a

---

reifying his dramaturgical approach. That is, in everyday life, Messinger argues, persons are not really engaged in the conscious employment of stagecraft to project identities. It is our position that in certain situations—those, for example, that are depicted in this paper—Goffman's normative model constitutes in fact an empirical description of social reality. Beyond this, we would suggest that increasingly American society is evolving into one where its social members are consciously engaged in the employment of stagecraft to construct and sustain identities. For a general discussion on the construction and maintenance of identity, see Anselm Strauss, *Mirrors and Masks*, Glencoe: The Free Press, 1959.

[7] See Alfred Schutz, "Commonsense and Scientific Interpretations of Human Action," in *Collected Papers, I*, edited by Maurice Natanson, The Hague: Martinus Nijhoff, 1962; also Harold Garfinkel, *Studies in Ethnomethodology*, Englewood Cliffs, N.J.: Prentice-Hall, 1967.

boner or a gaffe, his partners in the interaction disattend from these minor failings, make light of them, or accept without criticism an apology offered. Without such exercises of tact social interaction would be a treacherous state of affairs, always fraught with potentialities for unrelieved embarrassment, destruction of the mutually established sense of reality, or unresolvable questions of identity. In short, without such rules, humans would be immobilized for interaction in ordinary life.[8]

As adults, humans need little instruction in these rules. Rather, they serve as "background expectancies" or the taken-for-granted features of everyday life that are known in common by all *bona fide* members of the society. Such rules are problematic for children and often unknown to aliens, who in the processes of socialization and acculturation come to adopt and employ them as part of their own routine perspectives and as signs that they are indeed becoming full-fledged members of the society. Continuous violation of such rules by a person might earn him a label "troublemaker," or a stigma "Don't invite him; he always makes me uncomfortable," or render him eligible for clinical investigation. Onstage, however, such rules are relaxed, and individuals may legitimately become engrossed in slips that destroy the projected reality.

The dramatic stage is operating properly when its inhabitants successfully communicate to an audience a contrived construction of reality—the plot. The theater, unlike a confidence game and many small group experiments, demands that the audience engage in a voluntary deception: "the actor acts what he is not and the audience knows this."[9] However, the audience exacts a heavy price for this self-deception—nothing less than role perfection itself. "If the actor is good, he must be able to convince both audience and himself of the reality of his performance. When he succeeds, all ties to such non-play realities as his *other* roles are cut off, and he has reached the highest achievement of his profession."[10] Although role segmentation appears to be a feature of all urban industrial

---

[8] For a general discussion, see Erving Goffman, "Fun in Games," in *Encounters*, Indianapolis, Indiana: Bobbs-Merrill, 1961.

[9] Odd Ramsoy, *Social Groups as Systems and Subsystems*. N.Y.: Free Press of Glencoe, 1963, p. 53.

[10] *Ibid.*

societies,[11] nowhere is it perfected so well as on the dramatic stage, where for the duration of the performance, and sometimes beyond, actor and character must merge.

Within the framework of the theatrical stage, then, slips and flaws are seriously attended; and unlike most offstage encounters in everyday life, performances are expected to occur with qualities of perfection not ordinarily achieved. Since total congruency is assumed as the definition of the theatrical situation, the rules of tact and disattendance prevailing under ordinary conditions are revoked and rules requiring perfection substituted. And since stage actors know that they will be judged in accordance with these extraordinary rules of conduct during a performance, they are apprehensive.

Our contention is that stage fright arises precisely from the fact that the contrived performance differs from ordinary life in one crucial respect: the rules requiring tact and disattendance from slips are revoked, and thus the actor must mobilize that perfection of verbal and muscular control not usually expected in everyday life. In short, by studying the dramatic stage—its characteristics and its attendant anxieties—we can call attention to its equivalents in ordinary life to learn more about the conditions that generate stage fright in normal relationships.

THE DRAMATIC FRAME AND STAGE FRIGHT

The theater provides and demands a frame of meaning[12] whereby the audience engages in voluntary self-deception. Once the audience enters into this frame, it will—for the duration of the performance—accept as real the events portrayed within the frame.

There are virtually no limits to the self-deceiving reality that the audience will accept once it has entered the dramatic frame.

[11] Louis Wirth, "Urbanism as a Way of Life," *American Journal of Sociology*, 44 (July, 1938), pp. 1–24. The point, of course, was made earlier by Georg Simmel, "The Metropolis and Mental Life," in *Sociology of Georg Simmel*, edited by Kurt Wolff, New York: The Free Press, 1950, pp. 413–414.

[12] On the concept of "frame" or "frame of meaning," see Goffman, "Fun in Games," *op. cit.*

Thus, an "unworthy scaffold" is transformed into the battle grounds of Agincourt, and we accept for a time the reality construed for us by the speaker of the prologue in Henry V:

> Think when we talk of horses, that you see them,
> Printing their proud hoofs i' th' receiving earth:
> For 'tis your thoughts that now must deck our Kings . . .[13]

Limitations on the dramatic frame, then, are not set by the imaginative capacities of the audience. Rather they are set by the scenario itself. The scenario sets the limits within which the actors conduct themselves. Necessarily, the scenario requires a compression of time and space so that the duration and place of the drama can be enacted in a few hours on a stage. Onstage the entire range of action is admitted into the frame of meaningful events. Every gesture—a scratch, a tic, a lurching forward—is open not merely to observation, but more importantly to interpretation. Each action, verbal and physical, is an element of dramatic reality being communicated during the performance.

From the point of view of the audience each actor is negotiating the identity of a character. The audience is in a state of hyper-consciousness, which alerts it to scrutinize each gesture for its apparent and subtle characterological meaning. Detecting some element of puzzlement or incongruity, the audience is triggered into an even more enhanced state of watchfulness.

One slip or small mishap can weaken the entire dramatic reality, leaving the audience tense. The audience is aware of frame danger and waits for rescue, or a failure of rescue, to occur. During this period, some in the audience may give audial recognition to their state of awareness by "flooding out," laughing, gasping, or catcalling. Once a slip occurs, the actor is tensed and his heightened anxiety can lead to just what he does not desire—yet another slip. That is, audience tenseness can be communicated to the performers leading to a further raising of anxiety levels and more errors. Thus the very first slip must be avoided. The requirement for mobilization of self to avoid the first slip is what lies at the heart of stage fright.

---

[13] We are grateful to Erving Goffman for suggesting this example.

Otherwise put, the stage requires what we shall call the "rule of congruency." According to this rule each act and object present in the performance must be accounted for in terms of that performance.[14] Each actor must be on guard to communicate in character, while the audience gleans character identity from each staged action or interprets some of them as noticeable and disconfirming slips.

The theatrical frame, we are suggesting, has certain properties that lend themselves to both actor and audience becoming spontaneously engrossed in errors and mishaps. Aside from the rule of congruency, consider that what happens onstage is knowingly rehearsed. The audience's anticipation of a perfect performance is rooted in the everyday expectation that when people can rehearse what they are going to do, they ought to do it better than under conditions of spontaneity. The preacher in his pulpit, for instance, is expected to perform better under this circumstance than when appearing in ordinary encounters. The opportunity to practice in private what will be performed in public is assumed to provide the opportunity for perfection.

Actors themselves recognize the value of rehearsal in reducing the chance for errors onstage and in discovering for themselves the identity of the character to be portrayed. Lynn Fontanne reports that after the regular rehearsals at the theater, she rehearses again at home with her costar husband Alfred Lunt:

[We] work and work at home and slowly you get into the character of the person you are playing—the walk, the gestures . . . gradually I become more and more acquainted with her and then as the days go by I sink deeper and deeper into her, discovering traits and things about her I did not know existed when I began to rehearse.[15]

An even more extreme version of the actor's attempt to merge himself with the character to be portrayed is found in the example of Edwin Booth. He would not only mentally construct exactly how

[14] This point is fully developed by Goffman, *Presentation of Self in Everyday Life*, *op. cit.*, pp. 3–76.

[15] Lewis Funke and John E. Booth, *Actors Talk About Acting, II*, New York: Avon, 1961, p. 35.

the character looked and felt but also how the other characters looked and felt. When portraying Shylock, a particularly difficult role for which he worked years to master, he could not stand to have the actress playing Jessica standing in the wings within his range of vision:

> I go into that scene with a clear picture of Jessica. My own flesh and blood has betrayed me . . . I am deserted . . . I am hopeless—alone. I charge my voice with Shylock's agony, and then look up and see you— my daughter—standing [in the wings] before me, come back to me. My picture breaks up! I lose the scene![16]

And Sidney Poitier forces himself to study the social, economic, religious, political and psychological background of a character in order to appear spontaneous. Speaking of the school of acting he subscribes to, he reports that

> instead of employing the Stanislavsky Method for two hours a night in a theatre, I employ it for two or three months in the preparation of that work, so that when I go on the stage, or in front of a camera, my function becomes organic and instant and natural, spontaneous and full, because I have a frame of reference for every want, every need, every desire that is registered on my emotion boards.[17]

For all its vaunted virtues, however, rehearsal does not eliminate stage fright. Seasoned actors as well as neophytes suffer from pre-performance anxieties, a fact which sometimes comes as a shock (as well as a source of stage fright itself) to new thespians. Thus Gladys Swarthout recalls her first case of stage fright arising out of her discovery of pre-performance anxiety on the part of a basso of considerable renown:

> I was cast as *Siebel* in "Faust," opposite Chaliapin's *Mephisto*; and waiting in the wings to go on for the *Garden Scene*. I saw Chaliapin pacing the floor, ashen green under his make-up, and moaning to himself. I thought, of course, that the great basso was ill, and hurried to summon the stage manager. He laughed at me.

---

[16] Quoted in Garff B. Wilson, *A History of American Acting*, Bloomington: Indiana University Press, 1966, p. 77.
[17] Funke, *Actors Talk About Acting, I, op. cit.*, p. 206.

"Ill?" he said, "He's not ill; he's *nervous*. He gets like that every time, just before he goes on. Half dead of stage fright."[18]

That frequency of performance alone does not eliminate stage fright suggests that we must look further into the nature of stage performance to ferret out the complex etiology of this phenomenon.

THE STAGE AS AN ENVIRONMENT

The stage is determinedly eventful: it is a particular form of interaction in which the location of persons and objects is fixed by pre-established rules. Because the stage is, in this sense, an ecological environment, its rules of relevance differ from that of ordinary life. We may distinguish the crucial relevances for the stage under the headings "territories," "props," and "body."[19]

Territories

Staged dramas require that the actor performs in the most dramatically advantageous position available to the character that he is portraying. Ordinary life is never quite so exacting; an everyday encounter of considerable emotional significance may proceed without perfected locations for each interactant. On the stage, however, location is so important that chalked spots are often written on the stage floor to cue the actors to the proper position. Failure to position oneself properly or inability to move with poise to the right place at the right time are sources of anxiety for actors and causes for mirth or other frame-destructive reactions on the part of the audience.

The stage presents actors with an ecological problem only occasionally encountered in everyday life: namely, onstage the

[18] Heylbut, *op. cit.*, p. 12.
[19] Those concepts are employed by Gross and Stone, *op. cit.*, in their analysis of embarrassment.

actor must sustain the relationship required by the plot of the play between himself and the other characters—while simultaneously communicating to the ever-watchful but nonparticipating audience. The actor's precise location on the stage is thus often crucial. Not only must he talk to the conversational partner of the scene, but also audibly and visually for the audience to see what he means. Since not only sound but also facial gesture (and especially that of the eyes and mouth) communicate, the actor has to be both audially and visually available to the audience. Stage fright in this sense occurs when an actor imagines that he will—or in fact does—commit an ecological *faux pas* and is unable immediately to rescue himself from the damage.

Props

The stage is an arena of illusion in which both actors and audience agree to accept what is on the stage as actually being what it represents for the duration of the performance. Thus the "box" composed of wood, metal and wire represents the rooms of Willy Loman's home in Arthur Miller's *Death of a Salesman*. But it is precisely because the stage has transformed wood and wire into a temporarily working representation of reality that stage performances are hazardous. Ordinarily a door can be slammed without the walls of the house collapsing, stairs can be ascended without giving way beneath the weight of the person upon them, and ceilings can be expected to retain their horizontal stability at their pre-established height. On the stage, however, none of these can simply be taken for granted. The actor portraying the outraged husband may be expected to storm out of the room, slamming the door behind him, and leaving his wife weeping; but the slammed door should communicate only his anger, not sound the death knell of the house itself. The illusion of the prop-contrived reality must be maintained throughout the performance. Actions that suggest or reveal the actual nature of the props constitute frame destruction of the most irretrievable sort. To destroy the illusion here is to destroy all.

The problems related to managing prop failure are greater today than in the past. Until the middle of the nineteenth century stages were almost entirely set by elaborately painted wings and drops. But thereafter the so-called "box" setting supplemented or replaced wings, introducing an interior setting composed of three walls and a ceiling and giving the illusion of an actual room.[20] The painted wings and drops undoubtedly left more to the imagination and taxed the transformation capacities of the audience more than the "box." But with the stage settings coming more and more closely to approximate a taken-for-granted reality, the failure to use those settings properly and the ever-present possibility of accidents threaten to break up an illusion that is too well established. Thus, the technological and artistic advances in setting the stage impose an even more precarious fragility on the illusion at precisely the moment that it becomes most realistic. Destruction of what the audience could easily see was make-believe did not destroy as much as the collapse of the absolutely correct imitation decor which the audience admired as "real."

A word must be said about furniture and identity. Furniture is intimately connected with the life-style and self-image of the person who owns it. Even in everyday life stumbling over one's sofa, slipping on one's rug, or falling down one's staircase are sources of embarrassment, involving a symbolic discreditation of one's own identity.

But on the stage an unexpected fall is more than a momentary loss of poise or a mildly disconfirming note of self. To the audience such an act ought to communicate something, and if it is the actor's rather than the character's clumsiness that has been displayed, the character suffers a severely damaging blow. If the fall cannot be immediately integrated into the play the audience will either recognize it as a slip and react accordingly, or await the revelation of the message that the fall telegraphed. In everyday life a host may laughingly apologize to his guest for stumbling over his own footstool, and regular interaction may then proceed as if the incident had not occurred. But even if an actor successfully ad libs to cover for his carelessness to save the immediate scene, the audience is likely to glean an unintended clue to the character that he is portraying, a clue which they believe ought to have some future

---

[20] Wilson, *op. cit.*, pp. 107–108.

payoff. Thus, stage actors must develop motor controls onstage of a much higher order than those required offstage.

Besides such fixed props as doors and walls, movable objects (or chattels) present a source of danger not usually experienced in everyday life. In every social situation there is some kind of equipment to manipulate. Ordinarily the ability to start or stop, move, or control the action of the equipment regularly associated with one's environment is a signal of self. In this respect social actors formulate at least two general but extreme orientations toward the equipment one regularly handles: first, there is a high order of skill presumed to lodge in the individual primarily because of the frequency with which he handles the item; or second, there is a very low order of skill, approximating motor incapacity or extreme clumsiness and also indicating a character type which seems unable to master the mechanical world. And for most persons, it is believed, the handling of everyday pieces of equipment—automobiles, cigarette lighters, ashtrays, keys and coins—falls into a broad middle range, efficient enough to admit of being able to operate in the modern world with only occasional flaws and failures.

On the stage, however, handling movable and mechanical equipment presents problems far more extraordinary than their offstage counterparts. Objects that are to be picked up, moved, discovered, or destroyed must be available for use at the correct time and in the right place. While in an actual living room the search for an ashtray or a notebook might not interrupt ongoing proceedings, a similar search onstage—unless part of the plot—must not occur. Indeed, should an object necessary to the plot of a play be misplaced, the actor must not only make do without it but also contrive a suitable subterfuge to avoid audience awareness of the error.

Stage fright with respect to props may take the form of motor incapacity. The normal musculature appears to be frozen, and the actor is immobilized. Or he might get an attack of "the shakes," preventing appropriate handling of quite ordinary items, such as cigarette lighters, glasses, or telephones. Immobilization or shakiness may accelerate and exacerbate the original fear so that the anticipated flaw becomes realized. This in turn may generate a generalized fear which creates the very conditions for continuous errors and heightened fears.

Onstage, even clothing can serve as a source of danger. All clothing worn on the stage is officially a costume, that is, a garment appropriate to the character portrayed and not necessarily suitable to the actor wearing it. The actor must solve the problem of suiting the manner of its wear to the character, not to himself. In everyday life, of course, clothing can come undone, tear, or—by body movement—conceal or disclose aspects of the body and emotional states. Onstage the actor must keep clothing under perfect control not only in the ordinary sense of wear and tear, but also in the manner of its display.

When everyday dress in a society changes so that one kind of costume is relegated to "costume drama" and no longer worn otherwise, the vulnerability of actors to errors in its wearing increases. Thus the wearing of armor, chain mail and helmets in contemporary performances of Shakespearean dramas presents problems of stylistic and muscular control over the worn material which in everyday life is not part of the actor's repertoire.

Body

In addition to the perfection of his stage location and handling of props, the actor has to control all those physical and vocal peculiarities that in everyday life are part of his own personal character, but which may be intrusive or discrediting to the character he is portraying onstage.

Thus in everyday concerns the frame of self-presentation assumes a wide variety of imperfections that are disattended, especially if they are irrelevant to the central features of one's role performance. A doctor's nervous tic is ruled out as irrelevant to his performance in removing a wart from the patient's foot; a lawyer's obesity bears no relation to his defense of an accused shop lifter; and a physics teacher's limp does not prevent him from lecturing on astronomy. But the nervous tic of the stage doctor, the excessive weight of the stage lawyer, and the limp of the stage professor are rich in inferential meaning—which the audience expects to be revealed to them. The doctor's nervous tic is but an external sign of his evil designs; the lawyer's fatness indicates a generally jolly disposition temporarily held in abeyance as he manfully defends his client; the professor's limp will eventually "explain" his interest in space exploration, a compensation for mobility interference on earth.

In short, to present a visible imperfection without explanation is to create frame confusion in the story line. While such imperfections may be tolerated as such during the early portions of the drama, if they remain unexplained (or uninterpretable) at the end, audiences will experience a sense of incompleteness, mystification, or even fraud: the imperfection was presented; therefore, it should have been accounted for in the drama.

Although in everyday life people will accept (albeit grudgingly sometimes) that looks deceive, an audience will not so easily acquiesce to that proposition. Type casting meets the audience's desire to have congruency between appearance and reality. And this includes, of course, congruence in the relation of feigned appearance and the final curtain revelation of who the character "really" was.

The history of acting is replete with limitations of body. Edwin Forrest, whose massive, muscular physique gave him a Herculean appearance chose roles suited to that body type. In contrast, Edwin Booth, a man of graceful, slender physique, rejected the physically demanding roles chosen by Forrest for those that were endowed with an intellectual, spiritual or poetic quality. Booth aptly summed up the limitations of body type on acting when he remarked, "It is rather safe to assume that actors establish their school upon their physique—for one must cover up what one cannot physically do."[21]

A special case of complex and confused relationships between physical appearance and social reality arises in racially conscious societies. In the past American Negro actors have been relegated to a large assortment of stereotyped "Negro" roles. Negroes who wished to widen their repertoire and to include traditional "white" roles had to leave the country for such opportunity,[22] or might

[21] *Ibid.*, p. 7.
[22] Thus the distinguished nineteenth century Negro Shakespearean actor Ira Aldridge could not win an audience in the United States, but he succeeded admirably in England and Ireland. See Richard Bardolph, *The Negro Vanguard*, New York: Vintage, 1961, p. 79.

"pass" as whites if they were sufficiently light-skinned. But when racial barriers are relaxed the appearance of Negroes in conventional white roles sometimes occasions mirth or amazement. Thus a Negro child, upon seeing a Negro Santa Claus for the first time, remarked to her mother: "That sure is a funny Santa Claus. I mean he's not *white*."[23]

Special problems of performance anxiety—relating to identity, stereotypes and social consequences—face Negro actors in times of transition in racial relations. These problems and anxieties, though probably affecting the performance, extend beyond it into controversies over what kind of status visibility Negroes should exhibit on stage and screen. Thus Hattie McDaniels replied to an attack on her for accepting Hollywood roles as a domestic: "It is better getting $7,000 a week playing a servant than $7 a week *being* one."[24] And Negro film star Sidney Poitier has been accused of building his successful career by sacrificing his screen sexuality and manliness (and by symbolic extension, the manliness of all Negro males in America).[25] The portrayal of racially stigmatized people by members of their own racial group results in anxieties having to do with appropriate and socially tactful (and also tactical) representation.

Beyond physical appearance and the control of physical or cultural stigmas is body movement itself. Onstage the body must be in readiness to act the part, and perfect control of its movements must be maintained throughout the performance. In everyday life individuals can retire from the social scene to restore or repair the body and then return to regular activities. For actors onstage, however, this can only be done surreptitiously and at some hazard to the play itself. In addition, offstage, the movement of arms, legs, head and trunk need not be in perfect coordination with the role being enacted; onstage, it must be.

[23] Reported in Herb Caen's column, *The San Francisco Chronicle*, December 19, 1967, p. 27.
[24] Langston Hughes, "The Negro and American Entertainment," in *The American Negro Reference Book*, edited by John P. Davis, Englewood Cliffs, N.J.: Prentice-Hall, p. 847.
[25] See Calvin C. Hernton, *White Papers for White Americans*, Garden City, N.Y.: Doubleday, 1966, pp. 53–70.

AUDIENCE STAGE FRIGHT

Kingsley Davis tells the story of a mother who, after viewing a college play in which her daughter had a part, was asked how she enjoyed the play; she responded by saying that she was too worried over her daughter's presence onstage to pay any attention to the play.[26] In other words, a member of the audience was experiencing stage fright.

Audience stage fright arises from a sense of fusion of personalities or the imputation of representational character to a particular performance. Persons involved in intimate relations may experience stage fright when one member of the group must perform alone. The fusion of identities that characterizes their intimacy lends itself to an altruistic expression of fear for the other's performance. This empathic anxiety is likely to occur whenever intimate groups are physically or socially copresent before a hyperconscious audience but unable to assist one another. Thus the parent who must watch his own child witness death unaided for the first time, the reluctant pimp who listens silently to his favorite girl's screams as she is being roughly handled in the next room by a sadistic customer, and the friend who introduces a parvenu into a new circle may experience a special form of empathic audience stage fright.

Persons bearing tribal stigmas[27] or under some form of collective oppression are likely to regard any one of their number as a symbol for the whole group. For such persons any public performance by a group member is a potential source of embarrassment or even danger and is thus likely to generate in them a special form of audience stage fright.[28] A tradition of prejudice and discrimination undermines a sense of absolute individualism that a member of the oppressed group might otherwise have developed. The result is a kind of collective psychic disadvantage that finds its most acute

[26] Kingsley Davis, *Human Society*, New York: Macmillan, 1948, p. 295.

[27] See Erving Goffman, *Stigma*, Englewood Cliffs, N.J.: Prentice-Hall Spectrum, 1963.

[28] Goffman, *ibid.*, distinguished between the person with an overt stigma (the discredited), who suffers the plight of tension-management, and the person with a covert stigma (the discreditable), who suffers the plight of information control. In terms of the present paper, both kinds of stigma and their attendant anxieties are but special instances of the more general notion of stage fright.

form in anxious self-consciousness whenever a fellow member is in the limelight.

In America the psychically underprivileged groups include Jews, Negroes and homosexuals. Hence we sometimes find Jews wondering anxiously if its "good for the Jews" if a Jewish family signals its middle-class status by celebrating Christmas or joining the Unitarian church;[29] Negro college presidents wincing with excruciating social agony when Negro students sit at the gate of a university munching watermelon;[30] and covert homosexuals manfully attempting to hide their embarrassment when a wrist-flapping fairy minces in public.[31]

Another kind of audience stage fright arises when the audience becomes apprehensive that it will unceremoniously be converted to performers. In recent dramatic innovations—plays such as Peter Weiss' *Marat/Sade*—the audience is threatened by the performers' movements between acts and may sense that it might be made part of the drama itself.[32] This makes for both a more zestful night of theater and heightened audience uneasiness. A similar kind of uneasiness prevails when night club comedians famous for their sharp and incisive repartee move into an audience and engage individuals at random in witty but cutting conversation. Comedians of this type generate a pervasive fear among certain members of the audience that they are helplessly trapped while being looked over for just those traits that make them an easy mark for the jester's mirth. It is this sense of social nakedness combined with knowledge of being scrutinized that transforms the audience members into stage performers and generates performance anxiety.

[29] Louis Wirth, *The Ghetto*, Chicago: University of Chicago Press, 1956, pp. 37, 260–261; Judith R. Kramer and Seymour Leventman, *Children of the Gilded Ghetto*, New Haven: Yale University Press, 1961, pp. 92–94; Kurt Lewin, "Self Hatred Among Jews," in *Race Prejudice and Discrimination*, edited by Arnold Rose, New York: Knopf, 1953, pp. 321–332.

[30] See LeRoi Jones, "Philistinism and the Negro Writer" in *Anger and Beyond*, edited by Herbert Hill, New York: Harper and Row, 1966, pp. 51–52; see also E. Franklin Frazier, *Black Bourgeoisie*, Glencoe, Ill.: The Free Press, 1957, pp. 226–227.

[31] Many instances are reported in G. Westwood, *A Minority*, London: Longmans, Green and Co., 1960.

[32] In some plays, such as Pirandello's *Six Characters in Search of an Author*, the line between illusion and reality is stretched to its limits, creating a kind of generalized audience anxiety.

Common arenas for audience anxiety are all those settings in which a person of authority is privileged to command instant public performances from any one of an aggregate of underlings. School-teachers, for example, sometimes discover or create enormous performance anxiety among their pupils by looking them over carefully and then calling upon one to recite.[33] Typical of the reactions of persons experiencing this kind of stage fright is an attempt—often unsuccessful—to appear nondescript, coupled with an anxious desire to be invisible.[34] Audience anxiety of the type herein described is often apprehension of an impending and involuntary degradation ceremony.[35]

Audience anxiety is also generated by watching what is morally unwatchable. Some persons having attended a dramatic presentation of Eugene O'Neill's *Long Day's Journey Into Night*, Edward Albee's *Who's Afraid of Virginia Woolf?*, or Michael McClure's *The Beard* experienced acute self-consciousness combined with intense anxiety. These plays present elements of life that are so deeply personal that one has the feeling that he is an unwitting witness to scenes that should remain private.

Offstage the same feelings are experienced when individuals find themselves observers at a ceremony that propriety demands should be conducted without any others present than the participants. A sense of heightened, anxious self-consciousness occurs, for example, when a dinner guest finds himself privy to a heated quarrel between the host and his wife. Again, as when at certain plays, he feels he shouldn't be there at all. But the fact that one is present during an unwatchable encounter creates a dilemma of choice over discreet departure or delicate deportment. Any act

[33] For a piquant example, see Willard Waller, *The Sociology of Teaching*, N.Y.: Science Edition, John Wiley, 1965, pp. 329–332.

[34] Certain categories of persons—the Japanese are an outstanding example—apparently have a feeling of audience stage fright most of the time and attempt to cultivate a permanent sense of composure to cope with it. See George De Vos, "A Comparison of the Personality Differences in Two Generations of Japanese Americans by Means of the Rorschach Test, "*Nagoya Journal of Medical Science*, 17 (August, 1954), especially pp. 252–261; see also William Caudill, "Japanese American Personality and Acculturation," *Genetic Psychology Monographs*, 45 (1952), pp. 3–102.

[35] See Harold Garfinkel, "Conditions of Successful Degradation Ceremonies," *American Journal of Sociology*, 61 (March, 1956), pp. 420–424.

during such a situation constitutes an interference in the ongoing quarrel—even a polite, "Excuse me, I think I'll be going," has the disadvantage of converting the self-conscious observer into a performer in the very social drama from which he wishes to withdraw. Silent inaction, however, is also disconcerting; in such situations one cannot escape the feeling that everyone present should be accounted for, and is, in fact, somehow performing anyway (or about to perform), albeit inadequately and without rehearsal. The stage fright described here is that experienced by a person who, from the point of view of the quarreling couple, may be receiving non-person treatment, but who finds this role situationally and emotionally uncomfortable.

A related form of audience anxiety arises among persons watching pornographic films. The scenes depicted on the screen are those for which, when performed offscreen, no witnesses are morally permitted. The question causing alarm and acute self-consciousness in the audience is how to behave in the presence of activities which are, like intimate family quarrels and defecation, socially defined as unwitnessable. Audience activity here usually constitutes an arduous attempt at calmness and composure. Sometimes special coping mechanisms will be employed as when, for example, a person sensing impending loss of self-control will stammer out a light joke, or will attempt to shift the meaning of the cinematic event from the erotic to the technical or scientific, commenting on the anatomical elements or sociological significance of the film. Anxieties are likely to be even greater if the film showing is designed as a test of moral character, as it often is during college fraternity initiations, and the all-male audience knows or fears that composure will be tested by a command to stand as soon as the film is over.

STAGE FRIGHT IN EVERYDAY LIFE

Stage fright is likely to be a feature of a situation during the *critical performance* of a claimed identity. Typically the occasion for this is a testing situation in which the identity claimed will be recognized and legitimated by persons in a position to provide some reward or payoff, such as admission into the circle of those who have established their claim to the identity, a new job or promotion, or the hand of a girl in marriage. Persons about to perform at such times not infrequently experience stage fright, even if the task itself is one with which they are quite familiar and is one which they perform with skill and *savoir-faire* on non-critical occasions.

A nice example is provided in the fear evinced by a prize-winning teenage Negro poet, performing for the first time before a Southern white audience at a house party:

> Toward the end of the long afternoon, it was proposed that the young writers read their poems. Once again I was plunged into sweaty-palmed agony. My torment only increased as the first two readers read their poems like seasoned professionals, or so it seemed to me. When my turn came I tried to beg off, but the additional attention focused upon me only increased my discomfort and I plunged in, at first reading too fast and almost inaudibly but finally recollecting some of the admonitions my teacher had dinned into my head in preparation for "recitations" before Negro school and church audiences as far back as the second grade. I had not realized how long a poem it was when I was writing it and I was squirmingly conscious of certain flaws and failures which had never before loomed so large.[36]

Critical performances are usually those that test the relationship between rehearsal and stage performance. Off the dramatic stage they include the first full-fledged engagement of a person with the activities with which he identifies himself. For an entrepreneur the test is whether he can actually meet his first payroll; for a doctor, whether he can diagnose his first patient; for a young husband, whether he can sexually satisfy his new wife.

When the critical performance occurs in the presence of higher-status others, the lower-status person is likely to experience anxiety over whether and in what manner he should acknowledge the real differences that separate him from the higher-status person. The problem is further complicated when the higher-status person commands the status inferior to, in effect, be "at ease." In such

---

[36] M. Carl Holman, "The Afternoon of a Young Poet," in *Anger and Beyond, op. cit.*, p. 150.

situations the status inferior tends to experience a kind of "frame confusion" whereby he is never sure whether the interaction he is engaged in is something other than what the status superior says it is. Thus when a monarch goes among his people and urges them to honestly tell him their grievances, when a school principal invites the students in for a "gloves off" chat, or when the colonel requests that his lieutenant candidly evaluate the colonel's battle plan—in each situation, the status inferior experiences uncertainty, anxiety and identity confusion.

On some occasions the tables are turned and higher-status persons are critically tested in the presence of inferiors. Such occasions generate a particularly acute anxiety since the performance occurs before an attentive, even hyperconscious audience, seeking to discover a single flaw by which they can discredit not only the performer himself, but also the status group which he represents and, by extension, the entire social order.

At such times the performer experiences an excruciating awareness that upon his shoulders, for a few moments, there rests history itself. George Orwell, serving as a British colonial officer, describes such an occasion when, one day, he realizes that he must resolutely and without sign of fear and in full view of the subject people kill an elephant that had gone on a rampage:

Here was I, the white man with his gun, standing in front of the unarmed native crowd—seemingly the leading actor in the piece; but in reality I was only an absurd puppet pushed to and fro by the will of those yellow faces behind. I perceived in this moment that when the white man turns tyrant it is his own freedom that he destroys. He becomes a sort of hollow, posing dummy, the conventionalized figure of a sahib. For it is the condition of his rule that he shall spend his life in trying to impress the "natives," and so in every crisis he has to do what the "natives" expect of him. He wears a mask, and his face grows to fit it. I had got to shoot the elephant. A sahib has got to act like a sahib; he has got to appear resolute, to know his own mind and do definite things. To come all this way, rifle in hand, with two thousand people marching at my heels, and then to trail feebly away, having done nothing—no, that was impossible. The crowd would laugh at me. And my whole life, every white man's life in the East, was one long struggle not to be laughed at.

The sole thought in my mind was that if anything went wrong those two thousand Burmans would see me pursued, caught, trampled on . . . And if that happened it was quite probable that some of them would laugh. That would never do.[37]

Besides critical performances and interaction with status superiors and inferiors, problems of stage fright emerge during "first time" situations. That is, some performances must be carried off smoothly without prior rehearsal. The problem for those engaged in the activity is how to give off an air of dexterity and grace without having had any experience.

Consider a child's attendance at his first horror film when accompanied by "sophisticated" peers who have seen such films before. The boy's fear is specifically stage fright rather than general anxiety because he is conscious of being under careful surveillance by his friends who he believes are seeking to uncover, beneath his air of carefree nonchalance, some sign that he is in fact the cowering child they suspect. His voice, manner, gestures and style will be carefully studied for just those flaws that throw into relief his suspected "real" identity. Any incongruity—a trembling hand, for example—may mar his performance and undermine his identity claim. Similar anxieties and their attendant interactional features are found among those viewing for the first time pornographic films.

While many activities combine first time performance with expectations of skill and savoir-faire, we must distinguish between those that are linked by knowledge and rehearsal to be followed by a testing performance and those for which knowledge is available but practice forbidden. Thus, as an example of the first point, lawyers with first cases have not only their general law background but also experience in moot court. But at least two activities often require smooth performances with no previous experience: surrendering one's virginity and death. Each is, so to speak, for the first and last time.[38]

---

[37] George Orwell, "Shooting an Elephant," *Shooting an Elephant and Other Essays*, Garden City, N.Y.: Doubleday Anchor, 1954, pp. 159-160.

[38] In a sense this is not strictly accurate. Both the presence of virginity and the absence of life are socially defined and may vary within and between societies and classes. Moreover, both virgin status and death can be feigned. We are here concerned with the actor's orientation toward his situation and in each of these instances, we believe, the actors are experiencing a never-before, never-again situation.

Yet the manner of the performance is crucial since upon it may hang the fate of a relationship or the moral history of a life. Although virginity may excuse a bride from skill in her first attempts at sexual intercourse, apprehension and fear may be taken as a sign of lack of love or as indifference. Where virginity is culturally important, a woman undergoes stage fright precisely because of the special scrutiny with which her wedding night performance will be judged.

Death, too, often invokes an unrehearsed performance[39] before doctors, executioners, relatives and history. In other words, in the moments before it occurs a person may become frightened not only at the prospects of what death itself entails, but at the meaning of his own terminal performance. Executions profoundly tax the principal actors' capacities to cope with performance anxiety. The noble bearing of a condemned man just before his execution may win him plaudits that outweigh the heinous crime for which he has been sentenced.[40] For some men, then, nothing becomes them like their deaths, and their fears over just this may generate stage fright. Thus persons condemned to hang sometimes express fear that the loss of sphincter control concomitant with rope strangulation is too embarrassing to bear.

Certain roles—for example, the "understudy" and the parvenu —are vulnerable to the plight of stage fright to the extent that they share structural similarities with "first time" situations. The understudy, both onstage and in everyday life, is aware that many stand ready to challenge his credentials to give a performance. Thus, when a substitute teacher appears, students become active in testing the credibility of her identity claim. And to buoy up the stage confidence of the substitute teacher, the school principal and others make special efforts to reassure the "understudy" of her capacities to handle the situation. Among professional actors, the ritual everywhere is to offer the understudy moral support and boost confidence with flowers and good wishes to "break a leg."

[39] Two studies of dying are worthy of mention in this respect. Barney Glaser and Anselm Strauss, *Awareness of Dying*, Chicago: Aldine, 1965; *Time for Dying*, Chicago: Aldine, 1968. See also David Sudnow, *Passing On*, Englewood Cliffs, N.J.: Prentice-Hall, 1967.

[40] See Erving Goffman, "Where the Action Is," in *Interaction Ritual*, Garden City, N.J.: Doubleday Anchor, 1967, especially pp. 229–233.

Stage fright over claimed identity also arises for parvenus. Parvenus, aware of the precariousness of their identity claims, will frequently plan or search for coping mechanisms that hide their identity-betraying stage fright. Moreover, societies in which traditional values or legal norms are in transitional or fluctuating states provide numerous situations for trying out new identities under hazardous conditions. First-time users of marijuana, for example, who are not familiar with or sure about the emotional control measures available to them when high, fear that their mental state will be visible to disapproving non-users.[41] In general, contemporary society is systematically producing a vast assortment of parvenu statuses, making stage fright a more common problem in everyday life.[42]

COPING STRATEGIES

With respect to stage fright, three general kinds of coping strategies are available. First, there are those strategies that prevent stage fright from emerging. Here is the place for rehearsals and practice. But we have already noted that in some situations—

[41] See Howard S. Becker, *Outsiders*, N.Y.: The Free Press, 1963, pp. 41–58.

[42] The civil rights movement has generated many new statuses and the attendant anxieties in their performances. Consider the personal description (Merril Proudfoot, *Diary of a Sit-In*, New Haven: College and University Press, 1964, pp. 1–2) of stage fright by a white college professor attempting his first sit-in in the company of a Negro student:

When I made that promise to Robert Becker three months ago, I did not expect that I would ever have to keep it. Yet at 11:15 this morning I found myself —a white, bespectacled college professor at the usually conservative age of thirty-six—advancing to my baptism of fire as a sit-in demonstrator! With me was Robert Becker, a tall dignified Negro youth who is president of the student body of our college. As we approached the basement lunch counter in Rich's, the city's largest department store, Becker showed no fear; I was secretly terrified. . . .

The seat of my personality had shifted to the solar plexus. "Could I possibly be the fellow, I who gets nervous indigestion when I have to make an announcement in chapel, who has got himself involved in this situation?" I was asking myself. "Now have you got enough nerve to go through with it, or are you going to let your student understand that you are a coward?" I sauntered in after Becker, trying to look like an ordinary customer, but I could not have felt more self-conscious had my skin been coal-black.

executions, wedding nights for virgins, and so on—no practice can occur and thus, in the absence of this coping device, we may expect some overt evidence of stage fright. Aside from rehearsals, stage fright may be nipped in the bud, so to speak, by anxiety-reducing redefinitions of the performance situation. Nudist camps, for example, try to relieve patrons and visitors of undue concern about their unclothed state by establishing rules prohibiting staring, sex talk, body contact, and nude dancing.[43]

The second kind of strategy for coping with stage fright is that which contains it and prevents it from erupting into behavior that may disrupt a performance or discredit the identity of the performer. One technique for reducing the effects of stage fright on performer and audience is for the performer to disarm both by lightly calling attention to his own anxieties. Thus, the new bank manager, making his maiden speech before the toastmaster's club, may begin by saying that his knees are knocking so loudly that he wonders if his voice can be heard. Other small, self-deprecating remarks by speakers act to reduce tension and save face by inviting audience sympathy.

A related coping device is the performer's employment of a confederate to buoy up sagging stage confidence. The simplest example is that in which a mother or tutor instructs a novice performer to fix his gaze on her all during the performance with an implied promise that a confidence-maintaining countenance will be returned throughout. A more subtle employment of the same technique is the use of a friend as an agent of silent collusive communication in moments of stress, so that the anxious performer knows that there is at least one person in the audience who by his facial expression and eye contact will supply him with moral support.

Beyond interpersonal techniques are all those physical objects that may be used to hide the presence of stage fright from an audience. A lectern prevents the audience from seeing the trembling hands and quivering knees of the public speaker. Some lecturers confess to an inordinate anxiety whenever they know that they will have to perform without the protections afforded by this wooden

[43] See Martin S. Weinberg, "The Nudist Management of Respectability," in *Deviance and Respectability*, edited by Jack Douglas, N.Y.: Basic Books, 1970, pp. 375–403.

barrier. In a similar sense a teacher may be relieved of the anxiety that her pupils are allowing their eyes to wander to the body regions exposed to them when she sits behind her desk by having the front of the desk covered; but a young mini-skirted lady may suffer in silent agony when she is afforded no equal protection at a cocktail party and must remember to always cross her legs when seated. The presence or absence of a screen by which a performer may hide the most manifest signs of his own anxieties or those portions of the anatomy which when scrutinized subject him or her to embarrassment constitutes a major element in the generation or inhibition of stage fright itself.[44]

A third kind of coping strategy involves employing rescue devices when stage fright has manifested itself in such a manner that the performance has been disrupted. Sometimes the restorative measures are not employed by the immobilized performer himself, but by fellow performers or the audience. Thus when one stage actor has "frozen" and cannot carry off his part, another actor may quickly construct lines to "save" the scene. Similarly, in a wedding ceremony, the usher whose hands are trembling so that he cannot light the altar candles may be assisted by a priest, altar-boy, or guest. At times the entire audience restores the confidence of a totally frightened performer by a spontaneous sympathetic approval. A remarkable exhibition of this occurred in the film *Tales of Manhattan* when the overweight novice orchestra conductor, frightened about his own debut, ripped his tuxedo jacket in the first raise of the baton. Totally demoralized he sat down at the podium and wept, until the swallow-tailed audience silently removed their own jackets and urged him by their applause to begin again.

The experienced actor knows that he can often rescue a potentially disastrous scene by an ad lib, a joke, or some other hasty but effective scissors-and-paste over the cracked theatrical frame. Indeed, it is for this reason, probably, that the experienced stage actor suffers less anxiety over his own stage fright than the tyro performer or neophyte. The experienced actor, however, may be

---

[44] For a general discussion of screening devices and other "involvement shields," see Erving Goffman, *Behavior in Public Places*, New York: The Free Press of Glencoe, 1963, pp. 176–178 and *passim*.

motivated by concerns other than the salvage of a scene when he employs ad libs and new constructions within the characterological portrayal. To begin with, he may ad lib to add zest to his performance. If lines are too well anticipated, an actor learns, the performance may become flat.

Beyond the attainment of zest, ad libs and improvisations may be used to test the poise of fellow actors during the course of the drama itself. Examples of such situations are the stage Romeo who whispers to Juliet that she has bad breath or who bites her lip in the tragic kissing scene; the stage Peter who proclaims, *sotto voce*, that the matzo is stale while accepting the dramatic communion in the Passion Play; or the "joke" said to be continually employed by Caruso in *Madame Butterfly* of concealing a raw egg in his palm before shaking hands with his costar.

Ad libs and other innovative activities on the stage, then, can have a variety of functions beyond that of saving the performance. They can indicate an actor's poise under pressure, a test of his *sang-froid* (his "coolness," to use a contemporary idiom).[45] In this sense, *ad libs* and improvisations on the stage can be a cause for as well as a rescue from slips and errors. And the actor who must anticipate his own ability to present or respond to the unexpected onstage, can suffer stage fright therefrom. The actor knows he must put on a performance for his fellow actor as an infrastructure to the performance he does for the audience; that is, a frame of action is placed within the larger frame of dramatic presentation. In terms of its total consequences, to fail in the inner frame may be quite as disastrous as to fail in the outer one. In short, coping devices are often two-edged swords.

CONCLUSIONS

Within the framework of the theatrical stage, slips and flaws are seriously attended, and unlike most offstage encounters in everyday life, performances are expected to occur with qualities of

[45] See Stanford M. Lyman and Marvin B. Scott, "Coolness in Everyday Life," in *Sociology and Everyday Life, op. cit.*, pp. 93–101, reprinted as Chapter 6 in this book.

perfection not ordinarily achieved. Since total congruency is assumed as the definition of the theatrical situation, the rules of conduct prevailing under conditions of fragmented congruency— that is, the rules of conduct to which ordinary persons ordinarily subscribe—are revoked and rules requiring perfection substituted instead. And since stage actors know that they will be judged in accordance with these extraordinary rules of conduct during a performance, they are apprehensive. Consequently, the actor, as Sir Alec Guinness has observed, is totally exposed: "He's vulnerable from head to toe, his total personality is exposed to critical judgment —his intellect, his bearing, his whole appearance. In short, his ego."[46]

Stage fright is also a phenomenon of everyday life. We may expect stage fright to emerge whenever an event or performance itself is important. Importance is usually socially defined although there are idiosyncratic variations and individual innovations in the defining process. In general, however, we may expect that jockeys will experience greater performance anxiety when riding in the Kentucky Derby than in ordinary races; that a Jewish mother will be more acutely self-conscious at her son's Bar Mitzvah than on any other Saturday in the synagogue; and that a young man will more likely exhibit stage fright on his wedding night than on subsequent occasions of sexual intercourse with his wife.

A more complex situation generating stage fright involves the social composition of the audience. As a hypothesis we may suggest that both dramatic and social actors will experience a heightened sense of stage fright in proportion to the social status and valuable rewards available from the audience. To mention an extreme case of this point, we might expect the war hero to show greater anxiety at the ceremony in which he received the Congressional Medal of Honor than on the battlefield where he carried out the deeds to merit it.[47] In addition to the status and power of an audience, there is the question of its size. For some persons a performance that can be carried out with grace and skill before a few becomes impossible in front of seated hundreds.

[46] Runke, *op. cit.*, p. 20.

[47] For a case in point, see Ralph G. Martin, *Boy from Nebraska*, New York: Harper and Brothers, 1946, p. 198.

Neophytes and the neophyte status is another strategic research site for the study of stage fright. The neophyte is about to perform for the first time in a role that calls for certain skills never yet publicly tested. Neophytes, unlike experienced performers, are unaware of the relationship between rehearsal and performance, and thus cannot know what connection exists between their private practicing and their public performance. In addition, there are some situated neophyte statuses: for example, wedding nights for virgins, for which perfect performance may be expected without any prior rehearsal. Rehearsal or not, the neophyte status may be perceived as one characterized by apprehension based upon the expectation of perfection in a never-before-performed task.

Besides the neophyte status, there are those categories of persons whose identity is potentially discreditable and who, therefore, have a vested interest in masking the stigmatizable elements of their self-presentation.[48] Examples include ex-mental patients, passing homosexuals, and professional check forgers.[49] Such types, unlike ordinary persons, must be alive to those elements in their daily and regular performances which might give them away. And it is among such discreditable types that heightened apprehensiveness is to be found as well, perhaps, as strategies for coping with flaws in behavior.

Such persons are commonly labeled as "paranoids."[50] Thus homosexuals, sensitive Negroes and cripples exhibit anxieties about their image and their fate suggesting that a pervasive fear governs their lives. This fear, we contend, is stage fright of the same order as that experienced by dramatic actors in the theater and social actors in unusual situations. But in the case of the stigmatized, the fear is permanent, based on the continuous feeling of being onstage as a performer—always under surveillance, everywhere being looked over for just those tell-tale slips that will betray the identity which

---

[48] Goffman, *Stigma, op. cit.*

[49] For the case of the check forger, see Edwin H. Lemert, *Human Deviance, Social Problems, and Social Control*, Englewood Cliffs, N.J.: Prentice-Hall, 1967, pp. 109–134.

[50] For further discussion, see Marvin B. Scott and Stanford M. Lyman, "Paranoia, Homosexuality and Game Theory," *Journal of Health and Social Behavior*, 9 (September, 1968), pp. 179–187, reprinted as Chapter 3 in this book.

he has voluntarily assumed or which he has involuntarily acquired.

But one need not look to extreme cases to witness stage fright in everyday life. Much of the so-called anxiety of the modern age is essentially due to stage fright. We live in a pluralistic society where increasingly identity claims are made problematic. In other words, we are suggesting that our society is evolving into one where individuals are continually being faced with the necessity of mobilizing their interactional performances, a society where individuals are aware that their identity claims are being temporarily honored—until further notice. If so, the twin plights of tension management and mobilization of the self for purposes of information control become a problem not only for the stigmatized but increasingly for all men. And the coping mechanisms already alluded to appear to us as becoming dominant features of interpersonal relations.

What we are suggesting finally is that the age-old debate between art and life is more complex than has been recognized. For most, the sense of artistic performance is experienced occasionally and briefly; for a few it is a matter of professional skills, experienced in settings clearly marked out as theater; but for some, especially the stigmatized, art does not imitate life, but becomes it. And a pervasive fear haunts those for whom their very existence is theater.

8

On the time track

Man's mortality forces him to organize and allocate his energy according to that most scarce resource—time.[1] Social and cultural conventions carve out time segments from the raw, existential world, providing direction-giving tracks of meaning upon which man travels through life. Human existence is in effect a journey upon a complex network of time tracks.

Time tracks are temporal periods employed by individuals, groups, and whole cultures to designate the beginnings or the termination of things. To take a culturally universal example, the span of life and its benchmarked periods such as childhood, adolescence, adulthood, and old age are time tracks experienced as part of the human condition.

---

[1] The philosophical and psychological study of time is so vast that merely to list those sources that we consulted would be excessively space-consuming. Mention should be made, however, of the very useful source with an excellent bibliography: *The Voices of Time*, edited by J. T. Fraser, N.Y.: Braziller, 1966. Here let us note only those sociological works which served as the immediate source and inspiration for the present paper: Barney Glaser and Anselm Strauss, *Time for Dying*, Chicago: Aldine, 1968; Erving Goffman, "Where the Action Is," in *Interaction Ritual*, Garden City, N.Y.: Doubleday, 1968; Everett Hughes, "Cycles, Turning Points, and Careers," in *Men and Their Work*, Glencoe: The Free Press, 1958; Wilbert E. Moore, *Man, Time and Society*, N.Y.: Wiley, 1963; Alfred Schutz, *Collected Papers*, The Hague: Martinus Nijhoff, 1962, 1964, Vols. I and II. See especially his essays, "Making Music Together," "Mozart and the Philosophers," and "Tiresias, or Our Knowledge of Future Events." Schutz's

The time track concept presupposes that social actors conceive of periods as characterized by a dominant event or type of event, activity or type of activity, thought or category of thought. Thus, American historians have treated the twelve-year period from 1865 to 1877 as The Tragic Era,[2] and they have apparently accepted F. Scott Fitzgerald's announcement that the Jazz Age, which had begun with the May Day riots of 1919, had come to a close with the stock market crash of October, 1929.[3]

But time tracks are not the sole possession of historians nor do they arise only in the creative imagination of perceptive writers. One of the ubiquitous dimensions of ordinary life, they are recognized as major elements of careers, as crucial factors in family life, and as routine parts of everyday occasions. Moving from one track to another is sometimes celebrated by a rite of passage; travelling along others is sometimes abruptly halted. Some people know just what time tracks they are on, how long they last, and when to change from one to another; others are startled by their discovery of a track, ignorant of its length, and confused about change. In any case, since social behavior takes place on time tracks, any social system may be conceived as an arrangement of time-specific activities.

Briefly put, our purpose is to present the major analytical features of time tracks and to suggest a conceptual scheme for their study. Hopefully, this preliminary enterprise will sensitize future researchers to the historicity of social phenomena, the rhythms of activities, and the tempos of life.

---

work on the subject of time represents a finely developed synthesis of the contributions of Bergson and Husserl. While Schutz's work has been the most influential on our thinking about time, the immediate inspiration for the present effort was Julius A. Roth, *Timetables*, Indianapolis: Bobbs-Merrill, 1963. Aside from the above-mentioned works, we have been continuously influenced by those two classic gems: W. F. Cottrell, "Of Time and the Railroader," *American Sociological Review*, 4 (April, 1939), 190–198; and Pitirim Sorokin and Robert K. Merton, "Social Time: A Methodological and Functional Analysis," *American Journal of Sociology*, 42 (March, 1937) 615–629.

[2] See, for instance, Claude G. Bowers, *The Tragic Era*, Boston: Houghton-Mifflin, 1929.

[3] F. Scott Fitzgerald, "Echoes of the Jazz Age," *The Crack Up*, N.Y.: New Directions, 1956, 13–22.

ANALYTIC FEATURES OF TIME TRACKS

In thinking about "time," we have found two pairs of sensitizing concepts useful—"humanistic-fatalistic" and "continuous-episodic."[4]

The first pair of concepts to be examined measures events and their passage along a *humanistic-fatalistic* dimension.[5] By humanistic time tracks we refer to the complex subjective experience that activities are governed by personal decision, are entered into with a sense of mastery or control, and are exhibited through self expression. By fatalistic time tracks we refer to the subjective experience that these activities are matters of obligation or compulsion, are outside the active domination of the social actor, and are vehicles of coercive or conformist rather than individual expression. Social arrangements generate the experience that is defined as humanistic or fatalistic.

Persons on fatalistic time tracks find themselves suffering the inconveniences of time. Activities in which they are involved seem like slavery. Terms like "rat race," commonly applied to obligatory activities in bureaucratic settings, apprehend the subjective sense of fatalism sensed in some occupations. While all individuals may experience events or activities fatalistically sometimes, certain segments of society are more likely to perceive their very existence in fatalistic terms. In original Calvinism, as Max Weber pointed out, life itself was defined as predetermined by God's will; neither man's deeds nor his wishes could change the inevitable outcome.[6] Apart from the belief in fatalism derived from cultural definitions are situations and settings that tend to induce the same subjective sense. The urban Negro poor, inmates of various kinds, and persons in disastrous but unbreakable marriages are but some of the most

[4] For a discussion of the uses of paired concepts in sociology, see Reinhard Bendix and Bennett Berger, "Images of Society and Problems of Concept Formation in Sociology," in *Symposium on Sociological Theory*, Evanston: Harper, Row, Peterson, 1959, 92–118.

[5] For a discussion of humanism and fatalism which parallels our own and which we have adapted to our purposes, see David Matza, *Delinquency and Drift*, N.Y.: Wiley, 1964.

[6] Max Weber, *The Protestant Ethic and the Spirit of Capitalism*, N.Y.: Scribners, 1930.

noticeable social groups that experience their life situations as fatalistic.

One response to the anxious and frustrating awareness of being on a fatalistic time track is the attempt to gamble with fate by seeking to alter the seemingly inevitable. This involves the conversion of fatalistic to humanistic time tracks. In general the individual will attempt to place himself in a particular relation to time—a relation in which he can subjectively experience both personal freedom and active control over events. One manifestation of this phenomenon involves taking risks. Flaunting fate and history's directive, a man may allow the free play of his impulses to disorganize the predicted, frustrate the dictated, or wreak havoc in the ordered world. Thus, the fatalistic adolescent abandons his destiny to a rumble; the frustrated middle-class youth tests the limits of mind and body with powerful drugs; the inmate challenges the powerful staff to a fight; and the wife trapped in a "hollow shell" marriage takes a lover, or in desperation attempts suicide.

Much activity undertaken by those on fatalistic time tracks is defined by others as deviant behavior. This behavior, however, may be viewed as the conversion of anxiety-ridden fatalism to "courageous" humanism. The "little man" who robs a bank seizes the initiative from destiny. For robbing a bank activates the community. The robber provides a cause for activity on the part of others and thus converts himself from object to subject, from puppet to puppeteer. In general any infraction invites a counteraction[7]— and this counteraction is the very evidence needed to know that, for the moment, one controls destiny.

Adventures—bankrobbing is an extreme example—are relevant for the analysis of humanistic-fatalistic time tracks because of the unique manner in which they relocate individuals in time and because they provide unusual opportunities for the reduction of alienation.[8] One especially important element in the adventure is its absolute separation from linear time and interconnected events. The adventure, as Simmel has observed, "is independent of the

[7] Matza, *op. cit.*

[8] Georg Simmel, "The Adventure," *Georg Simmel, 1858–1918*, edited by Kurt H. Wolff, Columbus: Ohio State University Press, 1959, 249–252.

'before' and 'after'; its boundaries are defined regardless of them."[9] Because of this fundamental disconnectedness, because of its existence in time and space *sui generis,* the adventure functions as a relief and respite to those on fatalistic time tracks. For its duration, the individual is freed from the dictated importunities of time, subjected to his own abilities, re-created as a potential master of the scene. Adventures thus make potential heroes of "little men," offering opportunities for enterprise and skill that fate has otherwise proscribed.

The adventure, unlike the seeming continuity of the rest of life, collapses the scene of action in time. Nowhere is this illustrated better than in gambling, a species of the adventure that throws further light on its peculiar qualities. In contrast to most of life's endeavors, the gambler challenges fate and experiences the outcome within the same spatio-temporal episode. The crucial point here is best seen if we compare the temporal qualities in the challenge of undertaking a new occupational career with those of undertaking a bet on a horse. In the former instance the resolution of the gamble may not be realized for many years;[10] in the latter, it is realized in less than two minutes. Five hundred dollars might be a month's wages, but a two-dollar bet on a promising daily double might earn an equivalent amount in a moment.[11] Gambling also involves a peculiar combination of chance and rationality not found in the same co-relationship in everyday life. Thus, there is a rationality in gambling that suggests a peculiar sense of mastery and control.[12] On the other hand, gambling provides the opportunity for an individual to draw chance from its apparent inaccessibility and harness it to his private ends.[13]

[9] *Ibid.,* 244.

[10] "The notion of career implies a great number of future expectations. These future expectations extend through the work lifetime of the individual. Indeed, longevity of experience is one of the norms of career." Lee Taylor, *Occupational Sociology,* N.Y.: Oxford University Press, 1968, 267.

[11] For a description of the daily double in the context of the sociology of gambling, see Marvin B. Scott, *The Racing Game,* Chicago: Aldine Press, 1968, 133–135.

[12] See Irving K. Zola, "Observations on Gambling in a Lower Class Setting," in *The Other Side,* edited by Howard S. Becker, N.Y.: Free Press of Glencoe, 1964, 247–260; and Scott, *op. cit.,* 116–119.

[13] Simmel, *op. cit.* 246.

In general, persons who sense they are on humanistic time tracks experience life as exhilarating and euphoric; those on fatalistic tracks, as deadening and dyseuphoric. The latter will seek humanization in some form. Treated as a phenomenon of modern times, adventurous activity has been simultaneously democratized and delegitimized ever since Calvinism imposed its puritanical doctrines on work and self.[14] Since then adventures are, in a general sense, achieved only vicariously in fantasy and fiction, or accepted when they occur among ordinary men as unexpected premiums in an otherwise humdrum life, as unusual opportunities for self-expression.

The second major dimension we refer to as *continuous-episodic* time tracks. The everyday phrases "long term" and "short term" apprehend some elements of this time track dimension. In general we may say that the length of a time track is inversely proportional to the pace of behavior associated with it. Thus, the occupational career is associated with a long term accumulation of merits and skills, a slow but steady building up of confidence and socio-occupational adeptness, and an inhibition of excessive spontaneous emotionality. By contrast episodes are characterized by an intensity of activity, a relaxation of controls and vigilance, and more frenetic behavior. The distinction can be seen if we compare the amorous affair with marriage.

A romantic affair has an episodic quality about it quite unlike marriage. "To be a lover is easier than to be a husband," wrote Balzac. "For it is far more difficult to show intelligence every day than to make pretty speeches from time to time." Love, as Simmel reminds us, encompasses a twofold aspect of the erotic. "It displays two standards of time: the momentarily climactic, abruptly subsiding passion; and the idea of something which cannot pass, an idea in which the mystical destination of two souls for one another and for a higher unity finds temporal expression."[15] The man who has made a career out of fleeting, intense, but short-lived affairs with women employs the rhetoric of a never-ending love in order to secure his immediate interests. Thus we learn that Casanova

---

[14] Jessie Bernard, "The Eudaemonists," in *Why Men Take Chances*, edited by Samuel Z. Klausner, Garden City: Doubleday Anchor, 1968, 27–34.

[15] Simmel, *op. cit.*, 252.

recorded in his memoires that he had intended to marry one or another of his many mistresses. But Simmel interprets this as but his immersion in the "rapture of the moment," an involvement that was so engrossing that "he wanted to enter into a future relationship which was impossible precisely because his temperament was oriented to the present."[16] The erotic moment, its flushed excitement, its beginning and end in a single episode, its promise and realization experienced in a single time period, stands in sharp contrast to marriage with its career-like duration and manifold aspects beyond the purely erotic.

Life is experienced as being both continuous and episodic. In one sense episodes punctuate continuous time tracks, providing them with benchmarks, calamities, surprises, beginnings and terminations.

Given these preliminary remarks, we may now detail certain other analytic features of time tracks.

To begin with, all time tracks are governed by norms of *pace* and *sequence*. Sometimes these norms are enforced by nature. An airplane pilot, for example, must go through a set of intervening steps between the time he sights the field and lands the plane. A failure at any point in this intervening sequence might lead to incontrovertible consequences. A less stringent but similar situation may arise in the advanced stages of courtship. A woman may demonstrate that she loves a man by permitting, at his request, sexual relations. Despite her permissive contentions, she may suddenly deny him sexual access because she had failed to take intervening contraceptive precautions. Such a denial, at a strategic juncture in their relationship, could—in the absence of an efficacious excuse—lose the man forever.

Courtship provides many illustrations of the operation of norms of pace and sequence. As two people become attached to one another the frequency of their meetings is expected to increase, the quality of their mutual involvement is expected to grow, and the nature of their intimacies escalate. Thus in the early stages of courting the couple may attend to a ritual of dining, dancing and, at first, light petting. Later, if the courtship is mutually gratifying,

[16] *Ibid.*, 246.

the preliminaries may be dispensed with and heavy petting resorted to from the beginning of each encounter.[17] Petting itself calls for a carefully handled progressive sequence, beginning first with hand-holding, moving on to kissing, and then extending to more intimate embraces, including the handling of private parts. Heavy petting may later become the play preceding intercourse. To exercise the pace too rapidly or to skip early stages is—at least among middle-class Americans—to risk being labeled a boor, ineligible for future entree into polite society.

Norms of pace and sequence can also be seen operating in the area of race and ethnic relations. The second generation of every immigrant group is expected to do better than its parent generation. Groups or segments of groups that have collectively failed in upward mobility suffer from the frustrations of "timetable failure."[18] The consequences of this sense of failure are varied. One result that has been made visible by the recent movements for desegregation in largely Polish and other Eastern European neighborhoods in mid-western cities is direct and violent aggression against other minority groups that appear to be surpassing them too rapidly.[19] In American

[17] For a general discussion, see Gerald R. Leslie, *The Family in Social Context*, N.Y.: Oxford, 1967, 465–624; and Ira L. Reiss, *The Social Context of Premarital Permissiveness*, N.Y.: Holt, Rinehart and Winston, 1967, 76–91.

[18] On the concept of "timetable failure," see Roth, *op. cit.*, 105–107, 116.

[19] For earlier and more quietistic discriminations against Negroes see, among many works, Arthur Evans Wood, *Hamtrack*, New Haven: College and University Press, 1955, 99, 238–239; Frank F. Lee, *Negro and White in a Connecticut Town*, New Haven: College and University Press, 1961, 63–65. For a study of Jewish opposition to school desegregation indicating that socioeconomic status was a factor in Jewish dispositions toward Negroes, see Kurt Lang and Gladys Engel Lang, "Resistance to School Desegregation," in Raymond J. Murphy and Howard Elinson, editors, *Problems and Prospects of the Negro Movement*, Belmont: Wadsworth, 1966, 145–158. On the other hand where class differences were not a factor and both Negroes and Jews had achieved a modicum of success, integration moved more smoothly. See Herbert J. Gans, *The Levittowners*, N.Y.: Pantheon, 1967, 172–173, 371–384. For the attitudes of various ethnic groups who have only achieved some success in intergenerational mobility, see Nathan Glazer and Daniel Patrick Moynihan, *Beyond the Melting Pot*, Cambridge: M.I.T. Press and Harvard University Press, 1963, 18–19, 70–71. That backlash is a phenomenon of timetable perceptions is indicated in the resentment toward Irish demands for more power within the Democratic Party in New York City in the 1880s. "Like the Negroes in the 1960's, the Irish in the 1880's were feeling the middle-class backlash,"; see Thomas N. Brown, *Irish-American Nationalism, 1870–1890*, Philadelphia: Lippincott, 1966, 139.

race relations as in courtship there is apparently a perceived pace and sequence in which both movement that is too rapid and movement that is too slow are regarded as untoward and unacceptable.

Individuals who violate norms of pace and sequence in face-to-face relations are often labeled "mentally ill."[20] Psychiatrists have categories for speed problems. Slow speech and body movement are taken as symptoms of depressive states, while the opposite behavior pattern is evidence of a manic condition. In evaluating speed of action as a sign of mental illness, the social situation is taken into account. An impression of severe mental illness is given, for example, "by the patient who is on the grounds when it begins to rain and who, unlike others caught outside, does not walk faster or pull his clothes more tightly about him. Since he does not have a fitting concern for his own physical welfare, it is an open question as to just what it is he is concerned with."[21] Other instances of pace disorientation indicate that social and historical contingencies make an important difference in designating such activity as normal, religious, or pathological. The steps of current dances in America resemble the dancing manias of the sixteenth century, but to do the former is not to open oneself seriously to the charge of collective madness. Rolling on the floor to the shouts and chants of certain religious groups is a sign of heavenly possession; similar behavior in a grocery store or a court room is testimony to insanity. Glossolalia among Pentecostalists is revered; among school children, it is a sign of severe speech disorder. In short, the physical pace of body movement and speech may be rated, contextually, according to its proximity or departure from acceptable norms. Sometimes being physically out of step is being psychologically out of step as well.

Norms of pace and sequence are frequently related to *age-specific* activities. For example, most industrial cultures suppose that people will enter school, complete their education, and get married within a certain age period. Although the exact age for any of these may not be specified an age-range is recognized beyond which completion of the activity becomes either problematic, remarkable, a

[20] Many examples are to be found in Erving Goffman, *Behavior in Public Places*, Glencoe: The Free Press, 1963.
[21] *Ibid.*, 77.

sign of deviance, or irrelevant for measurement of success. In the occupational sphere certain notions of when people are promising, up-and-coming, and has-beens are established by age or age ranges. An obvious example is the case of the professional athlete—boxer, football player, baseball player. For a while he occupies the status of a "comer" or a "promising rookie"; soon his designation—if he succeeds—is shifted to steady performer or star. But at a certain age (usually, but not always, by the late 30's) he is regarded as an old man of the game. He has come to the end of his occupational time track.

Age is also a crucial consideration in the career lines of many women. The airline stewardess, the fashion model, and the chorus girl—each knowing that she has only a few years to display her bodily talents to best advantage, finds herself being continually subject to marriage proposals. Should she turn down such proposals while still in a position to gain "exposure" to perhaps more rewarding marriage prospects? If she delays too long in accepting a proposal she runs the risk of coming to the end of her career with neither a saleable talent nor a secure marriage to see her through her less pulchritudinous years.

Age-specific considerations are particularly relevant to certain occupations that place a premium on precociousness. In certain career lines there are widespread beliefs about the crucial importance of establishing ability at an early age. It is held, for example, that Olympic swimmers, mathematicians, jockeys, and virtuoso violinists must demonstrate considerable skill in childhood or not be considered potential "greats" in their respective fields.

Among the many features of time tracks mention must be made of their degree of *determinateness* and *indeterminateness*. A jail sentence, a hitch in the army, and a college curriculum have high degrees of determinateness. Usually they are specified as having a particular temporal length, or the time-activity ratio is so evident that anyone can plan with a high degree of certainty on how long the activity will take or how long one must wait for the end. On the other hand, when the judge metes out an indeterminate prison sentence, when the army command decides that military service will extend for the duration of hostilities, or when the requirements for college matriculation change annually, the respective parties to these arrangements experience a sense of temporal unpredictability.

Determinateness is a feature of any time track when the notion of a "deadline" is invoked. Deadlines themselves have a flexibility which often involves crucial decisions by the relevant social actors. Thus a newspaper must be "put to bed" at a certain hour to meet the afternoon edition, but if a reporter shows up after the deadline with a "scoop" a decision has to be made whether the presses should be stopped. On the other hand, some deadlines are irrevocable. A bet on a horse must be placed before the horses break through the barrier. A player with a "sure thing" who arrives at the window after the horses have begun to run is simply "shut out" by the automatic locking of the mutuel machines. Still other deadlines are socially understood to be more flexible than they appear. A military ultimatum to an enemy to surrender by a certain time or face attack, or a statement by a suitor that he will give a girl exactly one year to fall in love with him before breaking off relations entirely are deadline threats that may not be taken at face value. The situation here is usually that of a specialized information game wherein the participants on each side will seek out independent evidence to confirm or deny the stated meaning of the threat.[22]

TIME TRACK MOVEMENT

Movement on time tracks may be analyzed by reference to the actions and beliefs associated with entering and terminating such tracks and with "side-tracking" and "switching tracks."

One issue that arises with respect to entering (or serving out) a specific time track is the actor's knowledge that he has done just that. Institutionalized time tracks are distinctive in that the individual is usually unambiguously informed that he has entered into (or failed to enter into) a temporal sequence of activity or activity states. The annual birthday party informs the middle-class child that he has entered into a new age-specific status; the commitment ceremony initiates the time track for the mentally ill; and the trial,

[22] See T. C. Schelling, *The Strategy of Conflict*, N.Y.: Oxford Galaxy, 1963, 35–43.

jury decision, and sentence begin the time track for the prisoner. Some time tracks, however, are suddenly thrust upon persons without ceremony or prior information. The man who wishes to change jobs but then discovers he has been contributing for years to a non-transferable pension fund finds that he has been on a time track that he can leave only at considerable financial cost. More dramatic time-track disclosures occur when a doctor informs his patient that he has only six months to live, or when a woman tells her lover that in eight months he will be a father.

Just as entering a time track may or may not be governed by ritual or information so also termination is sometimes marked by finalizing ceremonies. In the life-death time track the funeral is the usual terminating ritual. This ritual is crucial in providing the connecting link between the end of secular time and the beginning of sacred existence.

Other time tracks also have terminating rituals. Retirement from gainful employment in the white-collar occupations is usually ceremonialized by a luncheon and a token of appreciation. Tokens of course are important for their symbolic content; and transfer of tokens often indicates termination of the relationship, as when the girl returns the engagement ring, or when the soldier-turned-pacifist sends his military decorations to the government.

Time tracks differ with respect to the strict liability in role performance demanded of persons who have just entered or are about to leave. Women entering marriage are at the outset permitted many failures in the kitchen and in bed, but as the marriage goes on performances in both areas are expected to improve and mistakes are less often overlooked. By contrast, the army recruit is early required to give maximum effort to discipline and military etiquette; however, toward the end of his hitch he is granted more leeway. Early excellence is apparently required in time tracks that take up less than the whole of one's life, that are risky and connected to tasks governed by technique and intelligence, and that are subject to public scrutiny. Time tracks that encompass life itself, that are not so risky but rather involve a diffuse and untechnical orientation, and that are subject to private judgment seem to encourage gradual adjustment rather than instant mastery.

Still another element in the termination of time tracks involves the institutionalized modes of suspending rules that have previously been binding. The condemned prisoner, despised during the course of his imprisonment, is allowed to select a gourmet dinner and permitted certain other final requests on the eve of his execution. In some legal and social circles the words of a dying man are granted a greater measure of credence than at any other time in his life and his wishes and testament are given considerable weight. And on such social occasions as card parties, the *last* hand of poker is often settled by innovative game-specific criteria, and the players relax their usual role vigilance by betting poor hands.[23]

We may note finally that persons at the end of time tracks are sometimes called upon to mobilize maximum control over self. A most dramatic illustration is found in public executions. On such occasions an extraordinary display of appropriate character may recoup a lost moral identity. Thus both kings and killers are constrained to display aloof detachment or joking light-heartedness at the execution block. Death conduct in general is of such a morally significant nature that those who go to their deaths with cheerfulness and equanimity are often honored for lightening the emotional load on those who must witness their death and remember it.[24] Terminations of time tracks can be distinguished, then, according to those that end with passive acquiescence and little expressive activity on the part of the terminating party, or those that call upon him to display a character or "face" suited to the situation.

Between the entering and terminating of time tracks are periods we may call "side tracking." Three types of side tracking are prominent: *waiting, time out,* and *withdrawal.*

Waiting periods may be cyclical or linear. Cyclical periods are repetitive intermissions between a single type of activity. A remarkable example is provided by certain unemployed urban Negro men who bide their time until Thursday night, typically the suburban Negro maid's night off, whereupon they drive to the railroad station,

---

[23] For other aspects of card playing, see Irving Crespi, "The Social Significance of Card Playing as a Leisure Time Activity," in *Sociology and Everyday Life,* edited by Marcello Truzzi, Englewood Cliffs: Prentice Hall, 1968, 101–108.

[24] See Goffman, *Interaction Ritual, op. cit.*, 229–233. Many examples are provided in the essays collected in *Death and Identity,* edited by Robert Fulton, N.Y.: Wiley, 1965.

pick up one of the girls, and enjoy a night of revelry and profit.[25] The period between these Thursday nights is defined as "dead" time—a period of social inactivity. On a macrocosmic level, cyclical waiting may be sensed by the assimilated members of society who carefully observe benchmarks along the several trajectories toward assimilation traversed by different ethnic groups in order to know just when occupational equality and personal intimacy may be practiced for each group with social impunity.[26]

Linear waiting consists of a long stay in a state of meditative quiescence or anxious inaction until something expected occurs. For those who believe that earthly existence is but a prelude to a more meaningful afterlife, life itself may be experienced as nothing more than a linear waiting period. Some of the problems and processes of linear waiting are exemplified in the attitudes and actions of those who expect a millenium.

The problem of the meaning of innerwordly life and historical events for those awaiting a millenium is dramaturgically depicted in Clifford Odets' *Waiting for Lefty* and Samuel Beckett's *Waiting for Godot*. In the former, a play produced in 1935, a group of factory workers are waiting for Lefty, the chairman of their strike committee, to come and tell them what to do. While waiting each man recounts his biography, telling how he came to his present social position and indicating more or less uncertainty with respect to action or quiescence. A representative of management argues against any untoward deeds, but others wonder whether they should wait any longer since Lefty may never come. Lefty, symbolically representative of both the inevitable revolution and the revolutionary leader, eventually is found dead, and the workers are then galvanized to action. In true secular, chiliastic[27] form they shout that only

[25] For this example we are indebted to Horace Cayton.

[26] Thus one view of assimilation in America is that of a kind of "race" toward full scale citizenship in which the "runners" not only jog along at different rates but also begin from culturally different starting places, while the assimilated members of the society sit as "judges" awarding economic, political, and social "laurels" to each group as it crosses the "finish line." For a critique of various views of assimilation, see Milton M. Gordon, *Assimilation in American Life*: N.Y.: Oxford University Press, 1964.

[27] For a sociological discussion of the transformation of the millenial kingdom from its post-historic transcendence to its realization in the mundane world, a

one course is available now: "strike, strike, strike!"[28] If strident action on behalf of the inevitable outcome is one way to assuage doubt and make proper use of otherwise dead time for some on the waiting list of fate, others are moved to regard the whole of life as meaningless. In Beckett's *Waiting for Godot*, two tramps, waiting for their appointment with the never-defined Godot, talk on and on, argue, joke, but "Nothing happens, nobody comes, nobody goes, it's awful."[29] As Martin Esslin[30] points out, "The subject of the play is not Godot but waiting, the act of waiting is an essential aspect of the human condition." But if fate is uncertain, if grace is not necessarily attained by good work or deeds, if indeed fate itself is problematic, then waiting is absurd and the activities undertaken while waiting for the inevitable are equally absurd. Life is meaningless, a cruel joke, and perhaps afterlife is a chimera or an equally cruel joke. Godot may never come. But still Estragon and Vladimir wait. To realize the totality of their absurdity would be too horrible to contemplate. And if the future is both inevitable and ungovernable, one way to resolve both the terrible realization of life's meaninglessness and the awful but unknowable end is unmeditative routine; unreflective activity—a plunge into ceaseless motion that keeps man from thinking too much about what is past and what is to come.[31]

Beneath the awful contemplation of fateful waiting are the more mundane waiting periods on career and situational time tracks. Illustrations of these are found everywhere, and here we need but mention the familiar idea of being frozen in rank, trapped on a seniority list waiting for one's superior to die or retire, and—in situational time tracks—waiting for the next hand to be dealt in a game of cards, waiting for the movie to end so that serious petting may begin on a date, and so on.

---

transformation that began with the evolutionary energies of oppressed Christians posed against the church's insistence on an orthodoxy which denied wordly betterment, see Karl Mannheim, *Ideology and Utopia*, N.Y.: Harcourt, Brace, 1953, 190–197.

[28] See Arthur M. Schlesinger, Jr., *The Politics of Upheaval*, Boston: Houghton-Mifflin, 1960, 185–187, for a discussion of this play and its social context.

[29] Samuel Beckett, *Waiting for Godot*, London: Faber and Faber, 1959, 41.

[30] Martin Esslin, *The Theatre of the Absurd*, Garden City: Doubleday Anchor, 1961, 17.

[31] See Weber, *op. cit.*, 102–128.

A second type of side tracking is the phenomenon of *time out*. Time out refers to a respite in activities related to a specific time track, a period when rules and roles related to that track are relaxed or revoked. During this time-specific state contradictory or irrelevant behavior may be carried out with impunity.[32] Games of all kinds are characterized by either formalized or informal periods in which game play is suspended and unrelated activities or relaxation permitted; the same is true for work in modern settings, institutionalized in the coffee break. On the lifetime track the adventure, as Simmel defines it, is a time out period.

Of course time out on one kind of activity signals time in on another. Time out is used to differentiate the serious from the droll, the sacred from the profane, the impersonal from the intimate. And thus time out may include a switch in time tracks from the long-term to the episodic, from one kind of episode to another, from the fatalistic to the humanistic, and so on. Joking relationships and episodes illustrate the temporal change from one kind of activity state to another. In some social circles card playing requires a ruthless attention to the game throughout the play; but between deals players may relax their role seriousness and tease one another, relate anecdotes, and engage in other irrelevant and unserious acts.[33]

A third type of side-tracking is *withdrawal*. Withdrawal refers to acts of persons or groups who voluntarily retire from the time tracks they are traversing. Looked at from the point of view of the society in which they live, those who withdraw are challengers to social stability and the greater their degree of social visibility the greater their threat. The classic instance is the loving pair, who, should they become too involved with one another, withdraw from social responsibilities. Libidinal withdrawal and its societal dysfunctions is one of the classic explanations for the incest taboo.[34] The loving pair are a greater threat when they form the primary unit

---

[32] See Sherri Cavan, *Liquor License*, Chicago: Aldine, 1966, 10–13, 235–237.

[33] Erving Goffman, "Fun in Games" in *Encounters*, Indianapolis: Bobbs-Merrill, 1961, 37–48.

[34] See Talcott Parsons, "The Incest Taboo in Relation to Social Structure and the Socialization of the Child," *British Journal of Sociology*, 5 (June, 1954), 101–117; and Philip Slater, "Social Limitations on Libidinal Withdrawal," *American Journal of Sociology*, 68 (November, 1961) 296–311.

of an extended kinship complex that requires diffuse mutual responsibilities, and for this reason, romantic love is discouraged in such units.[35]

Further features of withdrawal and its threat to social order are indicated if we compare societal attitudes toward the "primitive" and the "hippie." When Europeans came in contact with Africans and Indians they designated them "primitives" and "savages" and imputed to them the characteristics of promiscuity, license, and amorality—the very characteristics which were feared and envied among themselves.[36] Savages threatened European civilization in that their alleged emphases on the subterranean and forbidden features of Western culture might tempt talented men to abandon the burden of civilization for the freedom of native life. Individual instances of men "going native"—the case of Gauguin is an outstanding example—were sufficiently prevalent to keep alive the fear that the West would be drained of its talented men.[37] Cloistered withdrawal, on the other hand, is always less of a threat to the social order since those who take this step are removed from public view and presumably exercise less of an inducement to those who remain within the mundane world. But public monasticism—withdrawal from culturally prescribed activities unaccompanied by physical removal—challenges the social order itself by its high visibility. In this sense the current "hippie" revolt, characterized by a refusal to carry out even the minimal requirements of the Protestant ethic concomitant with "colonization" on public territories, provides a threat and a seduction to social order similar to that of the "primitives" two centuries removed.[38] And thus we find

[35] See William J. Goode, "The Theoretical Importance of Love," *American Sociological Review*, 24 (February, 1959), 38–47.

[36] See Katherine George, "The Civilized West Looks at Primitive Africa: 1400–1800," *Isis*, 49 (March, 1958), 62–72.

[37] See Henri Baudet, *Paradise on Earth: Some Thoughts on European Images of Non-European Man*, New Haven: Yale University Press, 1965.

[38] For an interesting discussion of hippie morality and social structure, see Fred Davis, "Why All of Us May Be Hippies Someday," and Bennett Berger, "Hippie Morality—More Old Than New," both in *Trans-Action*, 5 (December, 1967), 10–18, 19–27. In an afterword to his article Berger writes (p. 27): "If one knew why the hippies are so consistently newsworthy, one would have the answer to a very important question. The hippies don't know. Only the media know, and they aren't telling." Our observations would suggest that the "newsworthiness"

police and other agencies seeking to limit hippie activity or remove them altogether from the social scene.[39] Withdrawal involves a kind of social regression,[40] and when it occurs, efforts will be made to bring back the individual or group that strays off the beaten path.

Withdrawal and the adventure have certain characteristics in common. Both proceed outside of given time tracks removing the person physically or vicariously from his spatio-temporal surroundings.[41] Moreover, either might proceed from the same kind of evaluation of ongoing social events—that they are distasteful or boring. However, withdrawal and the adventure have at least one difference in orientation: Withdrawal tends to move people inward and to localize their action; the adventure radiates outward and broadens the field and its consequences.

Sidetracking is often the motivation for *switching* time tracks. Switching tracks is facilitated when two or more tracks come in tandem and may be thought of as manifest and latent time tracks. For example, the policeman in following his own career comes into regular contact with criminals and their stratagems; moreover, because of his knowledge of the law and the mechanisms of detection employed by the police he may come to believe in his own ability

---

of the hippies arises because they combine within themselves a *withdrawal* from socially approved attitudes and behavior and a highly visible *public display* of that withdrawal. If they had simply become monks and disappeared behind the walls of a remote monastery they would have attracted but occasional attention. However, by being ever-present but not accounted for in society, they challenge "straights" either to justify their own existence beyond slavish habituation to the dictates of culture or to become hippies themselves.

[39] For an early account of the beat scene in New York, its structures, processes, and relations with the outer world, see Ned Polsky, *Hustlers, Beats and Others,* Chicago: Aldine 1967, 150–185.

[40] Note also that when it occurs as an individual phenomenon, withdrawal is taken as a sign of mental illness. The catatonic schizophrenic is perhaps the extreme instance since he appears to have withdrawn entirely from the communicative world. In this sense, see Michel Foucault, *Madness and Civilization,* New York: Pantheon, 1965, 98–100 and passim.

[41] One form of withdrawal involves the combination of physical presence and mental absence. Thus soldiers on the drill field might perform their duties mechanically while they mentally rehearse what they will do when they get their week-end pass; students may relax into reverie while seemingly paying attention to a lecture; and one partner in a sexual encounter might fantasize during intercourse, transforming it entirely from its gross reality. Episodic time tracks are especially subject to this form of withdrawal.

to mastermind the very types of crime he is supposed to prevent and switch from a career of law enforcement to one of lawbreaking. Similarly, airline stewardesses can easily become drug smugglers; accountants, embezzlers; and mailmen, runners for the numbers racket.

Perhaps some of the most clear-cut examples of track switching are found in the "bridging" occupations, such as servant, soldier, and sportsman—which provide through work experience "the conditions and opportunities for movement from one occupation or cluster of occupations to another."[42] The butlers in nineteenth-century England, and perhaps high-ranking domestic employees everywhere, were in a position to acquire knowledge, tastes, and secrets, enabling them to transfer from formal service to innkeeping, sponsorship in business enterprises, or formal partnership in or unofficial control over the estates they managed. Similarly, the military man moves from formal retirement in middle age to manage a munitions firm, and the professional athlete becomes a sportscaster, or opens a restaurant that trades on the owner's fame.

TIME PANIC

Time panic is produced when an individual or a group senses it is coming to the end of a track without having completed the activities or having gained the benefits associated with it, or when a routinized spatio-temporal activity set is abruptly brought to imminent closure before it is normally scheduled to end.

Episodic time panics are brought into being by a sudden catastrophe that threatens either damage or destruction to the immediate situation, or to life itself. Common among the former are all those slips, gaffes, boners and errors emanating either from the actor or audience, which interrupt a performance and threaten to discredit it. Self-rescue from such situations requires adept impromptu management combined with masterful *savoir faire*. These

---

[42] See L. Broom and J. H. Smith, "Bridging Occupations," *British Journal of Sociology*, 14 (December, 1963), 322.

abilities are characteristic of experienced stage performers, comedians, and sophisticates everywhere, and are usually signs of moral worth. Beyond threats to self and situation that remain entirely encapsulated within the original situation are those which threaten life or limb. Fires in theaters, stock market failures, and invasions without warning—because they threaten not only the immediate situation but also careers, plans, and human existence—often generate a profound sense of time panic.[43] For those in such situations it is the manifest realization of the shortness of time combined with the externally imposed necessity of unplanned acting that apparently coalesces into the kinds of behavior we ordinarily associate with panic in general.[44]

Another kind of episodic time panic occurs in those cultures that require persons, upon coming into one another's view, to acknowledge instantly by word or gesture their exact reciprocal status relationship. Japan is one such culture of this type in which individuals, upon meeting one another and even, sometimes, upon passing in the street, must signal by the temporal length and physical depth of their respective bows exactly what relation they bear to each other according to age, sex, occupations, and heritage.[45] The calculation must take place instantly and must rate the relative merits of each of the status criteria. No time is permitted to sort out the relative weights of the criteria, and eyes are expected to be kept down during the bow so that either mutual monitoring or gleaning of clues is socially prohibited. Yet it is a sign of boorishness to make an incorrect calculation and bow too low or not low enough, or remain stooped too long or not long enough. A related kind of time panic is experienced in America when one party to an encounter, characterized by rhythmic exchanges of "cutting" repartee, is unable to respond at the pace the occasion demands. Momentary

---

[43] For useful discussions, see the papers collected in *Panic Behavior*, edited by Duane P. Schultz, New York: Random House, 1964.

[44] See Neil J. Smelser, *Collective Behavior*, Free Press of Glencoe, 1963.

[45] This point has been emphasized in conversations between Professor Shuichi Kato and Stanford M. Lyman. See Ruth Benedict, *The Chrysanthemum and the Sword*, Boston: Houghton-Mifflin, 1946, 47–48. Such time panics are not experienced by visitors to Japan and rarely experienced by Nisei, since the Japanese automatically exempt foreigners and culturally removed Japanese from this requirement of Japanese etiquette.

speechlessness is recognized by all present as a "loss" in the engagement. Panic is experienced at the very moment in which the response should occur, further unnerving the already disconcerted speaker so that his verbal response, when it actually does occur, nakedly reveals his loss of composure and face.

The instances of the Japanese bow and the rhythmic retort illustrate another feature of some time track terminations, namely, the characteristic of the "last chance." Last chances may be terminal and final, or recurrent, and structured to re-occur with each "play" of the particular time track. In any game, for example, the last event may be sensed by players and spectators as a last chance, but each new game permits that last chance to occur again. However, any sense of the last chance brings about either a steeled burst of emotional and physical control (e.g., when a tiring boxer prepares himself for the tenth round) or an abandonment of causation and calculation and the taking of reckless risks (e.g., when soldiers, hopelessly outnumbered, charge their opponents).

Many occurrences of time panic may be analyzed in terms of the "Rebecca," "Cinderella," and "Dracula" syndromes. By these we refer to panics generated by knowledge that the unchangeable past, the temporally specific future, and the spatio-temporally specific situation, respectively, impose unavoidable deadlines upon social actors. The Rebecca syndrome (so-called from the novel by Daphne du Maurier) refers to the belief that one's right to occupy a position (for instance, that of a second wife) is conditional upon living out the promise of the previous incumbent—a person who is now dead or absent, but whose ideas and activities exercise an inordinate influence on current affairs and whose wishes, yearnings, and goals must be brought to fruition.[46] Panic may set in when the surrogate "Rebecca" begins to feel that she cannot fulfill her obligations in the time allotted to her, and that she will thus soon forfeit her right to that position. Examples of this phenomenon are not only found among second wives, but also in social movements, when the charismatic leader who roused the people to action against injustice is replaced by the bureaucratic leader who must carry forward the former's promises.

[46] For a general discussion, see Alvin W. Gouldner, *Patterns of Industrial Bureaucracy*, Glencoe: Free Press, 1954, 79–83.

If panic sets in because of imposition from the past for those suffering as "Rebeccas," it is the imminent future deadline that threatens a Cinderella,[47] and a need to be at a certain place by a specific time that threatens those on a "Dracula" cycle.[48] Some statuses are limited to a certain time period so that their validity expires when the period is over. Persons in rented or borrowed clothing provide an example; so long as they keep their attire they may give off the status associated with it. But should the time for its return coincide with a crucial moment of impression management, time panic may set in. Similarly, a person disguised as someone else may be discovered if he does not carry off his purpose before those in a position to unmask him arrive, or before his make-up wears off because of natural decay.[49] As the time for discovery comes closer and closer with the proposed deed still uncompleted, panic may set in. Finally, consider the case of the excessively self-conscious crippled, maimed, or otherwise disfigured person who temporarily hides his stigmatic appearance in the unlit movie house, enjoying the film in the security that darkness provides, until a glance at his watch tells him that in one minute the picture will end, lights go on, and his deformed body be on public display. In his panic at the imagined imminent shamefulness of self-display he may behave in such a manner as to call even more attention to himself than his appearance alone would have aroused.

The Dracula syndrome is an extension of that described under the Cinderella rubric. Here not only time but place and ritual state count as well. Colostomy provides a nice example, since persons so afflicted must periodically retire to a private place for physical repair or suffer possible degradation and embarrassment. Similarly,

[47] On the Cinderella syndrome, see Erving Goffman, *Stigma*, Englewood Cliffs: Prentice-Hall Spectrum, 1963, 90.

[48] The term is derived from the Victorian gothic novel by Bram Stoker about a vampire who had to return each dawn to his casket or suffer total disintegration by the power of the sun's rays.

[49] The case of John Howard Griffin is instructive. After having darkened his skin chemically in order to pass as a Negro, his attempt to return to white society was impeded by the fact that for a few weeks after he had removed the outer dye he was subject to excessive darkening by the rays of the sun. For a while he could only depend on being white at night. See John Howard Griffin, *Black Like Me*, New York: Signet, 1962, 118–119.

persons whose protection from social importunities is secured by uniforms and other visible status symbols—such as nuns, priests, military officers, and psychiatrists in asylums—may suffer a peculiar panic when they find themselves suddenly vulnerable because they are in mufti and separated in time and space from their uniforms. Finally, the secretive drug addict in need of a "fix" may suffer terrible panic when, trapped in a situation permitting no escape, he realizes that what has begun as only a gnawing feeling from within will soon give way to uncontrollable emotional states and physical symptoms indicative of his hidden affliction. Persons who are on the "Dracula" track experience "life on a leash"[50] since their movements and engagements must constantly be modified by the need to return to a private place for physical repair or social restoration.

CONCLUSION

Time tracks are products of cultural definitions; they conceive of life as divided into temporally specific, qualitatively different event activities. Some of these tracks are institutionalized so that knowledge of them is part of any socialized individual's taken-for-granted world. Thus in any society we may speak of an officially approved time track cycle. In Occidental cultures since the sixteenth century there is a sense of socially preferred temporal divisions between work and leisure, education and career, unseriousness and gravity. Social time, as Sorokin and Merton observed more than thirty years ago, "in contrast to the time of astronomy, is qualitative and not purely quantitative." Its qualities "serve further to reveal the rhythms, pulsations, and beats of the societies in which they are found."[51]

Time tracks signal their point of departure and termination with some socially imbued occasion. Thus an education in medicine is begun with admission to a medical school and a commitment to spend four years as a student and apprentice practitioner. It is

[50] See Goffman, *Stigma, op. cit.*, 90.
[51] Sorokin and Merton, *op. cit.*

closed with a graduation ceremony and the awarding of the title "doctor" to those who have successfully carried out the commitments. The terms "pre-med," "medical student," "intern," and "resident" represent career stations on a linear time track which break calendar time into a set of time-specific activity stages leading to the terminal stage "doctor."

To understand the temporal outlook of any social actor one must comprehend which time track he is on and how that track measures the flow of time. The overseas Chinese sojourner conceives of time in terms of the years during which he must labor in the alien country in order to save enough money to rejoin his wife in the home village. In calendar time this might be from two to sixty-five years. For the contemporary Greek peasant the social calendar defines the period from sunup to sundown as work time; the period after sundown as time for gossip, visiting a coffeehouse, or ardent political debates.[52] For the "groom" who lives and works at the race track time "is measured not by the calendar but by the racing season. The past is punctuated by the emergence of a great horse, and the benchmarks of the passing of time are referred to as 'the year of Whirlaway, the year of Citation,' and so forth."[53] For the peoples of a pluralistic society there is no set clock; rather there are several personal and social calendars measuring the passing of life.

Moments of time are experienced as qualitatively uneven. Some are critical; others routine. Some are short and pleasurable; others long and filled with pain or anxiety. Some are full with a concretely identifiable plenitude; others are stretches of empty duration. Some are the stuff of the active life, goal-oriented, and instrumental in the attaining of an objective or expressive of mood or feeling; others are devoid of activity or feeling, a mere filling in between eventful moments. Thus time tracks divide life into feeling-activity states, and provide for man the crucial element of action or inaction in their broadest sense.

[52] See Dorothy Lee, *Freedom and Culture*, Englewood Cliffs: Spectrum Paper, 1959, 151.

[53] Scott, *op. cit.*, 72.

9

Conclusion:
Power, pluralism, and order

Machiavelli, the father of the Sociology of the Absurd, continually emphasized the role of power in the creation of social order. Power—the capacity to impose one's will upon the behavior of others[1]—has been neglected within the dominant theories of social order in American sociology. According to the functionalist approach, which at least one sociologist has claimed to be the only current mode of sociological inquiry,[2] the social order rests upon a normative system that legitimates not only social action but power itself. However, in terms of the Sociology of the Absurd, the issue of power may not be begged; rather power must be raised to its appropriate sociological significance. That significance arises precisely from the twin facts that power always *matters* in social relations, and that the gaining, holding, recognition, exercise, and consequences of power are always problematic. Like the social order, which functionalist sociology incorrectly assumes *a priori* to exist, power may neither be *assumed* nor *forgotten* in sociological analysis.

[1] Max Weber, *The Theory of Social and Economic Organization*, Glencoe: The Free Press, 1947, p. 152. (Translated by A.M.Henderson and Talcott Parsons. Edited by Talcott Parsons).

[2] Kingsley Davis, "The Myth of Functional Analysis as a Special Method in Sociology and Anthropology," *American Sociological Review*, 24 (December, 1959), pp. 757–772.

What is peculiarly significant about Machiavelli's theoretical ideas on power is that they were constructed in a social milieu that resembles contemporary society in one striking way: namely, its fundamental pluralism. The fragmentation of the peninsular principalities rendered Italy little more than a concept in Machiavelli's fertile brain; similarly, the fractionalization of modern societies into races, classes, and subcultures makes consensus unlikely and order problematic.

In these final pages, then, we wish to suggest the relationship of power to pluralism and its implications for the Sociology of the Absurd.

In pluralistic societies in which consensus on a wide range of matters cannot be presumed, social interaction is not likely to take an unambiguously predictable course.[3] Pluralism may entail differences in language,[4] differences in the identification of persons and objects,[5] and differences in the comprehension of concrete situations.[6]

The many groups and individuals that make up a pluralistic society do not possess equal power or authority.[7] In most societies, whether plural or not, we can speak of a power elite or a value-sharing oligarchy of elites governing the several sectors of society. The value pattern of the dominant elites tends to take precedence over all other value structures and moralities at least in all those situations in which individuals and groups find themselves in confrontation with these elites.[8] In such situations, when the encounter

---

[3] See Vilfredo Pareto, *The Mind and Society: A Treatise on General Sociology, Vol IV: The General Form of Society*, New York: Dover Publications, 1963, pp. 1511–1512.

[4] See Joshua A. Fishman, *et al.*, *Language Loyalty in the United States: The Maintenance and Perpetuation of Non-English Mother Tongues by American Ethnic and Religious Groups*, The Hague: Mouton and Co., 1966.

[5] Marshall H. Segall, Donald T. Campbell, and Melville Herskovitz, *The Influence of Culture on Visual Perception*, Indianapolis: Bobbs-Merrill, 1966.

[6] See Peter McHugh, *Defining the Situation: The Organization of Meaning in Social Interaction*, Indianapolis: Bobbs-Merrill, 1968.

[7] Cf. C. Wright Mills, *The Power Elite*, New York: Oxford University Press, 1956, and Arnold Rose, *The Power Structure: Political Process in American Society*, New York: Oxford University Press, 1967.

[8] The exception, of course, is when confrontation is established as a challenge to the power holders and their legitimacy.

involves an unequal power engagement between persons or collectivities sharing fundamentally different outlooks, there is the likelihood that not only will confusion or demoralization arise but also pain and deprivation. The latter are especially likely when the officially subordinate group fails to indicate acquiescence to the moral position of the power holders. Thus racial groups espousing a new *Weltanschauung*, youth groups in the process of developing innovative sex mores in lieu of those of their parents, and individuals adopting outlooks inconsistent with the prevailing dominant ethos are "troublesome" partners in a public or legal engagement precisely because they do not share the perspectives of their more powerful fellow interactants. Moreover, these social groups are likely to suffer injury in their engagements because they cannot control them—they lack the power of the elites who dominate public arenas.

Plural societies may be more or less compartmentalized, so that social contacts and the attendant opportunities for displays of relative power and resistance are more or less likely to occur. It is possible at least to imagine a plural society composed of groups who have no contact whatsoever with one another but who do acknowledge common membership in the same society. Such societies have been envisioned in the past[9] and in the present in South Africa[10] as the solution to problems of race contact and the protection of minorities, but they have rarely if at all been established. In such a society the lack of contact among groups presumably would reduce friction and related problems of value difference, but at the same time it could render the several groups relatively impotent with respect to the central power elite. Moreover, the establishment of such a society raises the following question: Which group or group of groups would provide the personnel and perspective of dominant authority?[11]

However, despite the wishes of nationalists and segregationists,

---

[9] See J. A. Laponce, *The Protection of Minorities*, Berkeley: University of California Press, 1960.

[10] Pierre van den Berghe, *South Africa: A Study in Conflict*, Berkeley: University of California Press, 1967.

[11] See Kingsley Davis, "American Society: Its Group Structure," *Contemporary Civilization 2*, Palo Alto: Scott, Foresman, 1961, pp. 171–187.

such perfect social and cultural *apartheid* is unlikely in modern societies because of the coexistence within them of independent cultural and social groups on the one hand and interdependent tasks on the other. Getting an education, preparing for an occupation, enjoying the fruits of one's labor, and seeking after or dispensing services provide opportunities for contact.[12] These contacts—crisscrossing social and cultural groups—promote the frequency of reciprocal violations of expectations and "political" struggles for dominance among groups. Thus black power movements in America raise again the Jewish question;[13] Catholic insistence on public legal enforcement of their religious views on birth control and abortion arouses the indignation of Protestants and non-believers;[14] and youth's demand for recognition of its rights to self-determination in sex activities, drug use, educational curricula and hiring of professors promotes reaction from religious leaders, doctors, school administrators, and a considerable number of adults in general.[15]

Finally, it is important to recognize that plural societies are not typically static. Two dimensions of their dynamics are salient for the analysis of power. The first, on which we have already touched, is their interdependency, a condition making it likely that socially and subculturally different groups will be thrown together in everyday affairs. The second is their tendency toward sociopolitical vicissitudes, changes in the relative status and power relations of several groups vis-à-vis one another. Plural societies in

[12] See Alain Locke and Berhard J. Stern, (Editors), *When Peoples Meet*, New York: Hynds, Hayden, and Eldredge, 1946; and Everett C. Hughes and Helen M. Hughes, *Where Peoples Meet*, Glencoe: Free Press, 1952.

[13] Cf. Earl Raab, "The Black Revolution and the Jewish Question," *Commentary*, 47 (January, 1969), pp. 23–33.

[14] See William J. Gibbons, S.J., "The Catholic Value System and Human Fertility," Kingsley Davis, "Value, Population, and the Supernatural: A Critique," United Church of Christ, "Responsible Parenthood and the Population Problem," all in William Petersen and David Matza, (Editors), *Social Controversy*, Belmont: Wadsworth, 1963, pp. 14–35.

[15] See, e.g., Jerry L. Avorn, *et al.*, *Up Against the Ivy Wall: A History of the Columbia Crisis*, New York: Atheneum, 1968. (Edited by Robert Freedman); Daniel Walker, *Rights in Conflict: The Violent Confrontation of Demonstrators and Police in the parks and streets of Chicago during the week of the Democratic National Convention of 1968*, New York: Signet, 1968; Free (Pseud. for Abbie Hoffman), *Revolution for the Hell of It*, New York: Dial Press, 1968; George Kennan, *Democracy and the Student Left*, New York, Bantam, 1968.

the modern era are not like the Estates of France during the *Ancien Regime*; rather, status groups might move from a less to a more respectable and powerful position in society. The two dynamic elements of pluralist society—their tendencies toward "horizontal" contacts among unlike groups and "vertical" redistributions of power and status—provide another problematic element for social life. Stable relations, unambiguous hierarchies, and predictable encounters are not likely to be characteristic of such a dynamic society.

PLURALISM AND THE SOCIOLOGY OF THE ABSURD

Recognizing the condition of pluralism and the reality of power, we may now take a retrospective look at the essays in this book to suggest some further directions for investigations, from the perspective of the Sociology of the Absurd.

In our discussion of game frameworks we noted that he who has the power can define the game being played as well as win out over less powerful players. However, it follows from our general analysis as well as the discussion of power and pluralism that the power relations of game players are by no means necessarily clear at the outset of a game. The power dimension may be subject to negotiation, hinged as it often is on identity negotiations, and, in general, subject to the rules of the exploitation game which we have described. Our modern day prince, the ordinary man, must establish and re-establish his power, and in the several circles in which he moves, he might find himself superordinate in one, subordinate in another, and confused with respect to just what power he holds in a third. Power is an existential variable in every game.

Our discussion of paranoia, homosexuality, and game theory is in fact predicated upon a power dimension that governs the essential labeling process by which a person is transformed into a deviant.[16] Not all labels "stick." If two strangers meet on the street,

[16] See Howard S. Becker, *The Outsiders*, New York: The Free Press of Glencoe, 1963, pp. 1–8.

get into an argument, and one calls the other "crazy," the likelihood of that appellation having a lasting effect is low indeed. On the other hand when a judge agrees with a lawyer and a psychiatrist that a defendant is "insane,"[17] that label is not only likely to adhere but also, and more important, to have consequences which could not have occurred unless the label had been legitimately affixed. The so-called "labeling" school of deviance is, in effect, a school engaged in a "political sociology"; and future research might focus not only on who labels, but on how the labeler is legitimated, and how, in turn the label is made to adhere to the putative deviant. In turn, the availability of power, persuasion, skill, and *savoir-faire* by which labeled deviants avoid the worst consequences of being labeled, lift the label from themselves, or manage their spoiled identities, needs further research built upon the excellent work that has already begun.

Accounts shore up fractured social relationships and mitigate, if they do not altogether prevent, the Hobbesian state of nature. In a pluralistic society the giving and receiving of accounts is distinctively modified by the presence of and contact with heterogeneous types. Differing social situations call for a situation ethics[18] whose general rules call for a special attention to and suggest the problematic nature of identities, the negotiation of which are underlying features of the presentation of excuses and justifications. When persons of African descent are willing to fight over whether they are "Negroes" or "Blacks";[19] when users of psychedelic drugs are regarded as victims of a debilitating disease or as the wave of the future;[20] when persons who have passed the age of thirty are regarded as experienced citizens or untrustworthy characters, then

---

[17] See Bernard L. Diamond, "With Malice Aforethought," *Archives of Criminal Psychodynamics*, II (Winter, 1957), pp. 1–45.

[18] Joseph Fletcher, *Situation Ethics: The New Morality*, Philadelphia: Westminster Press, 1966.

[19] See Warren L. d'Azevedo, "Race and the Negro," *Liberator* (December, 1968), pp. 4–11.

[20] See Herbert Blumer, *The World of Youthful Drug Use*, ADD Center Project, Final Report. Berkeley: School of Criminology, University of California, January, 1967; James T. Carey, *The College Drug Scene*, Englewood Cliffs: Prentice-Hall, 1968: J. L. Simmons, (Editor), *Marijuana: Myths and Realities*, North Hollywood, Calif.: Brandon House, 1967.

inter-group encounters with their attendant presentations of accounts are fraught with new difficulties.[21] Pluralism affects accounts by posing every man with problems of when, how, and in what manner to request and honor, or disallow, an account. Moreover, situations of account confusion are especially acute when one group is in transition from one status position to another and is undergoing a collective identity crisis. For everyman the management of respect and the maintenance of dignity becomes not only a central, but a potentially anxiety-provoking concern.

Territoriality, power, and pluralism are intricately connected. In a pluralistic society we may expect severe conflict over "public" and "home" territories as men remake their image of the vital habitat. We may see societies make startling re-examinations of what is vital and what is expendable, as men, or rather, national elites, re-define space in terms of air and "fire," rather than the traditional earth and water.[22] Control of territory is a major source of identity, and among persons and groups in status transition the territorial imperative may be uppermost in their minds. Thus, American Negroes have recently discovered the cherished values of the ghetto, university administrators fight students and legislatures for proprietary control over campus buildings, and "demilitarized zones" become the scenes of bloody battles. Space becomes an item of the environment due for persistent redefinition and struggles for stability.

With games more difficult, labels more dangerous, accounts more problematic, and territory less stable, risk becomes a feature of everyday life. The modern Machiavellian—that is, everyman— is more on his mettle than ever before to remain poised under the pressure of everyday affairs. Coolness, however, may not be simply a matter of will. For some it appears to be a natural gift, an element of charisma, in the literal sense; or it may be an accident of physico-cultural imputation; or it may be assiduously cultivated as an art. Moreover, its political consequences become more vital as opposed groups struggle for status and power. The new managerial elite of

[21] See J. L. Simmons and Barry Winograd, *It's Happening: A Portrait of the Youth Scene Today*, Santa Barbara: Marc-Laird Publications, 1966.
[22] See Raymond Aron, *Peace and War: A Theory of International Relations*, Garden City: Doubleday, 1966, pp. 181–210.

modern societies may find coolness in short supply as they become the power brokers among contending interests. The ability to maintain poise in the face of attempts to destroy it may become the single most important criterion in deciding the tenure of future holders of power in all administrative settings, replacing the more mundane and material skills that once held sway. And, as we have previously indicated, a prime test for the loss of cool is the manifestation of stage fright. Persons in leadership positions find their actions subject not only to moral but also to character examination. Fear and trembling in the face of pressure may be sufficient to cancel out the potential rewards of wise decisions. The avoidance of stage fright has thus become a crucial criterion of leadership.

Finally, let us note that power is a crucial feature in defining, maintaining, and switching time tracks. In a pluralist society, time tracks owe their subcultural legitimacy to the political acumen of the several elites who establish and maintain them. Work-time, playtime, and "banana time,"[23] not to mention "dead time," "hot time," and "time out" are temporal creatures of power holders and power brokerage. Some times are functions of space—as when physical barriers present opportunities for two or more time tracks to exist; others are functions of congregation and cultural difference —as when Chinese and Japanese tacitly agree to violate clock time at weddings, banquets, and other unserious activities, but to report to work on time; and still others are functions of negotiations—as when striking workers insist that a 10 a.m. coffee break is a *sine qua non* for their return to work. And on a macrocosmic level, the nature and measurement of time itself may be decided in the philosophical debates of contending anthropological schools of thought.[24] Although time seems to be a universal aspect of human existence, time tracks are products of power and persuasion, force and legitimation, strength and agreement.

[23] Donald F. Roy, " 'Banana Time'—Job Satisfaction and Informal Interaction," in Warren G. Bennes, *et al.*, *Interpersonal Dynamics: Essays and Readings in Human Interaction*, Homewood, Ill.: Dorsey Press, 1968 (Revised Edition), pp. 539–555.

[24] See the interesting discussion of time conceptions in anthropology in S. L. Washburn, "One Hundred Years of Biological Anthropology," in J. O. Brew (Editor), *One Hundred Years of Anthropology*, Cambridge: Harvard University Press, 1968, pp. 106–110.

CONCLUDING REMARKS

Let us restate our position. Functionalism takes social order for granted and confines its researches to the societal infrastructure. We hold that the basic problem of sociology—how is society possible?—is still a salient question. The Sociology of the Absurd re-establishes this question as the central concern of sociology and focuses attention on man as the creator of stable situations, the striver for his own interests, and the destroyer of specific social orders.

The study of power and order are intrinsically related. The course of action in any encounter will hinge upon the power relations of the interactants. In this sense, then, the ancient debate between Plato's Socrates and the ebullient Thrasymachus, as Ralf Dahrendorf has recently argued so forcefully, is not resolved on the side of Socrates. "Socrates became the first functionalist," writes Dahrendorf, "when he described justice as the state in which everybody does what he is supposed to do. . . ." But such a state does not exist, and even if it did, it would be "clearly a miserable state, a world without rebels or retreatists, without change, without liberty."[25] Socrates' humanism, like that of the functionalists and those opposed to Machiavelli's, is one mounted on a utopia, rather than one of this world. If we, as sociologists, are to come "out of utopia,"[26] we must agree, together with Merleau-Ponty's perceptive analysis of Machiavelli,[27] to build our discipline on an *innerworldly* humanism. Such a humanism recognizes both the reality of power and its "viscosity," and, with Dahrendorf, perceives justice "to be not an unchanging state of affairs, whether real or imagined, but the permanently changing outcome of the dialectic of power and resistance."[28]

[25] Ralf Dahrendorf, "In Praise of Thrasymachus," *Essays in the Theory of Society*, Stanford: Stanford University Press, 1968, p. 150.

[26] Ralf Dahrendorf, "Out of Utopia: Toward A Reorientation of Sociological Analysis," *Ibid.*, pp. 107–128.

[27] Maurice Merleau-Ponty, "A Note on Machiavelli," *Signs*, Evanston: Northwestern University Press, 1964, pp. 211–223.

[28] Dahrendorf, "In Praise of Thrasymachus," *loc. cit.* To us it appears that the chief exponent of modern functional analysis in sociology, Talcott Parsons, has adopted a view of power—at least in interpersonal relations—that is not too different from our own. See Talcott Parsons, "On the Concept of Power," and "On the Concept of Influence," *Sociological Theory and Modern Society*, New York: The Free Press, 1967, pp. 297–354, 355–382.